Web Development with Django Cookbook
Second Edition

Over 90 practical recipes to help you create scalable websites using the Django 1.8 framework

Aidas Bendoraitis

PUBLISHING

BIRMINGHAM - MUMBAI

Web Development with Django Cookbook
Second Edition

First published: October 2014

Second Edition: January 2016

Production reference: 1220116

Published by Packt Publishing Ltd.
Livery Place
35 Livery Street
Birmingham B3 2PB, UK.

ISBN 978-1-78588-677-5

www.packtpub.com

Credits

Author

Aidas Bendoraitis

Reviewers

Patrick Chan

Jake Kronika

Jorge Armin Garcia Lopez

Commissioning Editor

Dipika Gaonkar

Acquisition Editor

Nadeem N. Bagban

Content Development Editors

Arwa Manasawala

Sumeet Sawant

Technical Editor

Bharat Patil

Copy Editor

Vibha Shukla

Project Coordinator

Shweta H Birwatkar

Proofreader

Safis Editing

Indexer

Mariammal Chettiyar

Production Coordinator

Arvindkumar Gupta

Cover Work

Arvindkumar Gupta

About the Author

Aidas Bendoraitis has been professionally working with web technologies for over a decade. Over the past nine years at a Berlin-based company, studio 38 pure communication GmbH, he has developed a number of small-scale and large-scale Django projects—mostly in the cultural area—together with a creative team. At the moment, he is also working as a software architect at a London-based mobile startup, Hype.

Aidas regularly attends meetups of Django User Group Berlin, occasionally visits Django and Python conferences, and writes a weblog about Django: `http://djangotricks. blogspot.com/`.

I would like to thank my wife, Sofja, for her support and patience while I was writing this book, even during late evenings and weekends. I would also like to thank studio 38 pure communication GmbH and namely Reinhard Knobelspies for introducing Django to me nine years ago. Finally, I would like to thank Vilnius University in Lithuania for teaching the main programming concepts, without which I wouldn't be working in the positions I currently have.

About the Reviewers

Patrick Chan is a device and configuration management SME (subject matter expert), working in the telecommunication industry. His experience in Python has been instrumental in developing build systems that have not only increased developer productivity, but would also ensure operational reliability by automating software releases.

Jake Kronika is a passionate full-stack developer with over 20 years of experience. Jake's career grew alongside the evolution of the web development space. Starting with GeoCities and Angelfire, his skills have gradually expanded from simple HTML and copy and paste scripts to encapsulate a deep understanding of CSS. JavaScript skills that span core ECMAScript standards as well as numerous client-side libraries and powerful frameworks, such as Node.js and AngularJS; scripting languages including Python and PHP; and various databases, MySQL and PostgreSQL among them.

Jake is currently senior software engineer with CDK Global Digital Marketing wing and a PHP developer with Webkey LLC. Outside these roles, Jake also operates a sole proprietorship through which he provides services spanning the full spectrum of web administration, design, and development.

In addition to his professional career experience, Jake has acted as a reviewer for numerous other Packt titles, such as *Django JavaScript Integration: AJAX and jQuery* (2011), *jQuery UI 1.8: The User Interface Library for jQuery* (2011), *jQuery Tools UI Library* (2012), and *Developing Responsive Web Applications with AJAX and jQuery* (2014).

I would like to thank my family for their ongoing love and support.

Jorge Armin Garcia Lopez is a very passionate information security consultant from Mexico with more than seven years of experience in computer security, penetration testing, intrusion detection/prevention, malware analysis, and incident response. He is the head of GCS-CERT. He is also a security researcher at Cipher Storm Ltd and is the cofounder and CEO of the most important security conference in Mexico, called BugCON. He holds important security industry certifications such as OSCP, GCIA, and GPEN.

He loves reviewing code and books about information security and programming languages. He has worked on the books *Penetration Testing with Backbox*, *Penetration Testing with the Bash Shell*, *Learning OpenStack Networking (Neutron)*, *Django Essentials*, and *Getting Started with Django,* all by Packt Publishing.

www.PacktPub.com

Support files, eBooks, discount offers, and more

For support files and downloads related to your book, please visit www.PacktPub.com.

Did you know that Packt offers eBook versions of every book published, with PDF and ePub files available? You can upgrade to the eBook version at www.PacktPub.com and as a print book customer, you are entitled to a discount on the eBook copy. Get in touch with us at service@packtpub.com for more details.

At www.PacktPub.com, you can also read a collection of free technical articles, sign up for a range of free newsletters and receive exclusive discounts and offers on Packt books and eBooks.

https://www2.packtpub.com/books/subscription/packtlib

Do you need instant solutions to your IT questions? PacktLib is Packt's online digital book library. Here, you can search, access, and read Packt's entire library of books.

Why Subscribe?

- ▸ Fully searchable across every book published by Packt
- ▸ Copy and paste, print, and bookmark content
- ▸ On demand and accessible via a web browser

Free Access for Packt account holders

If you have an account with Packt at www.PacktPub.com, you can use this to access PacktLib today and view 9 entirely free books. Simply use your login credentials for immediate access.

Table of Contents

Preface   **v**

Chapter 1: Getting Started with Django 1.8   **1**

Introduction   2

Working with a virtual environment   2

Creating a project file structure   4

Handling project dependencies with pip   7

Making your code compatible with both Python 2.7 and Python 3   9

Including external dependencies in your project   12

Configuring settings for development, testing, staging,
and production environments   14

Defining relative paths in the settings   16

Creating and including local settings   17

Setting up STATIC_URL dynamically for Subversion users   19

Setting up STATIC_URL dynamically for Git users   20

Setting UTF-8 as the default encoding for MySQL configuration   22

Setting the Subversion ignore property   23

Creating the Git ignore file   26

Deleting Python-compiled files   28

Respecting the import order in Python files   29

Creating app configuration   30

Defining overwritable app settings   33

Chapter 2: Database Structure   **35**

Introduction   35

Using model mixins   36

Creating a model mixin with URL-related methods   37

Creating a model mixin to handle creation and modification dates   40

Creating a model mixin to take care of meta tags   42

Creating a model mixin to handle generic relations   45

Handling multilingual fields   50
Using migrations   56
Switching from South migrations to Django migrations   58
Changing a foreign key to the many-to-many field   59

Chapter 3: Forms and Views   **63**
Introduction   63
Passing HttpRequest to the form   64
Utilizing the save method of the form   66
Uploading images   68
Creating a form layout with django-crispy-forms   74
Downloading authorized files   79
Filtering object lists   83
Managing paginated lists   91
Composing class-based views   95
Generating PDF documents   98
Implementing a multilingual search with Haystack   105

Chapter 4: Templates and JavaScript   **115**
Introduction   115
Arranging the base.html template   116
Including JavaScript settings   119
Using HTML5 data attributes   122
Opening object details in a modal dialog   127
Implementing a continuous scroll   132
Implementing the Like widget   134
Uploading images by Ajax   141

Chapter 5: Custom Template Filters and Tags   **151**
Introduction   151
Following conventions for your own template filters and tags   152
Creating a template filter to show how many days have passed
since a post was published   153
Creating a template filter to extract the first media object   155
Creating a template filter to humanize URLs   157
Creating a template tag to include a template if it exists   158
Creating a template tag to load a QuerySet in a template   162
Creating a template tag to parse content as a template   166
Creating a template tag to modify request query parameters   169

Chapter 6: Model Administration   **175**
Introduction   175
Customizing columns on the change list page   175
Creating admin actions   180

Developing change list filters   **185**
Customizing default admin settings   **188**
Inserting a map into a change form   **192**

Chapter 7: Django CMS   205

Introduction   205
Creating templates for Django CMS   206
Structuring the page menu   210
Converting an app to a CMS app   214
Attaching your own navigation   216
Writing your own CMS plugin   219
Adding new fields to the CMS page   224

Chapter 8: Hierarchical Structures   231

Introduction   231
Creating hierarchical categories   233
Creating a category administration interface with django-mptt-admin   236
Creating a category administration interface with django-mptt-tree-editor   240
Rendering categories in a template   243
Using a single selection field to choose a category in forms   245
Using a checkbox list to choose multiple categories in forms   247

Chapter 9: Data Import and Export   253

Introduction   253
Importing data from a local CSV file   253
Importing data from a local Excel file   256
Importing data from an external JSON file   259
Importing data from an external XML file   264
Creating filterable RSS feeds   269
Using Tastypie to create API   274
Using Django REST framework to create API   278

Chapter 10: Bells and Whistles   285

Introduction   285
Using the Django shell   286
Using database query expressions   289
Monkey-patching the slugify() function for better
internationalization support   295
Toggling the Debug Toolbar   298
Using ThreadLocalMiddleware   301
Caching the method return value   304
Using Memcached to cache Django views   306
Using signals to notify administrators about new entries   308
Checking for missing settings   310

Chapter 11: Testing and Deployment   313
Introduction   313
Testing pages with Selenium   314
Testing views with mock   319
Testing API created using Django REST framework   323
Releasing a reusable Django app   329
Getting detailed error reporting via e-mail   333
Deploying on Apache with mod_wsgi   335
Setting up cron jobs for regular tasks   342
Creating and using the Fabric deployment script   345

Index   357

Preface

Django framework is relatively easy to learn and it solves many web-related questions, such as project structure, database object-relational mapping, templating, form validation, sessions, authentication, security, cookie management, internationalization, basic administration, interface to access data from scripts, and so on. Django is based on the Python programming language, where the code is clear and easy to read. Also, Django has a lot of third-party modules that can be used in conjunction with your own apps. Django has an established and vibrant community, where you can find source code, get help, and contribute.

Web Development with Django Cookbook - Second Edition will guide you through all the web development process with Django 1.8 framework. You will get started with the virtual environment and configuration of the project. Then, you will learn how to define the database structure with reusable components. The book will move on to the forms and views to enter and list the data. Then, you will continue with responsive templates and JavaScript to create the best user experience. After this, you will find out how to tweak administration in order to make the website editors happy. You will also learn how to integrate your own functionality in Django CMS. The next step will be to learn how to use hierarchical structures. You will find out that collecting data from different sources and providing data to others in different formats isn't as difficult as you thought. Then, you'll be introduced to some programming and debugging tricks. Finally, you will be shown how to test and deploy the project to a remote dedicated server.

In contrast to other Django books, this book will deal not only with the code of the framework itself, but also with some important third-party modules that are necessary for fully-equipped web development. Also, the book gives examples of rich user interfaces using Bootstrap frontend framework and jQuery JavaScript library.

What this book covers

Chapter 1, Getting Started with Django 1.8, guides you through the basic configuration that is necessary to start any Django project. It will cover topics such as the virtual environment, version control, and project settings.

Chapter 2, Database Structure, teaches how to write reusable pieces of code to use in your models. When you create a new app, the first thing to do is to define your models. Also, you will be asked how to manage the database schema changes using Django migrations.

Chapter 3, Forms and Views, shows you some patterns used to create the views and forms for your data.

Chapter 4, Templates and JavaScript, covers practical examples of using templates and JavaScript together. We will bring together templates and JavaScript as information is always presented to the user by rendered templates and in modern website, JavaScript is a must for a rich user experience.

Chapter 5, Custom Template Filters and Tags, explains how to create and use your own template filters and tags. As you will see, the default Django template system can be extended to match template developers' needs.

Chapter 6, Model Administration, guides you through extending the default administration with your own functionality as the Django framework comes with a handy pre-built model administration.

Chapter 7, Django CMS, deals with the best practices of using Django CMS, which is the most popular open source content management system made with Django, and adapting it to your project's requirements.

Chapter 8, Hierarchical Structures, shows that whenever you need to create a tree-like structure in Django, the `django-mptt` module comes in handy. This chapter shows you how to use it and set administration for hierarchical structures.

Chapter 9, Data Import and Export, demonstrates how to transfer data from and to different formats, as well as retrieve it from and provide it to different sources. This chapter deals with the management commands for data import and also APIs for data export.

Chapter 10, Bells and Whistles, shows some additional snippets and tricks useful in everyday web development and debugging.

Chapter 11, Testing and Deployment, teaches how to test your project and deploy it on the remote server.

What you need for this book

To develop with Django 1.8, you will need Python 2.7 or Python 3.4, the Pillow library for image manipulation, the MySQL database and MySQLdb bindings or PostgreSQL database, virtualenv to keep each project's Python modules separated, and Git or Subversion for version control.

All other specific requirements are separately mentioned in each recipe.

Who this book is for

If you have created websites with Django, but you want to sharpen your knowledge and learn some good approach for how to treat different aspects of web development, this book is for you. It is intended for intermediate and professional Django users who need to build projects that are multilingual, functional on devices of different screen sizes, and that scale over time.

Conventions

In this book, you will find a number of styles of text that distinguish between different kinds of information. Here are some examples of these styles, and an explanation of their meaning.

Code words in text, database table names, folder names, filenames, file extensions, pathnames, dummy URLs, user input, and Twitter handles are shown as follows: "If you just have one or two settings, you can use the following pattern in your `models.py` file."

A block of code is set as follows:

```
# magazine/__init__.py
# -*- coding: UTF-8 -*-
from __future__ import unicode_literals
default_app_config = "magazine.apps.MagazineAppConfig"
```

When we wish to draw your attention to a particular part of a code block, the relevant lines or items are set in bold:

```
# magazine/__init__.py
# -*- coding: UTF-8 -*-
from __future__ import unicode_literals
default_app_config = "magazine.apps.MagazineAppConfig"
```

Any command-line input or output is written as follows:

```
(myproject_env)$ python
>>> import sys
>>> sys.path
```

New terms and **important words** are shown in bold. Words that you see on the screen, in menus or dialog boxes for example, appear in the text like this: "For example, we added a phone icon to the **Phone** field and an @ sign for the **Email** field".

Warnings or important notes appear in a box like this.

Tips and tricks appear like this.

Reader feedback

Feedback from our readers is always welcome. Let us know what you think about this book—what you liked or may have disliked. Reader feedback is important for us to develop titles that you really get the most out of.

To send us general feedback, simply send an e-mail to feedback@packtpub.com, and mention the book title via the subject of your message.

If there is a topic that you have expertise in and you are interested in either writing or contributing to a book, see our author guide on www.packtpub.com/authors.

Customer support

Now that you are the proud owner of a Packt book, we have a number of things to help you to get the most from your purchase.

Downloading the example code

You can download the example code files for all Packt books you have purchased from your account at http://www.packtpub.com. If you purchased this book elsewhere, you can visit http://www.packtpub.com/support and register to have the files e-mailed directly to you.

Errata

Although we have taken every care to ensure the accuracy of our content, mistakes do happen. If you find a mistake in one of our books—maybe a mistake in the text or the code—we would be grateful if you would report this to us. By doing so, you can save other readers from frustration and help us improve subsequent versions of this book. If you find any errata, please report them by visiting http://www.packtpub.com/submit-errata, selecting your book, clicking on the **errata submission form** link, and entering the details of your errata. Once your errata are verified, your submission will be accepted and the errata will be uploaded on our website, or added to any list of existing errata, under the Errata section of that title. Any existing errata can be viewed by selecting your title from http://www.packtpub.com/support.

Piracy

Piracy of copyright material on the Internet is an ongoing problem across all media. At Packt, we take the protection of our copyright and licenses very seriously. If you come across any illegal copies of our works, in any form, on the Internet, please provide us with the location address or website name immediately so that we can pursue a remedy.

Please contact us at copyright@packtpub.com with a link to the suspected pirated material.

We appreciate your help in protecting our authors, and our ability to bring you valuable content.

Questions

You can contact us at questions@packtpub.com if you are having a problem with any aspect of the book, and we will do our best to address it.

1
Getting Started with Django 1.8

In this chapter, we will cover the following topics:

- ▶ Working with a virtual environment
- ▶ Creating a project file structure
- ▶ Handling project dependencies with pip
- ▶ Making your code compatible with both Python 2.7 and Python 3
- ▶ Including external dependencies in your project
- ▶ Configuring settings for development, testing, staging, and production environments
- ▶ Defining relative paths in the settings
- ▶ Creating and including local settings
- ▶ Setting up STATIC_URL dynamically for Subversion users
- ▶ Setting up STATIC_URL dynamically for Git users
- ▶ Setting UTF-8 as the default encoding for MySQL configuration
- ▶ Setting the Subversion ignore property
- ▶ Creating a Git ignore file
- ▶ Deleting Python-compiled files
- ▶ Respecting the import order in Python files
- ▶ Creating app configuration
- ▶ Defining overwritable app settings

Introduction

In this chapter, we will see a few good practices when starting a new project with Django 1.8 on Python 2.7 or Python 3. Some of the tricks introduced here are the best ways to deal with the project layout, settings, and configurations. However, for some tricks, you might have to find some alternatives online or in other books about Django. Feel free to evaluate and choose the best bits and pieces for yourself while digging deep into the Django world.

I am assuming that you are already familiar with the basics of Django, Subversion and Git version control, MySQL and PostgreSQL databases, and command-line usage. Also, I am assuming that you are probably using a Unix-based operating system, such as Mac OS X or Linux. It makes more sense to develop with Django on Unix-based platforms as the websites will most likely be published on a Linux server, therefore, you can establish routines that work the same while developing as well as deploying. If you are locally working with Django on Windows, the routines are similar; however, they are not always the same.

Working with a virtual environment

It is very likely that you will develop multiple Django projects on your computer. Some modules such as Python Imaging Library (or Pillow) and MySQLdb, can be installed once and then shared for all projects. Other modules such as Django, third-party Python libraries, and Django apps, will need to be kept isolated from each other. The virtualenv tool is a utility that separates all the Python projects in their own realms. In this recipe, we will see how to use it.

Getting ready

To manage Python packages, you will need `pip`. It is included in your Python installation if you are using Python 2.7.9 or Python 3.4+. If you are using another version of Python, install `pip` by executing the installation instructions at `http://pip.readthedocs.org/en/stable/installing/`. Let's install the shared Python modules Pillow and MySQLdb, and the virtualenv utility, using the following commands:

```
$ sudo pip install Pillow
$ sudo pip install MySQL-python
$ sudo pip install virtualenv
```

How to do it...

Once you have your prerequisites installed, create a directory where all your Django projects will be stored, for example, `virtualenvs` under your home directory. Perform the following steps after creating the directory:

1. Go to the newly created directory and create a virtual environment that uses the shared system site packages:

    ```
    $ cd ~/virtualenvs
    $ mkdir myproject_env
    $ cd myproject_env
    $ virtualenv --system-site-packages .
    New python executable in ./bin/python
    Installing setuptools…………. done.
    Installing pip……………done.
    ```

2. To use your newly created virtual environment, you need to execute the activation script in your current shell. This can be done with the following command:

    ```
    $ source bin/activate
    ```

    You can also use the following command one for the same (note the space between the dot and bin):

    ```
    $ . bin/activate
    ```

3. You will see that the prompt of the command-line tool gets a prefix of the project name, as follows:

    ```
    (myproject_env) $
    ```

4. To get out of the virtual environment, type the following command:

    ```
    $ deactivate
    ```

How it works...

When you create a virtual environment, a few specific directories (`bin`, `build`, `include`, and `lib`) are created in order to store a copy of the Python installation and some shared Python paths are defined. When the virtual environment is activated, whatever you have installed with `pip` or `easy_install` will be put in and used by the site packages of the virtual environment, and not the global site packages of your Python installation.

To install Django 1.8 in your virtual environment, type the following command:

```
(myproject_env) $ pip install Django==1.8
```

See also

▶ The *Creating a project file structure recipe*

▶ The *Deploying on Apache with mod_wsgi* recipe in *Chapter 11, Testing and Deployment*

Creating a project file structure

A consistent file structure for your projects makes you well-organized and more productive. When you have the basic workflow defined, you can get in the business logic quicker and create awesome projects.

Getting ready

If you haven't done this yet, create a `virtualenvs` directory, where you will keep all your virtual environments (read about this in the *Working with a virtual environment* recipe). This can be created under your home directory.

Then, create a directory for your project's environment, for example, `myproject_env`. Start the virtual environment in it. I would suggest adding the `commands` directory for local bash scripts that are related to the project, the `db_backups` directory for database dumps, and the `project` directory for your Django project. Also, install Django in your virtual environment.

How to do it...

Follow these steps in order to create a file structure for your project:

1. With the virtual environment activated, go to the project directory and start a new Django project as follows:

   ```
   (myproject_env)$ django-admin.py startproject myproject
   ```

   For clarity, we will rename the newly created directory as `django-myproject`. This is the directory that you will put under version control, therefore, it will have the `.git`, `.svn`, or similar directories.

2. In the `django-myproject` directory, create a `README.md` file to describe your project to the new developers. You can also put the pip requirements with the Django version and include other external dependencies (read about this in the *Handling project dependencies with pip* recipe). Also, this directory will contain your project's Python package named `myproject`; Django apps (I recommend having an app called `utils` for different functionalities that are shared throughout the project); a `locale` directory for your project translations if it is multilingual; a Fabric deployment script named `fabfile.py`, as suggested in the *Creating and using the Fabric deployment script* recipe in *Chapter 11, Testing and Deployment*; and the `externals` directory for external dependencies that are included in this project if you decide not to use pip requirements.

3. In your project's Python package, `myproject`, create the `media` directory for project uploads, the `site_static` directory for project-specific static files, the `static` directory for collected static files, the `tmp` directory for the upload procedure, and the `templates` directory for project templates. Also, the `myproject` directory should contain your project settings, the `settings.py` and `conf` directories (read about this in the *Configuring settings for development, testing, staging, and production environments* recipe), as well as the `urls.py` URL configuration.

4. In your `site_static` directory, create the `site` directory as a namespace for site-specific static files. Then, separate the separated static files in directories in it. For instance, `scss` for Sass files (optional), `css` for the generated minified Cascading Style Sheets, `img` for styling images and logos, `js` for JavaScript, and any third-party module combining all types of files such as the tinymce rich-text editor. Besides the `site` directory, the `site_static` directory might also contain overwritten static directories of third-party apps, for example, `cms` overwriting static files from Django CMS. To generate the CSS files from Sass and minify the JavaScript files, you can use the CodeKit or Prepros applications with a graphical user interface.

5. Put your templates that are separated by the apps in your templates directory. If a template file represents a page (for example, `change_item.html` or `item_list.html`), then directly put it in the app's template directory. If the template is included in another template (for example, `similar_items.html`), put it in the includes subdirectory. Also, your templates directory can contain a directory called `utils` for globally reusable snippets, such as pagination, language chooser, and others.

How it works...

The whole file structure for a complete project in a virtual environment will look similar to the following:

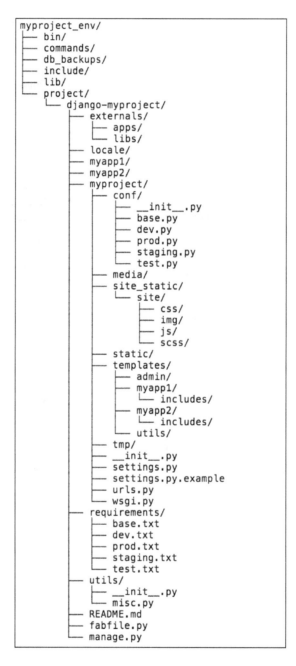

```
myproject_env/
├── bin/
├── commands/
├── db_backups/
├── include/
├── lib/
└── project/
    └── django-myproject/
        ├── externals/
        │   ├── apps/
        │   └── libs/
        ├── locale/
        ├── myapp1/
        ├── myapp2/
        ├── myproject/
        │   ├── conf/
        │   │   ├── __init__.py
        │   │   ├── base.py
        │   │   ├── dev.py
        │   │   ├── prod.py
        │   │   ├── staging.py
        │   │   └── test.py
        │   ├── media/
        │   ├── site_static/
        │   │   └── site/
        │   │       ├── css/
        │   │       ├── img/
        │   │       ├── js/
        │   │       └── scss/
        │   ├── static/
        │   ├── templates/
        │   │   ├── admin/
        │   │   ├── myapp1/
        │   │   │   └── includes/
        │   │   ├── myapp2/
        │   │   │   └── includes/
        │   │   └── utils/
        │   ├── tmp/
        │   ├── __init__.py
        │   ├── settings.py
        │   ├── settings.py.example
        │   ├── urls.py
        │   └── wsgi.py
        ├── requirements/
        │   ├── base.txt
        │   ├── dev.txt
        │   ├── prod.txt
        │   ├── staging.txt
        │   └── test.txt
        ├── utils/
        │   ├── __init__.py
        │   └── misc.py
        ├── README.md
        ├── fabfile.py
        └── manage.py
```

See also

- ▶ The *Handling project dependencies with pip* recipe
- ▶ The *Including external dependencies in your project* recipe
- ▶ The *Configuring settings for development, testing, staging, and production environments* recipe
- ▶ The *Deploying on Apache with mod_wsgi* recipe in *Chapter 11, Testing and Deployment*
- ▶ The *Creating and using the Fabric deployment script* recipe in *Chapter 11, Testing and Deployment*

Handling project dependencies with pip

The pip is the most convenient tool to install and manage Python packages. Besides installing the packages one by one, it is possible to define a list of packages that you want to install and pass it to the tool so that it deals with the list automatically.

You will need to have at least two different instances of your project: the development environment, where you create new features, and the public website environment that is usually called the production environment in a hosted server. Additionally, there might be development environments for other developers. Also, you may have a testing and staging environment in order to test the project locally and in a public website-like situation.

For good maintainability, you should be able to install the required Python modules for development, testing, staging, and production environments. Some of the modules will be shared and some of them will be specific. In this recipe, we will see how to organize the project dependencies and manage them with pip.

Getting ready

Before using this recipe, you need to have pip installed and a virtual environment activated. For more information on how to do this, read the *Working with a virtual environment* recipe.

How to do it...

Execute the following steps one by one to prepare pip requirements for your Django project:

1. Let's go to your Django project that you have under version control and create the `requirements` directory with these text files: `base.txt` for shared modules, `dev.txt` for development environment, `test.txt` for testing environment, `staging.txt` for staging environment, and `prod.txt` for production.

2. Edit `base.txt` and add the Python modules that are shared in all environments, line by line, for example:

```
# base.txt
Django==1.8
djangorestframework
-e git://github.com/omab/python-social-auth.
git@6b1e301c79#egg=python-social-auth
```

3. If the requirements of a specific environment are the same as in the `base.txt`, add the line including the `base.txt` in the requirements file of that environment, for example:

```
# prod.txt
-r base.txt
```

4. If there are specific requirements for an environment, add them as shown in the following:

```
# dev.txt
-r base.txt
django-debug-toolbar
selenium
```

5. Now, you can run the following command in order to install all the required dependencies for development environment (or analogous command for other environments), as follows:

```
(myproject_env)$ pip install -r requirements/dev.txt
```

How it works...

The preceding command downloads and installs all your project dependencies from `requirements/base.txt` and `requirements/dev.txt` in your virtual environment. As you can see, you can specify a version of the module that you need for the Django framework and even directly install from a specific commit at the Git repository for the `python-social-auth` in our example. In practice, installing from a specific commit would rarely be useful, for instance, only when having third-party dependencies in your project with specific functionality that are not supported in the recent versions anymore.

When you have many dependencies in your project, it is good practice to stick to specific versions of the Python modules as you can then be sure that when you deploy your project or give it to a new developer, the integrity doesn't get broken and all the modules function without conflicts.

If you have already manually installed the project `requirements` with pip one by one, you can generate the `requirements/base.txt` file using the following command:

```
(myproject_env)$ pip freeze > requirements/base.txt
```

There's more...

If you want to keep things simple and are sure that, for all environments, you will be using the same dependencies, you can use just one file for your requirements named `requirements.txt`, by definition:

```
(myproject_env)$ pip freeze > requirements.txt
```

To install the modules in a new environment simply call the following command:

```
(myproject_env)$ pip install -r requirements.txt
```

 If you need to install a Python library from other version control system or local path, you can learn more about pip from the official documentation at `http://pip.readthedocs.org/en/latest/reference/pip_install.html`.

See also

- ▸ The *Working with a virtual environment* recipe
- ▸ The *Including external dependencies in your project* recipe
- ▸ The *Configuring settings for development, testing, staging, and production environments* recipe

Making your code compatible with both Python 2.7 and Python 3

Since version 1.7, Django can be used with Python 2.7 and Python 3. In this recipe, we will take a look at the operations to make your code compatible with both the Python versions.

Getting ready

When creating a new Django project or upgrading an old existing project, consider following the rules given in this recipe.

How to do it...

Making your code compatible with both Python versions consists of the following steps:

1. At the top of each module, add `from __future__ import unicode_literals` and then use usual quotes without a `u` prefix for Unicode strings and a `b` prefix for bytestrings.

2. To ensure that a value is bytestring, use the `django.utils.encoding.smart_bytes` function. To ensure that a value is Unicode, use the `django.utils.encoding.smart_text` or `django.utils.encoding.force_text` function.

3. For your models, instead of the `__unicode__` method, use the `__str__` method and add the `python_2_unicode_compatible` decorator, as follows:

```python
# models.py
# -*- coding: UTF-8 -*-
from __future__ import unicode_literals
from django.db import models
from django.utils.translation import ugettext_lazy as _
from django.utils.encoding import \
    python_2_unicode_compatible


@python_2_unicode_compatible
class NewsArticle(models.Model):
    title = models.CharField(_("Title"), max_length=200)
    content = models.TextField(_("Content"))

    def __str__(self):
        return self.title

    class Meta:
        verbose_name = _("News Article")
        verbose_name_plural = _("News Articles")
```

4. To iterate through dictionaries, use `iteritems()`, `iterkeys()`, and `itervalues()` from `django.utils.six`. Take a look at the following:

```python
from django.utils.six import iteritems
d = {"imported": 25, "skipped": 12, "deleted": 3}
for k, v in iteritems(d):
    print("{0}: {1}".format(k, v))
```

5. When you capture exceptions, use the `as` keyword, as follows:

```python
try:
    article = NewsArticle.objects.get(slug="hello-world")
except NewsArticle.DoesNotExist as exc:
```

```
        pass
    except NewsArticle.MultipleObjectsReturned as exc:
        pass
```

6. To check the type of a value, use `django.utils.six`, as shown in the following:

```
from django.utils import six
isinstance(val, six.string_types) # previously basestring
isinstance(val, six.text_type) # previously unicode
isinstance(val, bytes) # previously str
isinstance(val, six.integer_types) # previously (int, long)
```

7. Instead of `xrange`, use `range` from `django.utils.six.moves`, as follows:

```
from django.utils.six.moves import range
for i in range(1, 11):
    print(i)
```

8. To check whether the current version is Python 2 or Python 3, you can use the following conditions:

```
from django.utils import six
if six.PY2:
    print("This is Python 2")
if six.PY3:
    print("This is Python 3")
```

How it works...

All strings in Django projects should be considered as Unicode strings. Only the input of `HttpRequest` and output of `HttpResponse` is usually in the UTF-8 encoded bytestring.

Many functions and methods in Python 3 now return the iterators instead of lists, which make the language more efficient. To make the code compatible with both the Python versions, you can use the six library that is bundled in Django.

Read more about writing compatible code in the official Django documentation at `https://docs.djangoproject.com/en/1.8/topics/python3/`.

Downloading the example code

You can download the example code files for all Packt books that you have purchased from your account at `http://www.packtpub.com`. If you purchased this book elsewhere, you can visit `http://www.packtpub.com/support` and register in order to have the files e-mailed directly to you.

Including external dependencies in your project

Sometimes, it is better to include external dependencies in your project. This ensures that whenever a developer upgrades third-party modules, all the other developers will receive the upgraded version in the next update from the version control system (Git, Subversion, or others).

Also, it is better to have external dependencies included in your project when the libraries are taken from unofficial sources, that is, somewhere other than **Python Package Index** (**PyPI**), or different version control systems.

Getting ready

Start with a virtual environment with a Django project in it.

How to do it...

Execute the following steps one by one:

1. If you haven't done this already, create an externals directory under your Django project `django-myproject` directory. Then, create the `libs` and `apps` directories under it.

    The `libs` directory is for the Python modules that are required by your project, for example, boto, Requests, Twython, Whoosh, and so on. The `apps` directory is for third-party Django apps, for example, django-cms, django-haystack, django-storages, and so on.

     I highly recommend that you create the `README.txt` files in the `libs` and `apps` directories, where you mention what each module is for, what the used version or revision is, and where it is taken from.

2. The directory structure should look something similar to the following:

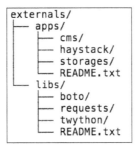

```
externals/
├── apps/
│   ├── cms/
│   ├── haystack/
│   ├── storages/
│   └── README.txt
└── libs/
    ├── boto/
    ├── requests/
    ├── twython/
    └── README.txt
```

3. The next step is to put the external libraries and apps under the Python path so that they are recognized as if they were installed. This can be done by adding the following code in the settings:

```python
# settings.py
# -*- coding: UTF-8 -*-
from __future__ import unicode_literals
import os
import sys

BASE_DIR = os.path.abspath(os.path.join(
    os.path.dirname(__file__), ".."
))

EXTERNAL_LIBS_PATH = os.path.join(
    BASE_DIR, "externals", "libs"
)
EXTERNAL_APPS_PATH = os.path.join(
    BASE_DIR, "externals", "apps"
)
sys.path = ["", EXTERNAL_LIBS_PATH, EXTERNAL_APPS_PATH] + \
    sys.path
```

How it works...

A module is meant to be under the Python path if you can run Python and import that module. One of the ways to put a module under the Python path is to modify the `sys.path` variable before importing a module that is in an unusual location. The value of `sys.path` is a list of directories starting with an empty string for the current directory, followed by the directories in the virtual environment, and finally the globally shared directories of the Python installation. You can see the value of `sys.path` in the Python shell, as follows:

```
(myproject_env)$ python
>>> import sys
>>> sys.path
```

When trying to import a module, Python searches for the module in this list and returns the first result that is found.

Therefore, we first define the `BASE_DIR` variable, which is the absolute path to one level higher than the `settings.py` file. Then, we define the `EXTERNAL_LIBS_PATH` and `EXTERNAL_APPS_PATH` variables, which are relative to `BASE_DIR`. Lastly, we modify the `sys.path` property, adding new paths to the beginning of the list. Note that we also add an empty string as the first path to search, which means that the current directory of any module should always be checked first before checking other Python paths.

 This way of including external libraries doesn't work cross-platform with the Python packages that have C language bindings, for example, `lxml`. For such dependencies, I would recommend using the pip requirements that were introduced in the *Handling project dependencies with pip* recipe.

See also

- The *Creating a project file structure* recipe
- The *Handling project dependencies with pip* recipe
- The *Defining relative paths in the settings* recipe
- The *Using the Django shell* recipe in *Chapter 10, Bells and Whistles*

Configuring settings for development, testing, staging, and production environments

As noted earlier, you will be creating new features in the development environment, test them in the testing environment, then put the website to a staging server to let other people to try the new features, and lastly, the website will be deployed to the production server for public access. Each of these environments can have specific settings and you will see how to organize them in this recipe.

Getting ready

In a Django project, we'll create settings for each environment: development, testing, staging, and production.

How to do it...

Follow these steps to configure project settings:

1. In `myproject` directory, create a `conf` Python module with the following files: `__init__.py`, `base.py` for shared settings, `dev.py` for development settings, `test.py` for testing settings, `staging.py` for staging settings, and `prod.py` for production settings.

2. Put all your shared settings in `conf/base.py`.

3. If the settings of an environment are the same as the shared settings, then just import everything from `base.py` there, as follows:

```
# myproject/conf/prod.py
# -*- coding: UTF-8 -*-
from __future__ import unicode_literals
from .base import *
```

4. Apply the settings that you want to attach or overwrite for your specific environment in the other files, for example, the development environment settings should go to `dev.py` as shown in the following:

```
# myproject/conf/dev.py
# -*- coding: UTF-8 -*-
from __future__ import unicode_literals
from .base import *
EMAIL_BACKEND = \
    "django.core.mail.backends.console.EmailBackend"
```

5. At the beginning of the `myproject/settings.py`, import the configurations from one of the environment settings and then additionally attach specific or sensitive configurations such as `DATABASES` or `API` keys that shouldn't be under version control, as follows:

```
# myproject/settings.py
# -*- coding: UTF-8 -*-
from __future__ import unicode_literals
from .conf.dev import *

DATABASES = {
    "default": {
        "ENGINE": "django.db.backends.mysql",
        "NAME": "myproject",
        "USER": "root",
        "PASSWORD": "root",
    }
}
```

6. Create a `settings.py.sample` file that should contain all the sensitive settings that are necessary for a project to run; however, with empty values set.

How it works...

By default, the Django management commands use the settings from `myproject/settings.py`. Using the method that is defined in this recipe, we can keep all the required non-sensitive settings for all environments under version control in the conf directory. Whereas, the `settings.py` file itself would be ignored by version control and will only contain the settings that are necessary for the current development, testing, staging, or production environments.

See also

▸ The *Creating and including local settings* recipe

▸ The *Defining relative paths in the settings* recipe

▸ The *Setting the Subversion ignore property* recipe

▸ The *Creating a Git ignore file* recipe

Defining relative paths in the settings

Django requires you to define different file paths in the settings, such as the root of your media, the root of your static files, the path to templates, the path to translation files, and so on. For each developer of your project, the paths may differ as the virtual environment can be set up anywhere and the user might be working on Mac OS X, Linux, or Windows. Anyway, there is a way to define these paths that are relative to your Django project directory.

Getting ready

To start with, open `settings.py`.

How to do it...

Modify your path-related settings accordingly instead of hardcoding the paths to your local directories, as follows:

```
# settings.py
# -*- coding: UTF-8 -*-
from __future__ import unicode_literals
import os

BASE_DIR = os.path.abspath(
```

```
        os.path.join(os.path.dirname(__file__), "..")
    )

    MEDIA_ROOT = os.path.join(BASE_DIR, "myproject", "media")

    STATIC_ROOT = os.path.join(BASE_DIR, "myproject", "static")

    STATICFILES_DIRS = (
        os.path.join(BASE_DIR, "myproject", "site_static"),
    )

    TEMPLATE_DIRS = (
        os.path.join(BASE_DIR, "myproject", "templates"),
    )

    LOCALE_PATHS = (
        os.path.join(BASE_DIR, "locale"),
    )

    FILE_UPLOAD_TEMP_DIR = os.path.join(
        BASE_DIR, "myproject", "tmp"
    )
```

How it works...

At first, we define `BASE_DIR`, which is an absolute path to one level higher than the `settings.py` file. Then, we set all the paths relative to `BASE_DIR` using the `os.path.join` function.

See also

▸   The *Including external dependencies in your project* recipe

Creating and including local settings

Configuration doesn't necessarily need to be complex. If you want to keep things simple, you can work with two settings files: `settings.py` for common configuration and `local_settings.py` for sensitive settings that shouldn't be under version control.

Getting ready

Most of the settings for different environments will be shared and saved in version control. However, there will be some settings that are specific to the environment of the project instance, for example, database or e-mail settings. We will put them in the `local_settings.py` file.

How to do it...

To use local settings in your project, perform the following steps:

1. At the end of `settings.py`, add a version of `local_settings.py` that claims to be in the same directory, as follows:

```python
# settings.py
# … put this at the end of the file …
try:
    execfile(os.path.join(
        os.path.dirname(__file__), "local_settings.py"
    ))
except IOError:
    pass
```

2. Create `local_settings.py` and put your environment-specific settings there, as shown in the following:

```python
# local_settings.py
DATABASES = {
    "default": {
        "ENGINE": "django.db.backends.mysql",
        "NAME": "myproject",
        "USER": "root",
        "PASSWORD": "root",
    }
}

EMAIL_BACKEND = \
    "django.core.mail.backends.console.EmailBackend"

INSTALLED_APPS += (
    "debug_toolbar",
)
```

How it works...

As you can see, the local settings are not normally imported, they are rather included and executed in the `settings.py` file itself. This allows you to not only create or overwrite the existing settings, but also adjust the tuples or lists from the `settings.py` file. For example, we add `debug_toolbar` to `INSTALLED_APPS` here in order to be able to debug the SQL queries, template context variables, and so on.

See also

- ▸ The *Creating a project file structure* recipe
- ▸ The *Toggling the Debug Toolbar* recipe in *Chapter 10, Bells and Whistles*

Setting up STATIC_URL dynamically for Subversion users

If you set `STATIC_URL` to a static value, then each time you update a CSS file, JavaScript file, or image, you will need to clear the browser cache in order to see the changes. There is a trick to work around clearing the browser's cache. It is to have the revision number of the version control system shown in `STATIC_URL`. Whenever the code is updated, the visitor's browser will force the loading of all-new static files.

This recipe shows how to put a revision number in `STATIC_URL` for subversion users.

Getting ready

Make sure that your project is under the subversion version control and you have `BASE_DIR` defined in your settings, as shown in the *Defining relative paths in the settings* recipe.

Then, create the `utils` module in your Django project, and also create a file called `misc.py` there.

How to do it...

The procedure to put the revision number in the `STATIC_URL` setting consists of the following two steps:

1. Insert the following content:

   ```
   # utils/misc.py
   # -*- coding: UTF-8 -*-
   from __future__ import unicode_literals
   ```

```
import subprocess

def get_media_svn_revision(absolute_path):
    repo_dir = absolute_path
    svn_revision = subprocess.Popen(
        'svn info | grep "Revision" | awk \'{print $2}\'',
        stdout=subprocess.PIPE, stderr=subprocess.PIPE,
        shell=True, cwd=repo_dir, universal_newlines=True)
    rev = svn_revision.communicate()[0].partition('\n')[0]
    return rev
```

2. Then, modify the `settings.py` file and add the following lines:

```
# settings.py
# … somewhere after BASE_DIR definition …
from utils.misc import get_media_svn_revision
STATIC_URL = "/static/%s/" % get_media_svn_revision(BASE_DIR)
```

How it works...

The `get_media_svn_revision()` function takes the `absolute_path` directory as a parameter and calls the `svn info` shell command in that directory to find out the current revision. We pass `BASE_DIR` to the function as we are sure that it is under version control. Then, the revision is parsed, returned, and included in the `STATIC_URL` definition.

See also

▶ The *Setting up STATIC_URL dynamically for Git users* recipe

▶ The *Setting the Subversion ignore property* recipe

Setting up STATIC_URL dynamically for Git users

If you don't want to refresh the browser cache each time you change your CSS and JavaScript files, or while styling images, you need to set `STATIC_URL` dynamically with a varying path component. With the dynamically changing URL, whenever the code is updated, the visitor's browser will force loading of all-new uncached static files. In this recipe, we will set a dynamic path for `STATIC_URL` when you use the Git version control system.

Getting ready

Make sure that your project is under the Git version control and you have `BASE_DIR` defined in your settings, as shown in the *Defining relative paths in the settings* recipe.

If you haven't done it yet, create the `utils` module in your Django project. Also, create a `misc.py` file there.

How to do it...

The procedure to put the Git timestamp in the `STATIC_URL` setting consists of the following two steps:

1. Add the following content to the `misc.py` file placed in `utils/`:

```python
# utils/misc.py
# -*- coding: UTF-8 -*-
from __future__ import unicode_literals
import subprocess
from datetime import datetime


def get_git_changeset(absolute_path):
    repo_dir = absolute_path
    git_show = subprocess.Popen(
        'git show --pretty=format:%ct --quiet HEAD',
        stdout=subprocess.PIPE, stderr=subprocess.PIPE,
        shell=True, cwd=repo_dir, universal_newlines=True,
    )
    timestamp = git_show.communicate()[0].partition('\n')[0]
    try:
        timestamp = \
            datetime.utcfromtimestamp(int(timestamp))
    except ValueError:
        return ""
    changeset = timestamp.strftime('%Y%m%d%H%M%S')
    return changeset
```

2. Then, import the newly created `get_git_changeset()` function in the settings and use it for the `STATIC_URL` path, as follows:

```python
# settings.py
# … somewhere after BASE_DIR definition …
from utils.misc import get_git_changeset
STATIC_URL = "/static/%s/" % get_git_changeset(BASE_DIR)
```

How it works...

The `get_git_changeset()` function takes the `absolute_path` directory as a parameter and calls the `git` show shell command with the parameters to show the Unix timestamp of the `HEAD` revision in the directory. As stated in the previous recipe, we pass `BASE_DIR` to the function as we are sure that it is under version control. The timestamp is parsed; converted to a string consisting of year, month, day, hour, minutes, and seconds; returned; and included in the definition of `STATIC_URL`.

See also

- ▶ The *Setting up STATIC_URL dynamically for Subversion users* recipe
- ▶ The *Creating the Git ignore file* recipe

Setting UTF-8 as the default encoding for MySQL configuration

MySQL is the most popular open source database. In this recipe, I will tell you how to set UTF-8 as the default encoding for it. Note that if you don't set this encoding in the database configuration, you might get into a situation where LATIN1 is used by default with your UTF-8 encoded data. This will lead to database errors whenever symbols such as € are used. Also, this recipe will save you from the difficulties of converting the database data from LATIN1 to UTF-8, especially when you have some tables encoded in LATIN1 and others in UTF-8.

Getting ready

Make sure that the MySQL database management system and the MySQLdb Python module are installed and you are using the MySQL engine in your project's settings.

How to do it...

Open the `/etc/mysql/my.cnf` MySQL configuration file in your favorite editor and ensure that the following settings are set in the sections: `[client]`, `[mysql]`, and `[mysqld]`, as follows:

```
# /etc/mysql/my.cnf
[client]
default-character-set = utf8

[mysql]
```

```
default-character-set = utf8

[mysqld]
collation-server = utf8_unicode_ci
init-connect = 'SET NAMES utf8'
character-set-server = utf8
```

If any of the sections don't exist, create them in the file. Then, restart MySQL in your command-line tool, as follows:

```
$ /etc/init.d/mysql restart
```

How it works...

Now, whenever you create a new MySQL database, the databases and all their tables will be set in UTF-8 encoding by default.

Don't forget to set this in all computers where your project is developed or published.

Setting the Subversion ignore property

If you are using Subversion for version control, you will need to keep most of the projects in the repository; however, some files and directories should only stay locally and not be tracked.

Getting ready

Make sure that your Django project is under the Subversion version control.

How to do it...

Open your command-line tool and set your default editor as nano, vi, vim or any other that you prefer, as follows:

```
$ export EDITOR=nano
```

 If you don't have a preference, I would recommend using nano, which is very intuitive and a simple text editor for the terminal.

Then, go to your project directory and type the following command:

```
$ svn propedit svn:ignore myproject
```

This will open a temporary file in the editor, where you need to put the following file and directory patterns for Subversion to ignore:

```
# Project files and directories
local_settings.py
static
media
tmp

# Byte-compiled / optimized / DLL files
__pycache__
*.py[cod]
*$py.class

# C extensions
*.so

# PyInstaller
*.manifest
*.spec

# Installer logs
pip-log.txt
pip-delete-this-directory.txt

# Unit test / coverage reports
htmlcov
.tox
.coverage
.coverage.*
.cache
nosetests.xml
coverage.xml
*.cover

# Translations
*.pot

# Django stuff:
*.log

# PyBuilder
target
```

Save the file and exit the editor. For every other Python package in your project, you will need to ignore several files and directories too. Just go to a directory and type the following command:

$ svn propedit svn:ignore .

Then, put this in the temporary file, save it, and close the editor, as follows:

```
# Byte-compiled / optimized / DLL files
__pycache__
*.py[cod]
*$py.class


# C extensions
*.so

# PyInstaller
*.manifest
*.spec

# Installer logs
pip-log.txt
pip-delete-this-directory.txt

# Unit test / coverage reports
htmlcov
.tox
.coverage
.coverage.*
.cache
nosetests.xml
coverage.xml
*.cover

# Translations
*.pot

# Django stuff:
*.log

# PyBuilder
target
```

How it works...

In Subversion, you need to define the ignore properties for each directory of your project. Mainly, we don't want to track the Python-compiled files, for instance, `*.pyc`. We also want to ignore `local_settings.py` that is specific for each environment, `static` that replicates collected static files from different apps, `media` that contains uploaded files and changes together with the database, and `tmp` that is temporarily used for file uploads.

 If you keep all your settings in a `conf` Python package as described in the *Configuring settings for development, testing, staging, and production environments* recipe, add `settings.py` to the ignored files too.

See also

▸ The *Creating and including local settings* recipe

▸ The *Creating the Git ignore file* recipe

Creating the Git ignore file

If you are using Git—the most popular distributed version control system—ignoring some files and folders from version control is much easier than with Subversion.

Getting ready

Make sure that your Django project is under the Git version control.

How to do it...

Using your favorite text editor, create a `.gitignore` file at the root of your Django project and put these files and directories there, as follows:

```
# .gitignore
# Project files and directories
/myproject/local_settings.py
/myproject/static/
/myproject/tmp/
/myproject/media/

# Byte-compiled / optimized / DLL files
__pycache__/
```

```
*.py[cod]
*$py.class

# C extensions
*.so

# PyInstaller
*.manifest
*.spec

# Installer logs
pip-log.txt
pip-delete-this-directory.txt

# Unit test / coverage reports
htmlcov/
.tox/
.coverage
.coverage.*
.cache
nosetests.xml
coverage.xml
*.cover

# Translations
*.pot

# Django stuff:
*.log

# Sphinx documentation
docs/_build/

# PyBuilder
target/
```

How it works...

The `.gitignore` file specifies the paths that should intentionally be untracked by the Git version control system. The `.gitignore` file that we created in this recipe will ignore the Python-compiled files, local settings, collected static files, temporary directory for uploads, and media directory with the uploaded files.

> If you keep all your settings in a `conf` Python package as described in the *Configuring settings for development, testing, staging, and production environments* recipe, add `settings.py` to the ignored files too.

See also

▶   The *Setting the Subversion ignore property* recipe

Deleting Python-compiled files

When you run your project for the first time, Python compiles all your `*.py` code in bytecode-compiled files, `*.pyc`, which are used later for execution.

Normally, when you change the `*.py` files, `*.pyc` is recompiled; however, sometimes when switching branches or moving the directories, you need to clean up the compiled files manually.

Getting ready

Use your favorite editor and edit or create a `.bash_profile` file in your home directory.

How to do it...

Add this alias at the end of `.bash_profile`, as follows:

```
# ~/.bash_profile
alias delpyc="find . -name \"*.pyc\" -delete"
```

Now, to clean the Python-compiled files, go to your project directory and type the following command in the command line:

```
$ delpyc
```

How it works...

At first, we create a Unix alias that searches for the `*.pyc` files and deletes them in the current directory and its children. The `.bash_profile` file is executed when you start a new session in the command-line tool.

See also

▸   The *Setting the Subversion ignore property* recipe

▸   The *Creating the Git ignore file* recipe

Respecting the import order in Python files

When you create the Python modules, it is good practice to stay consistent with the structure in the files. This makes it easier for other developers and yourself to read the code. This recipe will show you how to structure your imports.

Getting ready

Create a virtual environment and a Django project in it.

How to do it...

Use the following structure in a Python file that you create. Just after the first line that defines UTF-8 as the default Python file encoding, put the imports categorized in sections, as follows:

```
# -*- coding: UTF-8 -*-
# System libraries
from __future__ import unicode_literals
import os
import re
from datetime import datetime

# Third-party libraries
import boto
from PIL import Image

# Django modules
from django.db import models
from django.conf import settings

# Django apps
from cms.models import Page

# Current-app modules
from . import app_settings
```

How it works...

We have five main categories for the imports, as follows:

- System libraries for packages in the default installation of Python
- Third-party libraries for the additionally installed Python packages
- Django modules for different modules from the Django framework
- Django apps for third-party and local apps
- Current-app modules for relative imports from the current app

There's more...

When coding in Python and Django, use the official style guide for Python code, PEP 8. You can find it at `https://www.python.org/dev/peps/pep-0008/`.

See also

- The *Handling project dependencies with pip* recipe
- The *Including external dependencies in your project* recipe

Creating app configuration

When developing a website with Django, you create one module for the project itself and then, multiple Python modules called applications or apps that combine the different modular functionalities and usually consist of models, views, forms, URL configurations, management commands, migrations, signals, tests, and so on. The Django framework has application registry, where all apps and models are collected and later used for configuration and introspection. Since Django 1.7, meta information about apps can be saved in the `AppConfig` instance for each used app. Let's create a sample `magazine` app to take a look at how to use the app configuration there.

Getting ready

Either create your Django app manually or using this command in your virtual environment (learn how to use virtual environments in the *Working with a virtual environment* recipe), as follows:

```
(myproject_env)$ django-admin.py startapp magazine
```

Add some `NewsArticle` model to `models.py`, create administration for the model in `admin.py`, and put `"magazine"` in `INSTALLED_APPS` in the settings. If you are not yet familiar with these tasks, study the official Django tutorial at `https://docs.djangoproject.com/en/1.8/intro/tutorial01/`.

How to do it...

Follow these steps to create and use the app configuration:

1. First of all, create the `apps.py` file and put this content in it, as follows:

```python
# magazine/apps.py
# -*- coding: UTF-8 -*-
from __future__ import unicode_literals
from django.apps import AppConfig
from django.utils.translation import ugettext_lazy as _


class MagazineAppConfig(AppConfig):
    name = "magazine"
    verbose_name = _("Magazine")

    def ready(self):
        from . import signals
```

2. Then, edit the `__init__.py` file of the app and put the following content:

```python
# magazine/__init__.py
# -*- coding: UTF-8 -*-
from __future__ import unicode_literals
default_app_config = "magazine.apps.MagazineAppConfig"
```

3. Lastly, let's create a `signals.py` file and add some signal handlers there:

```python
# magazine/signals.py
# -*- coding: UTF-8 -*-
from __future__ import unicode_literals
from django.db.models.signals import post_save, post_delete
from django.dispatch import receiver
from django.conf import settings
from .models import NewsArticle


@receiver(post_save, sender=NewsArticle)
def news_save_handler(sender, **kwargs):
    if settings.DEBUG:
        print("%s saved." % kwargs['instance'])


@receiver(post_delete, sender=NewsArticle)
```

```
def news_delete_handler(sender, **kwargs):
    if settings.DEBUG:
        print("%s deleted." % kwargs['instance'])
```

How it works...

When you run an HTTP server or invoke a management command, `django.setup()` is called. It loads the settings, sets up logging, and initializes app registry. The app registry is initialized in three steps, as shown in the following:

- ▶ Django imports the configurations for each item from `INSTALLED_APPS` in the settings. These items can point to app names or configuration directly, for example,`"magazine"` or `"magazine.apps.NewsAppConfig"`.

- ▶ Django tries to import `models.py` from each app in `INSTALLED_APPS` and collect all the models.

- ▶ Finally, Django runs the `ready()` method for each app configuration. This method is a correct place to register signal handlers, if you have any. The `ready()` method is optional.

- ▶ In our example, the `MagazineAppConfig` class sets the configuration for the `magazine` app. The `name` parameter defines the name of the current app. The `verbose_name` parameter is used in the Django model administration, where models are presented and grouped by apps. The `ready()` method imports and activates the signal handlers that, when in DEBUG mode, print in the terminal that a `NewsArticle` was saved or deleted.

There is more...

After calling `django.setup()`, you can load the app configurations and models from the registry as follows:

```
>>> from django.apps import apps as django_apps
>>> magazine_app_config = django_apps.get_app_config("magazine")
>>> magazine_app_config
<MagazineAppConfig: magazine>
>>> magazine_app_config.models_module
<module 'magazine.models' from 'magazine/models.pyc'>
NewsArticle = django_apps.get_model("magazine", "NewsArticle")
```

You can read more about app configuration in the official Django documentation at `https://docs.djangoproject.com/en/1.8/ref/applications/`

See also

- ▸ The *Working with a virtual environment* recipe
- ▸ The *Defining overwritable app settings* recipe
- ▸ *Chapter 6, Model Administration*

Defining overwritable app settings

This recipe will show you how to define settings for your app that can be then overwritten in your project's `settings.py` or `local_settings.py` file. This is useful especially for reusable apps.

Getting ready

Either create your Django app manually or using the following command:

```
(myproject_env)$ django-admin.py startapp myapp1
```

How to do it...

If you just have one or two settings, you can use the following pattern in your `models.py` file. If the settings are extensive and you want to have them organized better, create an `app_settings.py` file in the app and put the settings in the following way:

```python
# models.py or app_settings.py
# -*- coding: UTF-8 -*-
from __future__ import unicode_literals
from django.conf import settings
from django.utils.translation import ugettext_lazy as _

SETTING1 = getattr(settings, "MYAPP1_SETTING1", u"default value")
MEANING_OF_LIFE = getattr(settings, "MYAPP1_MEANING_OF_LIFE", 42)
STATUS_CHOICES = getattr(settings, "MYAPP1_STATUS_CHOICES", (
    ("draft", _("Draft")),
    ("published", _("Published")),
    ("not_listed", _("Not Listed")),
))
```

Then, you can use the app settings in `models.py`, as follows:

```python
# models.py
# -*- coding: UTF-8 -*-
from __future__ import unicode_literals
from django.db import models
from django.utils.translation import ugettext_lazy as _

from .app_settings import STATUS_CHOICES

class NewsArticle(models.Model):
    # ...
    status = models.CharField(_("Status"),
        max_length=20, choices=STATUS_CHOICES
    )
```

If you want to overwrite the `STATUS_CHOICES` setting for just one project, you simply open `settings.py` and add the following:

```python
# settings.py
# ...
from django.utils.translation import ugettext_lazy as _
MYAPP1_STATUS_CHOICES = (
    ("imported", _("Imported")),
    ("draft", _("Draft")),
    ("published", _("Published")),
    ("not_listed", _("Not Listed")),
    ("expired", _("Expired")),
)
```

How it works...

The `getattr(object, attribute_name[, default_value])` Python function tries to get the `attribute_name` attribute from object and returns `default_value` if it is not found. In this case, different settings are tried in order to be taken from the Django project settings module, and if they are not found, the default values are assigned.

2
Database Structure

In this chapter, we will cover the following topics:

- ▶ Using model mixins
- ▶ Creating a model mixin with URL-related methods
- ▶ Creating a model mixin to handle creation and modification dates
- ▶ Creating a model mixin to take care of meta tags
- ▶ Creating a model mixin to handle generic relations
- ▶ Handling multilingual fields
- ▶ Using migrations
- ▶ Switching from South migrations to Django migrations
- ▶ Changing a foreign key to the many-to-many field

Introduction

When you start a new app, the first thing to do is create the models that represent your database structure. We are assuming that you have previously created Django apps or at least, you have read and understood the official Django tutorial. In this chapter, we will see a few interesting techniques that make your database structure consistent throughout different apps in your project. Then, we will see how to create custom model fields in order to handle internationalization of your data in the database. At the end of the chapter, we will see how to use migrations to change your database structure in the process of development.

Using model mixins

In object-oriented languages, such as Python, a mixin class can be viewed as an interface with implemented features. When a model extends a mixin, it implements the interface and includes all its fields, properties, and methods. Mixins in Django models can be used when you want to reuse the generic functionalities in different models multiple times.

Getting ready

First, you will need to create reusable mixins. Some typical examples of mixins are given later in this chapter. A good place to keep your model mixins is in the `utils` module.

 If you create a reusable app that you will share with others, keep the model mixins in the reusable app, for example, in the `base.py` file.

How to do it...

Open the `models.py` file of any Django app, where you want to use the mixins and type the following code:

```
# demo_app/models.py
# -*- coding: UTF-8 -*-
from __future__ import unicode_literals
from django.db import models
from django.utils.translation import ugettext_lazy as _
from django.utils.encoding import python_2_unicode_compatible
from utils.models import UrlMixin
from utils.models import CreationModificationMixin
from utils.models import MetaTagsMixin


@python_2_unicode_compatible
class Idea(UrlMixin, CreationModificationMixin, MetaTagsMixin):
    title = models.CharField(_("Title"), max_length=200)
    content = models.TextField(_("Content"))

    class Meta:
        verbose_name = _("Idea")
        verbose_name_plural = _("Ideas")

    def __str__(self):
        return self.title
```

How it works...

Django model inheritance supports three types of inheritance: abstract base classes, multi-table inheritance, and proxy models. Model mixins are abstract model classes with specified fields, properties, and methods. When you create a model such as `Idea`, as shown in the preceding example, it inherits all the features from `UrlMixin`, `CreationModificationMixin`, and `MetaTagsMixin`. All the fields of the abstract classes are saved in the same database table as the fields of the extending model. In the following recipes, you will learn how to define your model mixins.

Note that we are using the `@python_2_unicode_compatible` decorator for our `Idea` model. As you might remember from the *Making your code compatible with both Python 2.7 and Python 3* recipe in *Chapter 1, Getting Started with Django 1.8*, it's purpose is to make the `__str__()` method compatible with Unicode for both the following Python versions: 2.7 and 3.

There's more...

To learn more about the different types of model inheritance, refer to the official Django documentation available at `https://docs.djangoproject.com/en/1.8/topics/db/models/#model-inheritance`.

See also

  ▶ The *Making your code compatible with both Python 2.7 and Python 3* recipe in *Chapter 1, Getting Started with Django 1.8*

  ▶ The *Creating a model mixin with URL-related methods recipe*

  ▶ The *Creating a model mixin to handle creation and modification dates* recipe

  ▶ The *Creating a model mixin to take care of meta tags* recipe

Creating a model mixin with URL-related methods

For every model that has its own page, it is good practice to define the `get_absolute_url()` method. This method can be used in templates and also in the Django admin site to preview the saved object. However, `get_absolute_url()` is ambiguous as it returns the URL path instead of the full URL. In this recipe, we will see how to create a model mixin that allows you to define either the URL path or the full URL by default, generate the other out of the box, and take care of the `get_absolute_url()` method that is being set.

Getting ready

If you haven't done it yet, create the `utils` package to save your mixins. Then, create the `models.py` file in the `utils` package (alternatively, if you create a reusable app, put the mixins in the `base.py` file in your app).

How to do it...

Execute the following steps one by one:

1. Add the following content to the `models.py` file of your `utils` package:

```python
# utils/models.py
# -*- coding: UTF-8 -*-
from __future__ import unicode_literals
import urlparse
from django.db import models
from django.contrib.sites.models import Site
from django.conf import settings

class UrlMixin(models.Model):
    """
    A replacement for get_absolute_url()
    Models extending this mixin should have
    either get_url or get_url_path implemented.
    """
    class Meta:
        abstract = True

    def get_url(self):
        if hasattr(self.get_url_path, "dont_recurse"):
            raise NotImplementedError
        try:
            path = self.get_url_path()
        except NotImplementedError:
            raise
        website_url = getattr(
            settings, "DEFAULT_WEBSITE_URL",
            "http://127.0.0.1:8000"
        )
        return website_url + path
    get_url.dont_recurse = True

    def get_url_path(self):
```

```
    if hasattr(self.get_url, "dont_recurse"):
        raise NotImplementedError
    try:
        url = self.get_url()
    except NotImplementedError:
        raise
    bits = urlparse.urlparse(url)
    return urlparse.urlunparse(("", "") + bits[2:])
get_url_path.dont_recurse = True

def get_absolute_url(self):
    return self.get_url_path()
```

2. To use the mixin in your app, import it from the `utils` package, inherit the mixin in your model class, and define the `get_url_path()` method as follows:

```
# demo_app/models.py
# -*- coding: UTF-8 -*-
from __future__ import unicode_literals
from django.db import models
from django.utils.translation import ugettext_lazy as _
from django.core.urlresolvers import reverse
from django.utils.encoding import \
    python_2_unicode_compatible

from utils.models import UrlMixin

@python_2_unicode_compatible
class Idea(UrlMixin):
    title = models.CharField(_("Title"), max_length=200)

    # …

    get_url_path(self):
        return reverse("idea_details", kwargs={
            "idea_id": str(self.pk),
        })
```

3. If you check this code in the staging or production environment or run a local server with a different IP or port than the defaults, set `DEFAULT_WEBSITE_URL` in your local settings (without the trailing slash), as follows:

```
# settings.py
# …
DEFAULT_WEBSITE_URL = "http://www.example.com"
```

How it works...

The `UrlMixin` class is an abstract model that has three methods: `get_url()`, `get_url_path()`, and `get_absolute_url()`. The `get_url()` or `get_url_path()` methods are expected to be overwritten in the extended model class, for example, `Idea`. You can define `get_url()`, which is the full URL of the object, and then `get_url_path()` will strip it to the path. You can also define `get_url_path()`, which is the absolute path of the object, and then `get_url()` will prepend the website URL to the beginning of the path. The `get_absolute_url()` method will mimic the `get_url_path()` method.

 The rule of thumb is to always overwrite the `get_url_path()` method.

In the templates, use `<a href="{{ idea.get_url_path }}">{{ idea.title }}</a>` when you need a link of an object in the same website. Use `<a href="{{ idea.get_url }}">{{ idea.title }}</a>` for the links in e-mails, RSS feeds, or APIs.

The default `get_absolute_url()` method will be used in the Django model administration for the *View on site* functionality and might also be used by some third-party Django apps.

See also

- The *Using model mixins* recipe
- The *Creating a model mixin to handle creation and modification dates* recipe
- The *Creating a model mixin to take care of meta tags* recipe
- The *Creating a model mixin to handle generic relations* recipe

Creating a model mixin to handle creation and modification dates

It is a common behavior to have timestamps in your models for the creation and modification of your model instances. In this recipe, we will see how to create a simple model mixin that saves the creation and modification dates and times for your model. Using such a mixin will ensure that all the models use the same field names for the timestamps and have the same behavior.

Getting ready

If you haven't done this yet, create the `utils` package to save your mixins. Then, create the `models.py` file in the `utils` package.

How to do it...

Open the `models.py` file of your `utils` package and insert the following content there:

```python
# utils/models.py
# -*- coding: UTF-8 -*-
from __future__ import unicode_literals
from django.db import models
from django.utils.translation import ugettext_lazy as _
from django.utils.timezone import now as timezone_now


class CreationModificationDateMixin(models.Model):
    """
    Abstract base class with a creation and modification
    date and time
    """

    created = models.DateTimeField(
        _("creation date and time"),
        editable=False,
    )

    modified = models.DateTimeField(
        _("modification date and time"),
        null=True,
        editable=False,
    )

    def save(self, *args, **kwargs):
        if not self.pk:
            self.created = timezone_now()
        else:
            # To ensure that we have a creation data always,
            # we add this one
        if not self.created:
            self.created = timezone_now()

            self.modified = timezone_now()

            super(CreationModificationDateMixin, self).\
            save(*args, **kwargs)
        save.alters_data = True

    class Meta:
        abstract = True
```

How it works...

The `CreationModificationDateMixin` class is an abstract model, which means that extending model classes will create all the fields in the same database table, that is, there will be no one-to-one relationships that make the table difficult to handle. This mixin has two date-time fields and the `save()` method that will be called when saving the extended model. The `save()` method checks whether the model has no primary key, which is the case of a new not-yet-saved instance. In this case, it sets the creation date to the current date and time. If the primary key exists, the modification date is set to the current date and time.

Alternatively, instead of the `save()` method, you can use the `auto_now_add` and `auto_now` attributes for the created and modified fields, which will add creation and modification timestamps automatically.

See also

- The *Using model mixins* recipe
- The *Creating a model mixin to take care of meta tags* recipe
- The *Creating a model mixin to handle generic relations* recipe

Creating a model mixin to take care of meta tags

If you want to optimize your site for search engines, you need to not only set the semantic markup for each page but also the appropriate meta tags. For maximum flexibility, you need to have a way to define specific meta tags for each object, which has its own page on your website. In this recipe, we will see how to create a model mixin for the fields and methods related to the meta tags.

Getting ready

As seen in the previous recipes, make sure that you have the `utils` package for your mixins. Open the `models.py` file from this package in your favorite editor.

How to do it...

Put the following content in the `models.py` file:

```
# utils/models.py
# -*- coding: UTF-8 -*-
from __future__ import unicode_literals
from django.db import models
```

```python
from django.utils.translation import ugettext_lazy as _
from django.template.defaultfilters import escape
from django.utils.safestring import mark_safe

class MetaTagsMixin(models.Model):
    """
    Abstract base class for meta tags in the <head> section
    """
    meta_keywords = models.CharField(
        _("Keywords"),
        max_length=255,
        blank=True,
        help_text=_("Separate keywords by comma."),
    )
    meta_description = models.CharField(
        _("Description"),
        max_length=255,
        blank=True,
    )
    meta_author = models.CharField(
        _("Author"),
        max_length=255,
        blank=True,
    )
    meta_copyright = models.CharField(
        _("Copyright"),
        max_length=255,
        blank=True,
    )

    class Meta:
        abstract = True

    def get_meta_keywords(self):
        tag = ""
        if self.meta_keywords:
            tag = '<meta name="keywords" content="%s" />\n' %\
                escape(self.meta_keywords)
        return mark_safe(tag)

    def get_meta_description(self):
        tag = ""
        if self.meta_description:
            tag = '<meta name="description" content="%s" />\n' %\
```

```
        escape(self.meta_description)
    return mark_safe(tag)

def get_meta_author(self):
    tag = ""
    if self.meta_author:
        tag = '<meta name="author" content="%s" />\n' %\
            escape(self.meta_author)
    return mark_safe(tag)

def get_meta_copyright(self):
    tag = ""
    if self.meta_copyright:
        tag = '<meta name="copyright" content="%s" />\n' %\
            escape(self.meta_copyright)
    return mark_safe(tag)

def get_meta_tags(self):
    return mark_safe("".join((
        self.get_meta_keywords(),
        self.get_meta_description(),
        self.get_meta_author(),
        self.get_meta_copyright(),
    )))
```

How it works...

This mixin adds four fields to the model that extends from it: `meta_keywords`, `meta_description`, `meta_author`, and `meta_copyright`. The methods to render the meta tags in HTML are also added.

If you use this mixin in a model such as `Idea`, which is shown in the first recipe of this chapter, then you can put the following in the `HEAD` section of your detail page template to render all the meta tags:

```
{{ idea.get_meta_tags }}
```

You can also render a specific meta tag using the following line:

```
{{ idea.get_meta_description }}
```

As you may have noticed from the code snippet, the rendered meta tags are marked as safe, that is, they are not escaped and we don't need to use the safe template filter. Only the values that come from the database are escaped in order to guarantee that the final HTML is well-formed.

See also

- ▶ The *Using model mixins* recipe
- ▶ The *Creating a model mixin to handle creation and modification dates* recipe
- ▶ The *Creating a model mixin to handle generic relations* recipe

Creating a model mixin to handle generic relations

Besides normal database relationships such as a foreign-key relationship or many-to-many relationship, Django has a mechanism to relate a model to an instance of any other model. This concept is called generic relations. For each generic relation, there is a content type of the related model that is saved as well as the ID of the instance of this model.

In this recipe, we will see how to generalize the creation of generic relations in the model mixins.

Getting ready

For this recipe to work, you need to have the `contenttypes` app installed. It should be in the `INSTALLED_APPS` directory by default, as shown in the following:

```
# settings.py
INSTALLED_APPS = (
    # …
    "django.contrib.contenttypes",
)
```

Again, make sure that you have the `utils` package for your model mixins already created.

How to do it...

1. Open the `models.py` file in the `utils` package in a text editor and insert the following content there:

```
# utils/models.py
# -*- coding: UTF-8 -*-
from __future__ import unicode_literals
from django.db import models
from django.utils.translation import ugettext_lazy as _
from django.contrib.contenttypes.models import ContentType
from django.contrib.contenttypes import generic
```

```
from django.core.exceptions import FieldError


def object_relation_mixin_factory(
    prefix=None,
    prefix_verbose=None,
    add_related_name=False,
    limit_content_type_choices_to={},
    limit_object_choices_to={},
    is_required=False,
):
    """
        returns a mixin class for generic foreign keys using
        "Content type - object Id" with dynamic field names.
        This function is just a class generator

        Parameters:
        prefix : a prefix, which is added in front of the
            fields
        prefix_verbose :    a verbose name of the prefix, used
            to
                            generate a title for the field
                                column
                            of the content object in the Admin.
        add_related_name :  a boolean value indicating, that a
                            related name for the generated
                                content
                            type foreign key should be added.
                                This
                            value should be true, if you use
                                more
                            than one ObjectRelationMixin in
                                your model.

        The model fields are created like this:

        <<prefix>>_content_type :   Field name for the "content
            type"
        <<prefix>>_object_id :      Field name for the "object
            Id"
        <<prefix>>_content_object : Field name for the "content
            object"

    """
    p = ""
```

```python
if prefix:
  p = "%s_" % prefix

content_type_field = "%scontent_type" % p
object_id_field = "%sobject_id" % p
content_object_field = "%scontent_object" % p


class TheClass(models.Model):
  class Meta:
    abstract = True

if add_related_name:
  if not prefix:
    raise FieldError("if add_related_name is set to
      True,"
      "a prefix must be given")
    related_name = prefix
else:
  related_name = None


optional = not is_required

ct_verbose_name = (
  _("%s's type (model)") % prefix_verbose
  if prefix_verbose
  else _("Related object's type (model)")
)

content_type = models.ForeignKey(
  ContentType,
  verbose_name=ct_verbose_name,
  related_name=related_name,
  blank=optional,
  null=optional,
  help_text=_("Please select the type (model) for the
    relation, you want to build."),
  limit_choices_to=limit_content_type_choices_to,
)

fk_verbose_name = (prefix_verbose or _("Related
  object"))
```

```
object_id = models.CharField(
  fk_verbose_name,
  blank=optional,
  null=False,
  help_text=_("Please enter the ID of the related
    object."),
  max_length=255,
  default="",  # for south migrations
)
object_id.limit_choices_to = limit_object_choices_to
# can be retrieved by
# MyModel._meta.get_field("object_id").limit_choices_to

content_object = generic.GenericForeignKey(
  ct_field=content_type_field,
  fk_field=object_id_field,
)

TheClass.add_to_class(content_type_field, content_type)
TheClass.add_to_class(object_id_field, object_id)
TheClass.add_to_class(content_object_field,
  content_object)

return TheClass
```

2. The following is an example of how to use two generic relationships in your app (put
    this code in demo_app/models.py), as shown in the following:

```
# demo_app/models.py
# -*- coding: UTF-8 -*-
from __future__ import nicode_literals
from django.db import models
from utils.models import object_relation_mixin_factory
from django.utils.encoding import python_2_unicode_compatible

FavoriteObjectMixin = object_relation_mixin_factory(
    is_required=True,
)

OwnerMixin = object_relation_mixin_factory(
    prefix="owner",
    prefix_verbose=_("Owner"),
    add_related_name=True,
    limit_content_type_choices_to={
        'model__in': ('user', 'institution')
    },
```

```
            is_required=True,
        )

    @python_2_unicode_compatible
    class Like(FavoriteObjectMixin, OwnerMixin):
        class Meta:
            verbose_name = _("Like")
            verbose_name_plural = _("Likes")

        def __str__(self):
            return _("%(owner)s likes %(obj)s") % {
                "owner": self.owner_content_object,
                "obj": self.content_object,
            }
```

How it works...

As you can see, this snippet is more complex than the previous ones. The `object_relation_mixin_factory` object is not a mixin itself; it is a function that generates a model mixin, that is, an abstract model class to extend from. The dynamically created mixin adds the `content_type` and `object_id` fields and the `content_object` generic foreign key that points to the related instance.

Why couldn't we just define a simple model mixin with these three attributes? A dynamically generated abstract class allows us to have prefixes for each field name; therefore, we can have more than one generic relation in the same model. For example, the `Like` model, which was shown previously, will have the `content_type`, `object_id`, and `content_object` fields for the favorite object and `owner_content_type`, `owner_object_id`, and `owner_content_object` for the one (user or institution) who liked the object.

The `object_relation_mixin_factory()` function adds a possibility to limit the content type choices by the `limit_content_type_choices_to` parameter. The preceding example limits the choices for `owner_content_type` only to the content types of the `User` and `Institution` models. Also, there is the `limit_object_choices_to` parameter that can be used by custom form validation to limit the generic relations only to specific objects, for example, the objects with published status.

See also

▶ The *Creating a model mixin with URL-related methods* recipe

▶ The *Creating a model mixin to handle creation and modification dates* recipe

▶ The *Creating a model mixin to take care of meta tags* recipe

▶ The *Implementing the Like widget* recipe in *Chapter 4, Templates and JavaScript*

Handling multilingual fields

Django uses the internationalization mechanism to translate verbose strings in the code and templates. However, it's up to the developer to decide how to implement the multilingual content in the models. There are several third-party modules that handle translatable model fields; however, I prefer the simple solution that will be introduced to you in this recipe.

The advantages of the approach that you will learn about are as follows:

▶ It is straightforward to define multilingual fields in the database

▶ It is simple to use the multilingual fields in database queries

▶ You can use contributed administration to edit models with the multilingual fields without additional modifications

▶ If you need it, you can easily show all the translations of an object in the same template

▶ You can use database migrations to add or remove languages

Getting ready

Do you have the `utils` package created? You will now need a new `fields.py` file for the custom model fields there.

How to do it...

Execute the following steps to define the multilingual character field and multilingual text field:

1. Open the `fields.py` file and create the multilingual character field as follows:

```
# utils/fields.py
# -*- coding: UTF-8 -*-
from __future__ import unicode_literals
from django.conf import settings
from django.db import models
from django.utils.translation import get_language
from django.utils.translation import string_concat

class MultilingualCharField(models.CharField):

    def __init__(self, verbose_name=None, **kwargs):

        self._blank = kwargs.get("blank", False)
```

```python
    self._editable = kwargs.get("editable", True)

    super(MultilingualCharField, self).\
        __init__(verbose_name, **kwargs)

def contribute_to_class(self, cls, name,
    virtual_only=False):
    # generate language specific fields dynamically
    if not cls._meta.abstract:
        for lang_code, lang_name in settings.LANGUAGES:
            if lang_code == settings.LANGUAGE_CODE:
                _blank = self._blank
            else:
                _blank = True

            localized_field = models.CharField(
                string_concat(self.verbose_name,
                    " (%s)" % lang_code),
                        name=self.name,
                            primary_key=self.primary_key,
                            max_length=self.max_length,
                            unique=self.unique,
                            blank=_blank,
                            null=False,
                            # we ignore the null argument!
                            db_index=self.db_index,
                            rel=self.rel,
                            default=self.default or "",
                            editable=self._editable,
                            serialize=self.serialize,
                            choices=self.choices,
                            help_text=self.help_text,
                            db_column=None,
                            db_tablespace=self.db_tablespace
            )
            localized_field.contribute_to_class(
                cls,
                "%s_%s" % (name, lang_code),
            )

            def translated_value(self):
                language = get_language()
                val = self.__dict__["%s_%s" % (name, language)]
                if not val:
```

```
            val = self.__dict__["%s_%s" % \
              (name, settings.LANGUAGE_CODE)]
            return val

        setattr(cls, name, property(translated_value))
```

2. In the same file, add an analogous multilingual text field. The differing parts are highlighted in the following code:

```
class MultilingualTextField(models.TextField):

    def __init__(self, verbose_name=None, **kwargs):

        self._blank = kwargs.get("blank", False)
        self._editable = kwargs.get("editable", True)

        super(MultilingualTextField, self).\
            __init__(verbose_name, **kwargs)

    def contribute_to_class(self, cls, name,
        virtual_only=False):
        # generate language specific fields dynamically
        if not cls._meta.abstract:
            for lang_code, lang_name in settings.LANGUAGES:
                if lang_code == settings.LANGUAGE_CODE:
                    _blank = self._blank
                else:
                    _blank = True

                localized_field = models.TextField(
                    string_concat(self.verbose_name,
                        " (%s)" % lang_code),
                    name=self.name,
                    primary_key=self.primary_key,
                    max_length=self.max_length,
                    unique=self.unique,
                    blank=_blank,
                    null=False,
                    # we ignore the null argument!
                    db_index=self.db_index,
                    rel=self.rel,
                    default=self.default or "",
                    editable=self._editable,
                    serialize=self.serialize,
                    choices=self.choices,
```

```
                    help_text=self.help_text,
                    db_column=None,
                    db_tablespace=self.db_tablespace
                )
                localized_field.contribute_to_class(
                    cls,
                       "%s_%s" % (name, lang_code),
                )

          def translated_value(self):
              language = get_language()
              val = self.__dict__["%s_%s" % (name, language)]
              if not val:
                 val = self.__dict__["%s_%s" % \
                    (name, settings.LANGUAGE_CODE)]
                 return val

          setattr(cls, name, property(translated_value))
```

Now, we'll consider an example of how to use the multilingual fields in your app, as shown in the following:

1. First, set multiple languages in your settings:

```python
# myproject/settings.py
# -*- coding: UTF-8 -*-
# …
LANGUAGE_CODE = "en"

LANGUAGES = (
    ("en", "English"),
    ("de", "Deutsch"),
    ("fr", "Français"),
    ("lt", "Lietuvi kalba"),
)
```

2. Then, create the multilingual fields for your model, as follows:

```python
# demo_app/models.py
# -*- coding: UTF-8 -*-
from __future__ import unicode_literals
from django.db import models
from django.utils.translation import ugettext_lazy as _
from django.utils.encoding import \
    python_2_unicode_compatible

from utils.fields import MultilingualCharField
```

```
from utils.fields import MultilingualTextField

@python_2_unicode_compatible
class Idea(models.Model):
    title = MultilingualCharField(
        _("Title"),
        max_length=200,
    )
    description = MultilingualTextField(
        _("Description"),
        blank=True,
    )

    class Meta:
        verbose_name = _("Idea")
        verbose_name_plural = _("Ideas")

    def __str__(self):
        return self.title
```

How it works...

The example of Idea will create a model that is similar to the following:

```
class Idea(models.Model):
    title_en = models.CharField(
        _("Title (en)"),
        max_length=200,
    )
    title_de = models.CharField(
        _("Title (de)"),
        max_length=200,
        blank=True,
    )
    title_fr = models.CharField(
        _("Title (fr)"),
        max_length=200,
        blank=True,
    )
    title_lt = models.CharField(
        _("Title (lt)"),
        max_length=200,
        blank=True,
    )
```

```python
description_en = models.TextField(
    _("Description (en)"),
    blank=True,
)
description_de = models.TextField(
    _("Description (de)"),
    blank=True,
)
description_fr = models.TextField(
    _("Description (fr)"),
    blank=True,
)
description_lt = models.TextField(
    _("Description (lt)"),
    blank=True,
)
```

In addition to this, there will be two properties: `title` and `description` that will return the title and description in the currently active language.

The `MultilingualCharField` and `MultilingualTextField` fields will juggle the model fields dynamically, depending on your `LANGUAGES` setting. They will overwrite the `contribute_to_class()` method that is used when the Django framework creates the model classes. The multilingual fields dynamically add character or text fields for each language of the project. Also, the properties are created in order to return the translated value of the currently active language or the main language by default.

For example, you can have the following in the template:

```html
<h1>{{ idea.title }}</h1>
<div>{{ idea.description|urlize|linebreaks }}</div>
```

This will show the text in English, German, French, or Lithuanian, depending on the currently selected language. However, it will fall back to English if the translation doesn't exist.

Here is another example. If you want to have your `QuerySet` ordered by the translated titles in the view, you can define it as follows:

```python
qs = Idea.objects.order_by("title_%s" % request.LANGUAGE_CODE)
```

Using migrations

It is not true that once you have created your database structure, it won't change in the future. As development happens iteratively, you can get updates on the business requirements in the development process and you will need to perform database schema changes along the way. With the Django migrations, you don't need to change the database tables and fields manually, as most of it is done automatically using the command-line interface.

Getting ready

Activate your virtual environment in the command-line tool.

How to do it...

To create the database migrations, take a look at the following steps:

1. When you create models in your new `demo_app` app, you need to create an initial migration that will create the database tables for your app. This can be done using the following command:

   ```
   (myproject_env)$ python manage.py makemigrations demo_app
   ```

2. The first time that you want to create all the tables for your project, run the following command:

   ```
   (myproject_env)$ python manage.py migrate
   ```

   It executes the usual database synchronization for all apps that have no database migrations, and in addition to this, it migrates all apps that have the migrations set. Also, run this command when you want to execute the new migrations for all your apps.

3. If you want to execute the migrations for a specific app, run the following command:

   ```
   (myproject_env)$ python manage.py migrate demo_app
   ```

4. If you make some changes in the database schema, you have to create a migration for that schema. For example, if we add a new subtitle field to the `Idea` model, we can create the migration using the following command:

   ```
   (myproject_env)$ python manage.py makemigrations --name \
   subtitle_added demo_app
   ```

5. To create a data migration that modifies the data in the database table, we can use the following command:

   ```
   (myproject_env)$ python manage.py makemigrations --empty \
   --name populate_subtitle demo_app
   ```

This creates a skeleton data migration, which you need to modify and add data manipulation to it before applying.

6. To list all the available applied and unapplied migrations, run the following command:

    ```
    (myproject_env)$ python manage.py migrate --list
    ```

    The applied migrations will be listed with a `[X]` prefix.

7. To list all the available migrations for a specific app, run the following command:

    ```
    (myproject_env)$ python manage.py migrate --list demo_app
    ```

How it works...

Django migrations are instruction files for the database migration mechanism. The instruction files inform us which database tables to create or remove; which fields to add or remove; and which data to insert, update, or delete.

There are two types of migrations in Django. One is schema migration and the other is data migration. Schema migration should be created when you add new models, or add or remove fields. Data migration should be used when you want to fill the database with some values or massively delete values from the database. Data migrations should be created using a command in the command-line tool and then programmed in the migration file. Migrations for each app are saved in their `migrations` directories. The first migration will be usually called `0001_initial.py`, and the other migrations in our example app will be called `0002_subtitle_added.py` and `0003_populate_subtitle.py`. Each migration gets a number prefix that is automatically incremented. For each migration that is executed, there is an entry that is saved in the `django_migrations` database table.

It is possible to migrate back and forth by specifying the number of the migration to which we want to migrate to, as shown in the following:

```
(myproject_env)$ python manage.py migrate demo_app 0002
```

If you want to undo all the migrations for a specific app, you can do so using the following command:

```
(myproject_env)$ python manage.py migrate demo_app zero
```

 Do not commit your migrations to version control until you have tested the forward and backward migration process and you are sure that they will work well in other development and public website environments.

See also

▸ The *Handling project dependencies with pip and Including external dependencies in your project* recipes in *Chapter 1, Getting Started with Django 1.8*

▸ The *Changing a foreign key to the many-to-many field* recipe

Switching from South migrations to Django migrations

If you, like me, have been using Django since before database migrations existed in the core functionality, that is, before Django 1.7; you have, more than likely, used third-party South migrations before. In this recipe, you will learn how to switch your project from South migrations to Django migrations.

Getting ready

Make sure that all apps and their South migrations are up to date.

How to do it...

Execute the following steps:

1. Migrate all your apps to the latest South migrations, as follows:

   ```
   (myproject_env)$ python manage.py migrate
   ```

2. Remove `south` from `INSTALLED_APPS` in the settings.

3. For each app with South migrations, delete the migration files and only leave the `migrations` directories.

4. Create new migration files with the following command:

   ```
   (my_project)$ python manage.py makemigrations
   ```

5. Fake the initial Django migrations as the database schema has already been set correctly:

   ```
   (my_project)$ python manage.py migrate --fake-initial
   ```

6. If you have any circular foreign keys in the apps (that is, two models in different apps pointing to each other with a foreign key or many-to-many relation), separately apply the fake initial migrations to these apps:

   ```
   (my_project)$ python manage.py migrate --fake-initial demo_app
   ```

How it works...

There is no conflict in the database when switching to the new way of dealing with the database schema changes as the South migration history is saved in the `south_ migrationhistory` database table; whereas, the Django migration history is saved in the `django_migrations` database table. The only problem are the migration files that have different syntax and, therefore, the South migrations need to be completely replaced with the Django migrations.

Therefore, at first, we delete the South migration files. Then, the `makemigrations` command recognizes the empty `migrations` directories and creates new initial Django migrations for each app. Once these migrations are faked, the further Django migrations can be created and applied.

See also

- ▸ The *Using migrations* recipe
- ▸ The *Changing a foreign key to the many-to-many field* recipe

Changing a foreign key to the many-to-many field

This recipe is a practical example of how to change a many-to-one relation to many-to-many relation, while preserving the already existing data. We will use both schema and data migrations for this situation.

Getting ready

Let's consider that you have the `Idea` model with a foreign key pointing to the `Category` model, as follows:

```python
# demo_app/models.py
# -*- coding: UTF-8 -*-
from __future__ import unicode_literals
from django.db import models
from django.utils.translation import ugettext_lazy as _
from django.utils.encoding import python_2_unicode_compatible

@python_2_unicode_compatible
class Category(models.Model):
```

```
        title = models.CharField(_("Title"), max_length=200)

        def __str__(self):
            return self.title

@python_2_unicode_compatible
class Idea(models.Model):
    title = model.CharField(_("Title"), max_length=200)
    category = models.ForeignKey(Category,
        verbose_name=_("Category"),  null=True, blank=True)

        def __str__(self):
            return self.title
```

The initial migration should be created and executed using the following commands:

```
(myproject_env)$ python manage.py makemigrations demo_app
(myproject_env)$ python manage.py migrate demo_app
```

How to do it...

The following steps will teach you how to switch from a foreign key relation to many-to-many relation, while preserving the already existing data:

1. Add a new many-to-many field called `categories`, as follows:

   ```
   # demo_app/models.py
   @python_2_unicode_compatible
   class Idea(models.Model):
       title = model.CharField(_("Title"), max_length=200)
       category = models.ForeignKey(Category,
           verbose_name=_("Category"),
           null=True,
           blank=True,
       )
       categories = models.ManyToManyField(Category,
           verbose_name=_("Categories"),
           blank=True,
           related_name="ideas",
       )
   ```

2. Create and run a schema migration in order to add the new field to the database, as shown in the following:

   ```
   (myproject_env)$ python manage.py makemigrations demo_app \
   --name categories_added
   (myproject_env)$ python manage.py migrate demo_app
   ```

3. Create a data migration to copy categories from the foreign key to the many-to-many field, as follows:

```
(myproject_env)$ python manage.py makemigrations --empty \
--name copy_categories demo_app
```

4. Open the newly created migration file (demo_app/migrations/0003_copy_categories.py) and define the forward migration instructions, as shown in the following:

```python
# demo_app/migrations/0003_copy_categories.py
# -*- coding: utf-8 -*-
from __future__ import unicode_literals
from django.db import models, migrations


def copy_categories(apps, schema_editor):
    Idea = apps.get_model("demo_app", "Idea")
    for idea in Idea.objects.all():
        if idea.category:
            idea.categories.add(idea.category)


class Migration(migrations.Migration):

    dependencies = [
        ('demo_app', '0002_categories_added'),
    ]

    operations = [
        migrations.RunPython(copy_categories),
    ]
```

5. Run the following data migration:

```
(myproject_env)$ python manage.py migrate demo_app
```

6. Delete the foreign key field category in the models.py file:

```python
# demo_app/models.py
@python_2_unicode_compatible
class Idea(models.Model):
    title = model.CharField(_("Title"), max_length=200)
    categories = models.ManyToManyField(Category,
        verbose_name=_("Categories"),
        blank=True,
        related_name="ideas",
    )
```

7. Create and run a schema migration in order to delete the categories field from the database table, as follows:

```
(myproject_env)$ python manage.py schemamigration \
--name delete_category demo_app
(myproject_env)$ python manage.py migrate demo_app
```

How it works...

At first, we add a new many-to-many field to the `Idea` model. Then, we copy the existing relations from a foreign key relation to the many-to-many relation. Lastly, we remove the foreign key relation.

See also

- The *Using migrations* recipe
- The *Switching from South migrations to Django migrations* recipe

3

Forms and Views

In this chapter, we will cover the following topics:

- ▸ Passing HttpRequest to the form
- ▸ Utilizing the save method of the form
- ▸ Uploading images
- ▸ Creating form layout with django-crispy-forms
- ▸ Downloading authorized files
- ▸ Filtering object lists
- ▸ Managing paginated lists
- ▸ Composing class-based views
- ▸ Generating PDF documents
- ▸ Implementing a multilingual search with Haystack

Introduction

When the database structure is defined in the models, we need some views to let the users enter data or show the data to the people. In this chapter, we will focus on the views managing forms, the list view, and views generating an alternative output than HTML. For the simplest examples, we will leave the creation of URL rules and templates up to you.

Passing HttpRequest to the form

The first argument of every Django view is the `HttpRequest` object that is usually named `request`. It contains metadata about the request. For example, current language code, current user, current cookies, and current session. By default, the forms that are used in the views accept the GET or POST parameters, files, initial data, and other parameters; however, not the `HttpRequest` object. In some cases, it is useful to additionally pass `HttpRequest` to the form, especially when you want to filter out the choices of form fields using the request data or handle saving something such as the current user or IP in the form.

In this recipe, we will see an example of a form where a person can choose a user and write a message to them. We will pass the `HttpRequest` object to the form in order to exclude the current user from the recipient choices; we don't want anybody to write a message to themselves.

Getting ready

Let's create a new app called `email_messages` and put it in `INSTALLED_APPS` in the settings. This app will have no models, just forms and views.

How to do it...

To complete this recipe, execute the following steps:

1. Add a new `forms.py` file with the message form containing two fields: the recipient selection and message text. Also, this form will have an initialization method, which will accept the request object and then, modify `QuerySet` for the recipient's selection field:

```
# email_messages/forms.py
# -*- coding: UTF-8 -*-
from __future__ import unicode_literals
from django import forms
from django.utils.translation import ugettext_lazy as _
from django.contrib.auth.models import User

class MessageForm(forms.Form):
    recipient = forms.ModelChoiceField(
        label=_("Recipient"),
        queryset=User.objects.all(),
        required=True,
    )
    message = forms.CharField(
        label=_("Message"),
```

```
            widget=forms.Textarea,
            required=True,
    )

    def __init__(self, request, *args, **kwargs):
        super(MessageForm, self).__init__(*args, **kwargs)
        self.request = request
        self.fields["recipient"].queryset = \
            self.fields["recipient"].queryset.\
            exclude(pk=request.user.pk)
```

2. Then, create `views.py` with the `message_to_user()` view in order to handle the form. As you can see, the request object is passed as the first parameter to the form, as follows:

```python
# email_messages/views.py
# -*- coding: UTF-8 -*-
from __future__ import unicode_literals
from django.contrib.auth.decorators import login_required
from django.shortcuts import render, redirect

from .forms import MessageForm

@login_required
def message_to_user(request):
    if request.method == "POST":
        form = MessageForm(request, data=request.POST)
        if form.is_valid():
            # do something with the form
            return redirect("message_to_user_done")
    else:
        form = MessageForm(request)

    return render(request,
        "email_messages/message_to_user.html",
        {"form": form}
    )
```

How it works...

In the initialization method, we have the `self` variable that represents the instance of the form itself, we also have the newly added `request` variable, and then we have the rest of the positional arguments (`*args`) and named arguments (`**kwargs`). We call the `super()` initialization method passing all the positional and named arguments to it so that the form is properly initiated. We will then assign the `request` variable to a new `request` attribute of the form for later access in other methods of the form. Then, we modify the `queryset` attribute of the recipient's selection field, excluding the current user from the request.

In the view, we will pass the `HttpRequest` object as the first argument in both situations: when the form is posted, as well as when it is loaded for the first time.

See also

- ► The *Utilizing the save method of the form* recipe

Utilizing the save method of the form

To make your views clean and simple, it is good practice to move the handling of the form data to the form itself whenever possible and makes sense. The common practice is to have a `save()` method that will save the data, perform search, or do some other smart actions. We will extend the form that is defined in the previous recipe with the `save()` method, which will send an e-mail to the selected recipient.

Getting ready

We will build upon the example that is defined in the *Passing HttpRequest to the form* recipe.

How to do it...

To complete this recipe, execute the following two steps:

1. From Django, import the function in order to send an e-mail. Then, add the `save()` method to `MessageForm`. It will try to send an e-mail to the selected recipient and will fail silently if any errors occur:

```
# email_messages/forms.py
# -*- coding: UTF-8 -*-
from __future__ import unicode_literals
from django import forms
from django.utils.translation import ugettext,\
```

```
        ugettext_lazy as _
from django.core.mail import send_mail
from django.contrib.auth.models import User

class MessageForm(forms.Form):
    recipient = forms.ModelChoiceField(
        label=_("Recipient"),
        queryset=User.objects.all(),
        required=True,
    )
    message = forms.CharField(
        label=_("Message"),
        widget=forms.Textarea,
        required=True,
    )

    def __init__(self, request, *args, **kwargs):
        super(MessageForm, self).__init__(*args, **kwargs)
        self.request = request
        self.fields["recipient"].queryset = \
            self.fields["recipient"].queryset.\
            exclude(pk=request.user.pk)

    def save(self):
        cleaned_data = self.cleaned_data
        send_mail(
            subject=ugettext("A message from %s") % \
                self.request.user,
            message=cleaned_data["message"],
            from_email=self.request.user.email,
            recipient_list=[
                cleaned_data["recipient"].email
            ],
            fail_silently=True,
        )
```

2. Then, call the `save()` method from the form in the view if the posted data is valid:

```
# email_messages/views.py
# -*- coding: UTF-8 -*-
from __future__ import unicode_literals
from django.contrib.auth.decorators import login_required
```

```
from django.shortcuts import render, redirect

from .forms import MessageForm

@login_required
def message_to_user(request):
    if request.method == "POST":
        form = MessageForm(request, data=request.POST)
        if form.is_valid():
            form.save()
            return redirect("message_to_user_done")
    else:
        form = MessageForm(request)

    return render(request,
        "email_messages/message_to_user.html",
        {"form": form}
    )
```

How it works...

Let's take a look at the form. The `save()` method uses the cleaned data from the form to read the recipient's e-mail address and the message. The sender of the e-mail is the current user from the request. If the e-mail cannot be sent due to an incorrect mail server configuration or another reason, it will fail silently; that is, no error will be raised.

Now, let's look at the view. When the posted form is valid, the `save()` method of the form will be called and the user will be redirected to the success page.

See also

- ▶ The *Passing HttpRequest to the form* recipe
- ▶ The *Downloading authorized files* recipe

Uploading images

In this recipe, we will take a look at the easiest way to handle image uploads. You will see an example of an app, where the visitors can upload images with inspirational quotes.

Getting ready

Make sure to have Pillow or PIL installed in your virtual environment or globally.

Then, let's create a `quotes` app and put it in `INSTALLED_APPS` in the settings. Then, we will add an `InspirationalQuote` model with three fields: the `author`, `quote` text, and `picture`, as follows:

```python
# quotes/models.py
# -*- coding: UTF-8 -*-
from __future__ import unicode_literals
import os
from django.db import models
from django.utils.timezone import now as timezone_now
from django.utils.translation import ugettext_lazy as _
from django.utils.encoding import python_2_unicode_compatible


def upload_to(instance, filename):
    now = timezone_now()
    filename_base, filename_ext = os.path.splitext(filename)
    return "quotes/%s%s" % (
        now.strftime("%Y/%m/%Y%m%d%H%M%S"),
        filename_ext.lower(),
    )


@python_2_unicode_compatible
class InspirationalQuote(models.Model):
    author = models.CharField(_("Author"), max_length=200)
    quote = models.TextField(_("Quote"))
    picture = models.ImageField(_("Picture"),
        upload_to=upload_to,
        blank=True,
        null=True,
    )

    class Meta:
        verbose_name = _("Inspirational Quote")
        verbose_name_plural = _("Inspirational Quotes")

    def __str__(self):
        return self.quote
```

In addition, we created an `upload_to()` function, which sets the path of the uploaded picture to be something similar to `quotes/2015/04/20150424140000.png`. As you can see, we use the date timestamp as the filename to ensure its uniqueness. We pass this function to the `picture` image field.

How to do it...

Execute these steps to complete the recipe:

1. Create the `forms.py` file and put a simple model form there:

```python
# quotes/forms.py
# -*- coding: UTF-8 -*-
from __future__ import unicode_literals
from django import forms
from .models import InspirationalQuote

class InspirationalQuoteForm(forms.ModelForm):
    class Meta:
        model = InspirationalQuote
        fields = ["author", "quote", "picture", "language"]
```

2. In the `views.py` file, put a view that handles the form. Don't forget to pass the `FILES` dictionary-like object to the form. When the form is valid, trigger the save method as follows:

```python
# quotes/views.py
# -*- coding: UTF-8 -*-
from __future__ import unicode_literals
from django.shortcuts import redirect
from django.shortcuts import render
from .forms import InspirationalQuoteForm

def add_quote(request):
    if request.method == "POST":
        form = InspirationalQuoteForm(
            data=request.POST,
            files=request.FILES,
        )
        if form.is_valid():
            quote = form.save()
            return redirect("add_quote_done")
    else:
        form = InspirationalQuoteForm()
    return render(request,
        "quotes/change_quote.html",
        {"form": form}
    )
```

3. Lastly, create a template for the view in `templates/quotes/change_quote.`
   `html`. It is very important to set the `enctype` attribute to `multipart/form-data`
   for the HTML form, otherwise the file upload won't work:

```
{# templates/quotes/change_quote.html #}
{% extends "base.html" %}
{% load i18n %}

{% block content %}
    <form method="post" action="" enctype="multipart/form-data">
        {% csrf_token %}
        {{ form.as_p }}
        <button type="submit">{% trans "Save" %}</button>
    </form>
{% endblock %}
```

How it works...

Django model forms are forms that are created from models. They provide all the fields from
the model so you don't need to define them again. In the preceding example, we created a
model form for the `InspirationalQuote` model. When we save the form, the form knows
how to save each field in the database, as well as to upload the files and save them in the
media directory.

There's more

As a bonus, we will see an example of how to generate a thumbnail out of the uploaded
image. Using this technique, you could also generate several other specific versions of the
image, such as the list version, mobile version, and desktop computer version.

We will add three methods to the `InspirationalQuote` model (`quotes/models.py`).
They are `save()`, `create_thumbnail()`, and `get_thumbnail_picture_url()`. When
the model is being saved, we will trigger the creation of the thumbnail. When we need to
show the thumbnail in a template, we can get its URL using `{{ quote.get_thumbnail_`
`picture_url }}`. The method definitions are as follows:

```python
# quotes/models.py
# ...
from PIL import Image
from django.conf import settings
from django.core.files.storage import default_storage as storage
THUMBNAIL_SIZE = getattr(
    settings,
    "QUOTES_THUMBNAIL_SIZE",
    (50, 50)
```

```
    )

    class InspirationalQuote(models.Model):
        # ...
        def save(self, *args, **kwargs):
            super(InspirationalQuote, self).save(*args, **kwargs)
            # generate thumbnail picture version
            self.create_thumbnail()

        def create_thumbnail(self):
            if not self.picture:
                return ""
            file_path = self.picture.name
            filename_base, filename_ext = os.path.splitext(file_path)
            thumbnail_file_path = "%s_thumbnail.jpg" % filename_base
            if storage.exists(thumbnail_file_path):
                # if thumbnail version exists, return its url path
                return "exists"
            try:
                # resize the original image and
                # return URL path of the thumbnail version
                f = storage.open(file_path, 'r')
                image = Image.open(f)
                width, height = image.size

                if width > height:
                    delta = width - height
                    left = int(delta/2)
                    upper = 0
                    right = height + left
                    lower = height
                else:
                    delta = height - width
                    left = 0
                    upper = int(delta/2)
                    right = width
                    lower = width + upper

                image = image.crop((left, upper, right, lower))
                image = image.resize(THUMBNAIL_SIZE, Image.ANTIALIAS)

                f_mob = storage.open(thumbnail_file_path, "w")
                image.save(f_mob, "JPEG")
                f_mob.close()
```

```
            return "success"
        except:
            return "error"

    def get_thumbnail_picture_url(self):
        if not self.picture:
            return ""
        file_path = self.picture.name
        filename_base, filename_ext = os.path.splitext(file_path)
        thumbnail_file_path = "%s_thumbnail.jpg" % filename_base
        if storage.exists(thumbnail_file_path):
            # if thumbnail version exists, return its URL path
            return storage.url(thumbnail_file_path)
        # return original as a fallback
        return self.picture.url
```

In the preceding methods, we are using the file storage API instead of directly juggling the filesystem, as we could then exchange the default storage with Amazon S3 buckets or other storage services and the methods will still work.

How does the creating the thumbnail work? If we had the original file saved as `quotes/2014/04/20140424140000.png`, we are checking whether the `quotes/2014/04/20140424140000_thumbnail.jpg` file doesn't exist and, in that case, we are opening the original image, cropping it from the center, resizing it to 50 x 50 pixels, and saving it to the storage.

The `get_thumbnail_picture_url()` method checks whether the thumbnail version exists in the storage and returns its URL. If the thumbnail version does not exist, the URL of the original image is returned as a fallback.

See also

- The *Creating a form layout with django-crispy-forms* recipe

Creating a form layout with django-crispy-forms

The `django-crispy-forms` Django app allows you to build, customize, and reuse forms using one of the following CSS frameworks: Uni-Form, Bootstrap, or Foundation. The usage of `django-crispy-forms` is analogous to fieldsets in the Django contributed administration; however, it is more advanced and customizable. You define form layout in the Python code and you don't need to worry about how each field is presented in HTML. However, if you need to add specific HTML attributes or wrapping, you can easily do that too. Moreover, all the markup used by `django-crispy-forms` is located in the templates that can be overwritten for specific needs.

In this recipe, we will see an example of how to use `django-crispy-forms` with Bootstrap 3, which is the most popular frontend framework to develop responsive, mobile-first web projects.

Getting ready

To start with, execute the following tasks one by one:

Download the Bootstrap frontend framework from `http://getbootstrap.com/` and integrate CSS and JavaScript in the templates. Learn more about this in the *Arranging the base.html template* recipe in *Chapter 4, Templates and JavaScript*.

Install `django-crispy-forms` in your virtual environment using the following command:

```
(myproject_env)$ pip install django-crispy-forms
```

Make sure that `crispy_forms` is added to `INSTALLED_APPS` and then set `bootstrap3` as the template pack to be used in this project:

```
# conf/base.py or settings.py
INSTALLED_APPS = (
    # …
    "crispy_forms",
)
# …
CRISPY_TEMPLATE_PACK = "bootstrap3"
```

Let's create a `bulletin_board` app to illustrate the usage of `django-crispy-forms` and put it in `INSTALLED_APPS` in the settings. We will have a `Bulletin` model there with these fields: `bulletin_type`, `title`, `description`, `contact_person`, `phone`, `email`, and `image` as follows:

```python
# bulletin_board/models.py
# -*- coding: UTF-8 -*-
from __future__ import unicode_literals
from django.db import models
from django.utils.translation import ugettext_lazy as _
from django.utils.encoding import python_2_unicode_compatible

TYPE_CHOICES = (
    ('searching', _("Searching")),
    ('offering', _("Offering")),
)


@python_2_unicode_compatible
class Bulletin(models.Model):
    bulletin_type = models.CharField(_("Type"), max_length=20,
        choices=TYPE_CHOICES)

    title = models.CharField(_("Title"), max_length=255)
    description = models.TextField(_("Description"),
        max_length=300)

    contact_person = models.CharField(_("Contact person"),
        max_length=255)
    phone = models.CharField(_("Phone"), max_length=200,
        blank=True)
    email = models.EmailField(_("Email"), blank=True)

    image = models.ImageField(_("Image"), max_length=255,
        upload_to="bulletin_board/", blank=True)

    class Meta:
        verbose_name = _("Bulletin")
        verbose_name_plural = _("Bulletins")
        ordering = ("title",)

    def __str__(self):
        return self.title
```

How to do it...

Follow these steps:

1. Let's add a model form for the bulletin in the newly created app. We will attach a form helper to the form in the initialization method itself. The form helper will have the layout property that will define the layout for the form, as follows:

```python
# bulletin_board/forms.py
# -*- coding: UTF-8 -*-
from django import forms
from django.utils.translation import ugettext_lazy as _,\
    ugettext
from crispy_forms.helper import FormHelper
from crispy_forms import layout, bootstrap
from .models import Bulletin


class BulletinForm(forms.ModelForm):
    class Meta:
        model = Bulletin
        fields = ["bulletin_type", "title", "description",
        "contact_person", "phone", "email", "image"]

    def __init__(self, *args, **kwargs):
        super(BulletinForm, self).__init__(*args, **kwargs)

        self.helper = FormHelper()
        self.helper.form_action = ""
        self.helper.form_method = "POST"

        self.fields["bulletin_type"].widget = \
            forms.RadioSelect()
        # delete empty choice for the type
        del self.fields["bulletin_type"].choices[0]

        self.helper.layout = layout.Layout(
            layout.Fieldset(
                _("Main data"),
                layout.Field("bulletin_type"),
                layout.Field("title",
                    css_class="input-block-level"),
                    layout.Field("description",
                    css_class="input-blocklevel",
                    rows="3"),
                ),
```

```
        layout.Fieldset(
          _("Image"),
          layout.Field("image",
            css_class="input-block-level"),
          layout.HTML(u"""{% load i18n %}
            <p class="help-block">{% trans
              "Available formats are JPG, GIF, and PNG.
                Minimal size is 800 x 800 px." %}</p>
          """),
          title=_("Image upload"),
          css_id="image_fieldset",
        ),
        layout.Fieldset(
          _("Contact"),
          layout.Field("contact_person",
            css_class="input-blocklevel"),
          layout.Div(
            bootstrap.PrependedText("phone",
            """<span class="glyphicon glyphicon-
              earphone">
            </span>""",
              css_class="inputblock-level"),
            bootstrap.PrependedText("email", "@",
              css_class="input-block-level",
              placeholder="contact@example.com"),
            css_id="contact_info",
          ),
        ),
        bootstrap.FormActions(
          layout.Submit("submit", _("Save")),
        )
      )
```

2. To render the form in the template, we just need to load the `crispy_forms_tags` template tag library and use the `{% crispy %}` template tag as shown in the following:

```
{# templates/bulletin_board/change_form.html #}
{% extends "base.html" %}
{% load crispy_forms_tags %}

{% block content %}
    {% crispy form %}
{% endblock %}
```

3. Create the `base.html` template. You can do this according to the example in the *Arranging the base.html template* recipe in *Chapter 4, Templates and JavaScript*.

How it works...

The page with the bulletin form will look similar to the following:

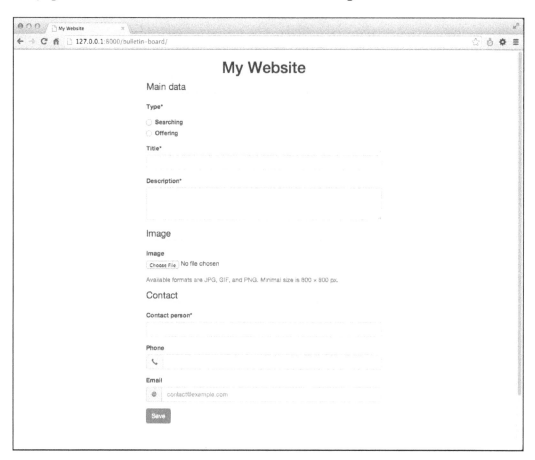

As you can see, the fields are grouped by fieldsets. The first argument of the `Fieldset` object defines the legend, the other positional arguments define the fields. You can also pass named arguments to define the HTML attributes for the fieldset; for example, for the second fieldset, we are passing `title` and `css_id` to set the `title` and `id` HTML attributes.

Fields can also have additional attributes passed by named arguments; for example, for the `description` field, we are passing `css_class` and `rows` to set the `class` and `rows` HTML attributes.

Besides the normal fields, you can pass HTML snippets as this is done with the help block for the image field. You can also have prepended text fields in the layout. For example, we added a phone icon to the **Phone** field and an @ sign for the **Email** field. As you can see from the example with the contact fields, we can easily wrap fields in the HTML `<div>` elements using the `Div` objects. This is useful when specific JavaScript needs to be applied to some form fields.

The `action` attribute for the HTML form is defined by the `form_action` property of the form helper. If you use the empty string as an action, the form will be submitted to the same view, where the form is included. The `method` attribute of the HTML form is defined by the `form_method` property of the form helper. As you know, the HTML forms allow the GET and POST methods. Finally, there is a `Submit` object in order to render the submit button, which takes the name of the button as the first positional argument and the value of the button as the second argument.

There's more...

For the basic usage, the given example is more than necessary. However, if you need a specific markup for the forms in your project, you can still overwrite and modify templates of the `django-crispy-forms` app as there is no markup hardcoded in the Python files, rather all the generated markup is rendered through the templates. Just copy the templates from the `django-crispy-forms` app to your project's template directory and change them as required.

See also

- The *Filtering object lists* recipe
- The *Managing paginated lists* recipe
- The *Downloading authorized files* recipe

Downloading authorized files

Sometimes, you might need to allow only specific people to download intellectual property from your website. For example, music, videos, literature, or other artistic works should be accessible only to the paid members. In this recipe, you will learn how to restrict image downloads only to the authenticated users using the contributed Django auth app.

Getting ready

To start, create the `quotes` app as in the *Uploading images* recipe.

How to do it...

Execute these steps one by one:

1. Create the view that will require authentication to download a file, as follows:

```python
# quotes/views.py
# -*- coding: UTF-8 -*-
from __future__ import unicode_literals
import os
from django.shortcuts import get_object_or_404
from django.http import FileResponse
from django.utils.text import slugify
from django.contrib.auth.decorators import login_required
from .models import InspirationalQuote


@login_required(login_url="my_login_page")
def download_quote_picture(request, quote_id):
    quote = get_object_or_404(InspirationalQuote,
        pk=quote_id)
    file_name, file_extension = os.path.splitext(
        quote.picture.file.name)
    file_extension = file_extension[1:]  # remove the dot
    response = FileResponse(
        quote.picture.file,
        content_type="image/%s" % file_extension
    )
    response["Content-Disposition"] = "attachment;" \
        " filename=%s---%s.%s" % (
        slugify(quote.author)[:100],
        slugify(quote.quote)[:100],
        file_extension
    )
    return response
```

2. Add the view to the URL configuration:

```python
# quotes/urls.py
# -*- coding: UTF-8 -*-
from __future__ import unicode_literals
from django.conf.urls import patterns, url

urlpatterns = patterns("",
    # …
    url(r'^(?P<quote_id>\d+)/download/$',
        "quotes.views.download_quote_picture",
```

```
                name="download_quote_picture"
        ),
    )
```

3. Then, we need to set the login view in project URL configuration. Note how we are also adding `login_helper` for `django-crispy-forms`:

```python
# myproject/urls.py
# -*- coding: UTF-8 -*-
from django.conf.urls import patterns, include, url
from django.conf import settings
from django.contrib import admin
from django.core.urlresolvers import reverse_lazy
from django.utils.translation import string_concat
from django.utils.translation import ugettext_lazy as _
from django.conf.urls.i18n import i18n_patterns
from crispy_forms.helper import FormHelper
from crispy_forms import layout, bootstrap


login_helper = FormHelper()
login_helper.form_action = reverse_lazy("my_login_page")
login_helper.form_method = "POST"
login_helper.form_class = "form-signin"
login_helper.html5_required = True
login_helper.layout = layout.Layout(
    layout.HTML(string_concat("""<h2 class="form-signin-
heading">""", _("Please Sign In"), """</h2>""")),
    layout.Field("username", placeholder=_("username")),
    layout.Field("password", placeholder=_("password")),
    layout.HTML("""<input type="hidden" name="next" value="{{ next
}}" />"""),
    layout.Submit("submit", _("Login"), css_class="btn-lg"),
)


urlpatterns = i18n_patterns("",
    # …
    url(r'login/$', "django.contrib.auth.views.login",
        {"extra_context": {"login_helper": login_helper}},
        name="my_login_page"
    ),
    url(r'^quotes/', include("quotes.urls")),
)
```

4. Let's create a template for the login form, as shown in the following:

```
{# templates/registration/login.html #}
{% extends "base.html" %}
{% load crispy_forms_tags %}

{% block stylesheet %}
    {{ block.super }}
    <link rel="stylesheet" href="{{ STATIC_URL }}site/css/login.
css">
{% endblock %}

{% block content %}
    <div class="container">
        {% crispy form login_helper %}
    </div>
{% endblock %}
```

5. Create the `login.css` file to add some style to the login form. Lastly, you should restrict the users from bypassing Django and downloading restricted files directly. To do so on an Apache web server, you can put the `.htaccess` file in the `media/quotes` directory with the following content if you are using Apache 2.2:

```
# media/quotes/.htaccess
Order deny,allow
Deny from all
```

You can put the following content if you are using Apache 2.4:

```
# media/quotes/.htaccess
Require all denied
```

How it works...

The `download_quote_picture()` view streams the picture from a specific inspirational quote. The `Content-Disposition` header that is set to `attachment` makes the file downloadable instead of being immediately shown in the browser. The filename for the file will be something similar to `walt-disney---if-you-can-dream-it-you-can-do-it.png`. The `@login_required` decorator will redirect the visitor to the login page if he or she tries to access the downloadable file without being logged in.

As we want to have a nice Bootstrap-style login form, we are using `django-crispy-forms` again and define a helper for the `login_helper` form. The helper is passed to the authorization form as an extra context variable and then used as the second parameter in the `{% crispy %}` template tag.

Depending on the CSS applied, the login form might look similar to the following:

See also

▸ The *Uploading images* recipe

▸ The *Creating a form layout with django-crispy-forms* recipe

Filtering object lists

In web development, besides views with forms, it is typical to have object-list views and detail views. List views can simply list objects that are ordered, for example, alphabetically or by creation date; however, that is not very user-friendly with huge amounts of data. For the best accessibility and convenience, you should be able to filter the content by all possible categories. In this recipe, we will see the pattern that is used to filter list views by any number of categories.

What we'll be creating is a list view of movies that can be filtered by genre, director, actor, or rating. It will look similar to the following with Bootstrap 3 applied to it:

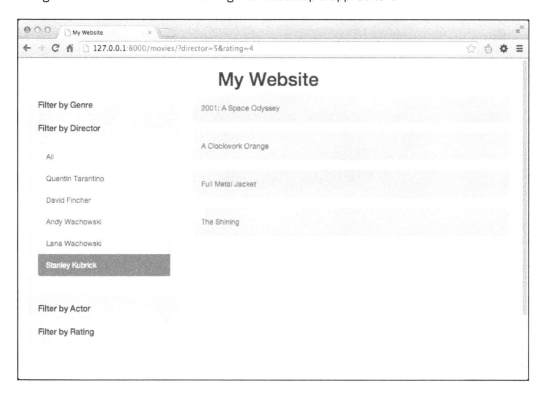

Getting ready

For the filtering example, we will use the `Movie` model with relations to genres, directors, and actors to filter by. It will also be possible to filter by ratings, which is `PositiveIntegerField` with choices. Let's create the `movies` app, put it in `INSTALLED_APPS` in the settings, and define the mentioned models in the new app, as follows:

```
# movies/models.py
# -*- coding: UTF-8 -*-
from __future__ import unicode_literals
from django.db import models
from django.utils.translation import ugettext_lazy as _
from django.utils.encoding import python_2_unicode_compatible

RATING_CHOICES = (
    (1, "★"),
    (2, "★★"),
    (3, "★★★"),
```

```
        (4, "★★★★"),
        (5, "★★★★★"),
)


@python_2_unicode_compatible
class Genre(models.Model):
    title = models.CharField(_("Title"), max_length=100)

    def __str__(self):
        return self.title


@python_2_unicode_compatible
class Director(models.Model):
    first_name = models.CharField(_("First name"), max_length=40)
    last_name = models.CharField(_("Last name"), max_length=40)

    def __str__(self):
        return self.first_name + " " + self.last_name


@python_2_unicode_compatible
class Actor(models.Model):
    first_name = models.CharField(_("First name"), max_length=40)
    last_name = models.CharField(_("Last name"), max_length=40)

    def __str__(self):
        return self.first_name + " " + self.last_name


@python_2_unicode_compatible
class Movie(models.Model):
    title = models.CharField(_("Title"), max_length=255)
    genres = models.ManyToManyField(Genre, blank=True)
    directors = models.ManyToManyField(Director, blank=True)
    actors = models.ManyToManyField(Actor, blank=True)
    rating = models.PositiveIntegerField(choices=RATING_CHOICES)

    def __str__(self):
        return self.title
```

How to do it...

To complete the recipe, follow these steps:

1. First of all, we create `MovieFilterForm` with all the possible categories to filter by:

```python
# movies/forms.py
# -*- coding: UTF-8 -*-
from __future__ import unicode_literals
from django import forms
from django.utils.translation import ugettext_lazy as _


from .models import Genre, Director, Actor, RATING_CHOICES

class MovieFilterForm(forms.Form):
    genre = forms.ModelChoiceField(
        label=_("Genre"),
        required=False,
        queryset=Genre.objects.all(),
    )
    director = forms.ModelChoiceField(
        label=_("Director"),
        required=False,
        queryset=Director.objects.all(),
    )
    actor = forms.ModelChoiceField(
        label=_("Actor"),
        required=False,
        queryset=Actor.objects.all(),
    )
    rating = forms.ChoiceField(
        label=_("Rating"),
        required=False,
        choices=RATING_CHOICES,
    )
```

2. Then, we create a `movie_list` view that will use `MovieFilterForm` to validate the request query parameters and perform the filtering for chosen categories. Note the `facets` dictionary that is used here to list the categories and also the currently selected choices:

```python
# movies/views.py
# -*- coding: UTF-8 -*-
from __future__ import unicode_literals
```

```python
from django.shortcuts import render
from .models import Genre, Director, Actor
from .models import Movie, RATING_CHOICES
from .forms import MovieFilterForm

def movie_list(request):
    qs = Movie.objects.order_by("title")

    form = MovieFilterForm(data=request.GET)

    facets = {
        "selected": {},
        "categories": {
            "genres": Genre.objects.all(),
            "directors": Director.objects.all(),
            "actors": Actor.objects.all(),
            "ratings": RATING_CHOICES,
        },
    }

    if form.is_valid():
        genre = form.cleaned_data["genre"]
        if genre:
            facets["selected"]["genre"] = genre
            qs = qs.filter(genres=genre).distinct()

        director = form.cleaned_data["director"]
        if director:
            facets["selected"]["director"] = director
            qs = qs.filter(directors=director).distinct()

        actor = form.cleaned_data["actor"]
        if actor:
            facets["selected"]["actor"] = actor
            qs = qs.filter(actors=actor).distinct()

        rating = form.cleaned_data["rating"]
        if rating:
            rating = int(rating)
            facets["selected"]["rating"] = (rating, dict(RATING_
CHOICES)[rating])
            qs = qs.filter(rating=rating).distinct()

    # Let's inspect the facets in the console
```

```
if settings.DEBUG:
    from pprint import pprint
    pprint(facets)

context = {
    "form": form,
    "facets": facets,
    "object_list": qs,
}
return render(request, "movies/movie_list.html",
    context)
```

3. Lastly, we create the template for the list view. We will use the `facets` dictionary here to list the categories and know which category is currently selected. To generate URLs for the filters, we will use the `{% modify_query %}` template tag, which will be described later in the *Creating a template tag to modify request query parameters* recipe in *Chapter 5, Custom Template Filters and Tags*. Copy the following code in the `templates/movies/movie_list.html` directory:

```
{# templates/movies/movie_list.html #}
{% extends "base_two_columns.html" %}
{% load i18n utility_tags %}

{% block sidebar %}
<div class="filters panel-group" id="accordion">
    <div class="panel panel-default">
        <div class="panel-heading">
            <h6 class="panel-title">
                <a data-toggle="collapse" data-parent="#accordion"
href="#collapseGenres">
                    {% trans "Filter by Genre" %}
                </a>
            </h6>
        </div>
        <div id="collapseGenres" class="panel-collapse collapse
in">
            <div class="panel-body">
                <div class="list-group">
                    <a class="list-group-item{% if not facets.
selected.genre %} active{% endif %}" href="{% modify_query "genre"
"page" %}">{% trans "All" %}</a>
                    {% for cat in facets.categories.genres %}
                        <a class="list-group-item{% if facets.
selected.genre == cat %} active{% endif %}" href="{% modify_query
"page" genre=cat.pk %}">{{ cat }}</a>
                    {% endfor %}
```

```
                    </div>
                </div>
            </div>
        </div>


    <div class="panel panel-default">
        <div class="panel-heading">
            <h6 class="panel-title">
                <a data-toggle="collapse" data-parent="#accordion"
href="#collapseDirectors">
                    {% trans "Filter by Director" %}
                </a>
            </h6>
        </div>
        <div id="collapseDirectors" class="panel-collapse
collapse">
            <div class="panel-body">
                <div class="list-group">
                    <a class="list-group-item{% if not facets.
selected.director %} active{% endif %}" href="{% modify_query
"director" "page" %}">{% trans "All" %}</a>
                    {% for cat in facets.categories.directors %}
                        <a class="list-group-item{% if facets.
selected.director == cat %} active{% endif %}" href="{% modify_
query "page" director=cat.pk %}">{{ cat }}</a>
                    {% endfor %}
                </div>
            </div>
        </div>
    </div>


    {# Analogously by the examples of genres and directors above,
add a filter for actors here… #}

    <div class="panel panel-default">
        <div class="panel-heading">
            <h6 class="panel-title">
                <a data-toggle="collapse" data-parent="#accordion"
href="#collapseRatings">
                    {% trans "Filter by Rating" %}
                </a>
            </h6>
        </div>
        <div id="collapseRatings" class="panel-collapse collapse">
            <div class="panel-body">
```

```
                        <div class="list-group">
                            <a class="list-group-item{% if not facets.
    selected.rating %} active{% endif %}" href="{% modify_query
    "rating" "page" %}">{% trans "All" %}</a>
                            {% for r_val, r_display in facets.categories.
    ratings %}
                                <a class="list-group-item{% if facets.
    selected.rating.0 == r_val %} active{% endif %}" href="{% modify_
    query "page" rating=r_val %}">{{ r_display }}</a>
                            {% endfor %}
                        </div>
                    </div>
                </div>
            </div>
        </div>
    {% endblock %}


    {% block content %}
    <div class="movie_list">
        {% for movie in object_list %}
            <div class="movie alert alert-info">
                <p>{{ movie.title }}</p>
            </div>
        {% endfor %}
    </div>
    {% endblock %}
```

4. Add a simple base template with two-column layout, as follows:

```
{# base_two_columns.html #}
{% extends "base.html" %}

{% block container %}
    <div class="container">
        <div class="row">
            <div id="sidebar" class="col-md-4">
                {% block sidebar %}
                {% endblock %}
            </div>
            <div id="content" class="col-md-8">
                {% block content %}
                {% endblock %}
            </div>
        </div>
    </div>
{% endblock %}
```

5. Create the `base.html` template. You can do that according to the example provided in the *Arranging the base.html template* recipe in *Chapter 4, Templates and JavaScript*.

How it works...

We are using the facets dictionary that is passed to the template context to know which filters we have and which filters are selected. To look deeper, the `facets` dictionary consists of two sections: the `categories` dictionary and the `selected` dictionary. The `categories` dictionary contains `QuerySets` or choices of all filterable categories. The `selected` dictionary contains the currently selected values for each category.

In the view, we check whether the query parameters are valid in the form and then drill down `QuerySet` of objects from the selected categories. Additionally, we set the selected values to the `facets` dictionary, which will be passed to the template.

In the template, for each categorization from the `facets` dictionary, we list all the categories and mark the currently selected category as active.

It is as simple as that.

See also

- The *Managing paginated lists* recipe
- The *Composing class-based views* recipe
- The *Creating a template tag to modify request query parameters* recipe in *Chapter 5, Custom Template Filters and Tags*

Managing paginated lists

If you have dynamically changing lists of objects or the amount of them is greater than 30, you will surely need pagination for the list. With pagination, instead of the full `QuerySet`, you provide a fraction of the dataset that is limited to a specific amount per page and you will also show the links to get to the other pages of the list. Django has classes to manage the paginated data, and we will see how to do that in this recipe for the example provided in the previous recipe.

Getting ready

Let's start with the forms and views of the `movies` app from the *Filtering object lists* recipe.

How to do it...

To add pagination to the list view of the movies, follow these steps:

1. First, import the necessary pagination classes from Django. We will add pagination management to the `movie_list` view just after filtering. Also, we will slightly modify the context dictionary by assigning `page` instead of the movie QuerySet to the object_list key:

```python
# movies/views.py
# -*- coding: UTF-8 -*-
from __future__ import unicode_literals
from django.shortcuts import render
from django.core.paginator import Paginator, EmptyPage,\
    PageNotAnInteger

from .models import Movie
from .forms import MovieFilterForm

def movie_list(request):
    paginate_by = 15
    qs = Movie.objects.order_by("title")
    # … filtering goes here…

    paginator = Paginator(qs, paginate_by)

    page_number = request.GET.get("page")
    try:
        page = paginator.page(page_number)
    except PageNotAnInteger:
        # If page is not an integer, show first page.
        page = paginator.page(1)
    except EmptyPage:
        # If page is out of range, show last existing page.
        page = paginator.page(paginator.num_pages)

    context = {
        # …
        "object_list": page,
    }
    return render(request, "movies/movie_list.html", context)
```

2. In the template, we will add pagination controls after the list of movies, as follows:

```html
{# templates/movies/movie_list.html #}
{% extends "base.html" %}
```

```
{% load i18n utility_tags %}

{% block sidebar %}
    {# … filters go here… #}
{% endblock %}

{% block content %}
<div class="movie_list">
    {% for movie in object_list %}
        <div class="movie alert alert-info">
            <p>{{ movie.title }}</p>
        </div>
    {% endfor %}
</div>

{% if object_list.has_other_pages %}
    <ul class="pagination">
        {% if object_list.has_previous %}
            <li><a href="{% modify_query page=object_list.
previous_page_number %}">&laquo;</a></li>
        {% else %}
            <li class="disabled"><span>&laquo;</span></li>
        {% endif %}
        {% for page_number in object_list.paginator.page_range %}
            {% if page_number == object_list.number %}
                <li class="active">
                    <span>{{ page_number }} <span class="sr-
only">(current)</span></span>
                </li>
            {% else %}
                <li>
                    <a href="{% modify_query page=page_number
%}">{{ page_number }}</a>
                </li>
            {% endif %}
        {% endfor %}
        {% if object_list.has_next %}
            <li><a href="{% modify_query page=object_list.next_
page_number %}">&raquo;</a></li>
        {% else %}
            <li class="disabled"><span>&raquo;</span></li>
        {% endif %}
    </ul>
{% endif %}
{% endblock %}
```

How it works...

When you look at the results in the browser, you will see the pagination controls similar to the following, added after the list of movies:

How do we achieve this? When the `QuerySet` is filtered out, we will create a `paginator` object passing `QuerySet` and the maximal amount of items that we want to show per page, which is 15 here. Then, we will read the current page number from the query parameter, `page`. The next step is to retrieve the current page object from `paginator`. If the page number is not an integer, we get the first page. If the number exceeds the amount of possible pages, the last page is retrieved. The page object has methods and attributes necessary for the pagination widget shown in the preceding screenshot. Also, the page object acts like `QuerySet` so that we can iterate through it and get the items from the fraction of the page.

The snippet marked in the template creates a pagination widget with the markup for the Bootstrap 3 frontend framework. We show the pagination controls only if there are more pages than the current one. We have the links to the previous and next pages, and the list of all page numbers in the widget. The current page number is marked as active. To generate URLs for the links, we use the {% modify_query %} template tag, which will be described later in the *Creating a template tag to modify request query parameters* recipe in *Chapter 5, Custom Template Filters and Tags*.

See also

- ▶ The *Filtering object lists* recipe
- ▶ The *Composing class-based views* recipe
- ▶ The *Creating a template tag to modify request query parameters* recipe in *Chapter 5, Custom Template Filters and Tags*

Composing class-based views

Django views are callables that take requests and return responses. In addition to the function-based views, Django provides an alternative way to define views as classes. This approach is useful when you want to create reusable modular views or combine views of the generic mixins. In this recipe, we will convert the previously shown function-based `movie_list` view to a class-based `MovieListView` view.

Getting ready

Create the models, form, and template similar to the previous recipes, *Filtering object lists* and *Managing paginated lists*.

How to do it...

1. We will need to create a URL rule in the URL configuration and add a class-based view. To include a class-based view in the URL rules, the `as_view()` method is used, as follows:

```
# movies/urls.py
# -*- coding: UTF-8 -*-
from __future__ import unicode_literals
from django.conf.urls import patterns, url
from .views import MovieListView
urlpatterns = patterns("",
    url(r'^$', MovieListView.as_view(), name="movie_list"),
)
```

2. Our class-based view, `MovieListView`, will inherit the Django `View` class and override the `get()` and `post()` methods, which are used to distinguish between the requests by GET and POST. We will also add the `get_queryset_and_facets()` and `get_page()` methods to make the class more modular:

```
# movies/views.py
# -*- coding: UTF-8 -*-
from django.shortcuts import render
from django.core.paginator import Paginator, EmptyPage,\
    PageNotAnInteger
from django.views.generic import View

from .models import Genre
from .models import Director
from .models import Actor
from .models import Movie, RATING_CHOICES
```

```
from .forms import MovieFilterForm

class MovieListView(View):
    form_class = MovieFilterForm
    template_name = "movies/movie_list.html"
    paginate_by = 15

    def get(self, request, *args, **kwargs):
        form = self.form_class(data=request.GET)
        qs, facets = self.get_queryset_and_facets(form)
        page = self.get_page(request, qs)
        context = {
            "form": form,
            "facets": facets,
            "object_list": page,
        }
        return render(request, self.template_name, context)

    def post(self, request, *args, **kwargs):
        return self.get(request, *args, **kwargs)

    def get_queryset_and_facets(self, form):
        qs = Movie.objects.order_by("title")

        facets = {
            "selected": {},
            "categories": {
                "genres": Genre.objects.all(),
                "directors": Director.objects.all(),
                "actors": Actor.objects.all(),
                "ratings": RATING_CHOICES,
            },
        }
        if form.is_valid():
            genre = form.cleaned_data["genre"]
            if genre:
                facets["selected"]["genre"] = genre
                qs = qs.filter(genres=genre).distinct()

            director = form.cleaned_data["director"]
            if director:
                facets["selected"]["director"] = director
                qs = qs.filter(
                    directors=director,
```

```
                    ).distinct()

            actor = form.cleaned_data["actor"]
            if actor:
                facets["selected"]["actor"] = actor
                qs = qs.filter(actors=actor).distinct()

            rating = form.cleaned_data["rating"]
            if rating:
                facets["selected"]["rating"] = (
                    int(rating),
                    dict(RATING_CHOICES)[int(rating)]
                )
                qs = qs.filter(rating=rating).distinct()
        return qs, facets

    def get_page(self, request, qs):
        paginator = Paginator(qs, self.paginate_by)

        page_number = request.GET.get("page")
        try:
            page = paginator.page(page_number)
        except PageNotAnInteger:
            # If page is not an integer, show first page.
            page = paginator.page(1)
        except EmptyPage:
            # If page is out of range,
            # show last existing page.
            page = paginator.page(paginator.num_pages)
        return page
```

How it works...

The following are the things happening in the get() method:

First, we create the form object passing the GET dictionary-like object to it. The GET object contains all the query variables that are passed using the GET method.

Then, the form is passed to the get_queryset_and_facets() method, which returns a tuple of the following two elements: the QuerySet and the facets dictionary respectively.

Then, the current request object and QuerySet is passed to the get_page() method, which returns the current page object.

Lastly, we create a context dictionary and render the response.

There's more...

As you see, the `get()`, `post()`, and `get_page()` methods are generic so that we could create a generic `FilterableListView` class with these methods in the `utils` app. Then, in any app that requires a filterable list, we could create a class-based view that extends `FilterableListView` and defines only the `form_class` and `template_name` attributes and the `get_queryset_and_facets()` method. This is how class-based views work.

See also

▸ The *Filtering object lists* recipe

▸ The *Managing paginated lists* recipe

Generating PDF documents

Django views allow you to create much more than just HTML pages. You can generate files of any type. For example, you can create PDF documents for invoices, tickets, booking confirmations, and so on. In this recipe, we will show you how to generate resumes (curriculum vitae) in the PDF format out of the data from the database. We will be using the Pisa xhtml2pdf library, which is very practical as it allows you to use HTML templates to make PDF documents.

Getting ready

First of all, we need to install the xhtml2pdf Python library in your virtual environment:

```
(myproject_env)$ pip install xhtml2pdf
```

Then, let's create a `cv` app containing a simple `CV` model with the `Experience` model that is attached to it through a foreign key. The `CV` model will have these fields: first name, last name, and e-mail. The `Experience` model will have these fields: the start date of a job, the end date of a job, company, position at that company, and the skills gained:

```python
# cv/models.py
# -*- coding: UTF-8 -*-
from __future__ import unicode_literals
from django.db import models
from django.utils.translation import ugettext_lazy as _
from django.utils.encoding import python_2_unicode_compatible

@python_2_unicode_compatible
class CV(models.Model):
    first_name = models.CharField(_("First name"), max_length=40)
    last_name = models.CharField(_("Last name"), max_length=40)
```

```
        email = models.EmailField(_("Email"))

        def __str__(self):
            return self.first_name + " " + self.last_name

@python_2_unicode_compatible
class Experience(models.Model):
    cv = models.ForeignKey(CV)
    from_date = models.DateField(_("From"))
    till_date = models.DateField(_("Till"), null=True, blank=True)
    company = models.CharField(_("Company"), max_length=100)
    position = models.CharField(_("Position"), max_length=100)
    skills = models.TextField(_("Skills gained"), blank=True)

    def __str__(self):
        till = _("present")
        if self.till_date:
            till = self.till_date.strftime("%m/%Y")
        return _("%(from)s-%(till)s %(pos)s at %(company)s") % {
            "from": self.from_date.strftime("%m/%Y"),
            "till": till,
            "pos": self.position,
            "company": self.company,
        }
    class Meta:
        ordering = ("-from_date",)
```

How to do it...

Execute the following steps to complete the recipe:

1. In the URL rules, let's create a rule for the view that will download a PDF document of a resume by the ID of the CV model, as follows:

    ```
    # cv/urls.py
    # -*- coding: UTF-8 -*-
    from __future__ import unicode_literals
    from django.conf.urls import patterns, url

    urlpatterns = patterns('cv.views',
        url(r'^(?P<cv_id>\d+)/pdf/$', "download_cv_pdf",
    name="download_cv_pdf"),
    )
    ```

2. Now, let's create the `download_cv_pdf()` view. This view renders an HTML template and then passes the rendered string to the `pisaDocument` PDF creator:

```python
# cv/views.py
# -*- coding: UTF-8 -*-
from __future__ import unicode_literals
try:
    from cStringIO import StringIO
except ImportError:
    from StringIO import StringIO
from xhtml2pdf import pisa

from django.conf import settings
from django.shortcuts import get_object_or_404
from django.template.loader import render_to_string
from django.http import HttpResponse

from .models import CV

def download_cv_pdf(request, cv_id):
    cv = get_object_or_404(CV, pk=cv_id)

    response = HttpResponse(content_type="application/pdf")
    response["Content-Disposition"] = "attachment; "\
        "filename=%s_%s.pdf" % (
            cv.first_name,
            cv.last_name
        )

    html = render_to_string("cv/cv_pdf.html", {
        "cv": cv,
        "MEDIA_ROOT": settings.MEDIA_ROOT,
        "STATIC_ROOT": settings.STATIC_ROOT,
    })
    pdf = pisa.pisaDocument(
        StringIO(html.encode("UTF-8")),
        response,
        encoding="UTF-8",
    )
    return response
```

3. Lastly, we will create the template with which the document will be rendered, as follows:

```
{# templates/cv/cv_pdf.html #}
<!DOCTYPE HTML>
<html>
  <head>
    <meta charset="utf-8" />
    <title>My Title</title>
    <style type="text/css">
      @page {
        size: "A4";
        margin: 2.5cm 1.5cm 2.5cm 1.5cm;
        @frame footer {
          -pdf-frame-content: footerContent;
          bottom: 0cm;
          margin-left: 0cm;
          margin-right: 0cm;
          height: 1cm;
        }
      }
      #footerContent {
        color: #666;
        font-size: 10pt;
        text-align: center;
      }
      /* … Other CSS Rules go here … */

    </style>
  </head>
  <body>
    <div>
      <h1>Curriculum Vitae</h1>
      <table>
        <tr>
          <td><p><b>{{ cv.first_name }} {{ cv.last_name
            }}</b><br />
            Contact: {{ cv.email }}</p>
          </td>
          <td align="right">
            <img src="{{ STATIC_ROOT
              }} /site/img/smiley.jpg"
                width="100" height="100" />
          </td>
        </tr>
```

```
      </table>

      <h2>Experience</h2>
        <table>
          {% for experience in cv.experience_set.all %}
            <tr>
              <td valign="top"><p>{{
                experience.from_date|date:"F Y" }} -
                {% if experience.till_date %}
                {{ experience.till_date|date:"F Y" }}
                {% else %}
                present
                {% endif %}<br />
                {{ experience.position }} at {{
                  experience.company }}</p>
              </td>
              <td valign="top"><p><b>Skills gained</b><br>
                {{ experience.skills|linebreaksbr }}
                <br>
                <br>
              </p>
              </td>
            </tr>
          {% endfor %}
        </table>
    </div>
    <pdf:nextpage>
      <div>
        This is an empty page to make a paper plane.
      </div>
      <div id="footerContent">
        Document generated at {% now "Y-m-d" %} |
        Page <pdf:pagenumber> of <pdf:pagecount>
      </div>
  </body>
</html>
```

How it works...

Go to model administration and enter a CV document. Then, if you access the document's URL at `http://127.0.0.1:8000/en/cv/1/pdf/`, you will be asked to download a PDF document that looks something similar to the following:

How does the view work? First, we load a curriculum vitae by its ID, if it exists, or raise the page not found error, if it doesn't. Then, we create the response object with the content type of the PDF document. We set the `Content-Disposition` header to `attachment` with the specified filename. This will force the browsers to open a dialog box prompting us to save the PDF document and suggesting the specified name for the file. Then, we render the HTML template as a string passing curriculum vitae object and the `MEDIA_ROOT` and `STATIC_ROOT` paths.

> Note that the `src` attribute of the `<img>` tag that is used for the PDF creation needs to point to the file in the filesystem or the full URL of the online image. Pisa xhtml2pdf will download the image and include it in the PDF document.

Then, we create a `pisaDocument` file with the UTF-8-encoded HTML as source and response object as the destination. The response object is a file-like object and `pisaDocument` writes the content of the document to it. The response object is returned by the view as expected.

Let's take a look at the HTML template that is used to create this document. The template has some unusual markup tags and CSS rules. If we want to have some elements on each page of the document, we can create CSS frames for that. In the preceding example, the `<div>` tag with the `footerContent` ID is marked as a frame, which will be repeated at the bottom of each page. In a similar way, we can have a header or background image for each page.

The following are the specific markup tags used in this document:

- The `<pdf:nextpage>` tag sets a manual page break
- The `<pdf:pagenumber>` tag returns the number of the current page
- The `<pdf:pagecount>` tag returns the total number of pages

The current version 0.0.6 of the Pisa xhtml2pdf library doesn't fully support all HTML tags and CSS rules. There are no publicly-accessible benchmarks to see what exactly is supported and at what level. Therefore, you would need to experiment in order to make a PDF document look like in the design requirements. However, this library is still mighty enough for customized layouts, which can be basically created just with the knowledge of HTML and CSS.

See also

- The *Managing paginated lists* recipe
- The *Downloading authorized files* recipe

Implementing a multilingual search with Haystack

One of the main functionalities of content-driven websites is a full-text search. Haystack is a modular search API that supports the Solr, Elasticsearch, Whoosh, and Xapian search engines. For each model in your project that has to be findable in the search, you need to define an index that will read out the textual information from the models and place it into the backend. In this recipe, you will learn how to set up a search with Haystack and the Python-based Whoosh search engine for a multilingual website.

Getting ready

In the beginning, let's create a couple of apps with models that will be indexed in the search. Let's create an `ideas` app containing the `Category` and `Idea` models, as follows:

```python
# ideas/models.py
# -*- coding: UTF-8 -*-
from __future__ import unicode_literals
from django.db import models
from django.utils.translation import ugettext_lazy as _
from django.core.urlresolvers import reverse
from django.core.urlresolvers import NoReverseMatch
from django.utils.encoding import python_2_unicode_compatible
from utils.models import UrlMixin
from utils.fields import MultilingualCharField, MultilingualTextField


@python_2_unicode_compatible
class Category(models.Model):
    title = MultilingualCharField(_("Title"), max_length=200)

    class Meta:
        verbose_name = _("Idea Category")
        verbose_name_plural = _("Idea Categories")

    def __str__(self):
        return self.title


@python_2_unicode_compatible
class Idea(UrlMixin):
    title = MultilingualCharField(_("Title"), max_length=200)
    subtitle = MultilingualCharField(_("Subtitle"), max_length=200,
blank=True)
```

```
    description = MultilingualTextField(_("Description"),
        blank=True)
    is_original = models.BooleanField(_("Original"))
    categories = models.ManyToManyField(Category,
        verbose_name=_("Categories"), blank=True,
        related_name="ideas")

    class Meta:
        verbose_name = _("Idea")
        verbose_name_plural = _("Ideas")

    def __str__(self):
        return self.title

    def get_url_path(self):
        try:
            return reverse("idea_detail", kwargs={"id": self.pk})
        except NoReverseMatch:
            return ""
```

The `Idea` model has multilingual fields, which means that there is supposed to be a translation of the content for each language.

Another app will be `quotes` from the *Uploading images* recipe with the `InspirationalQuote` model, where each quote can just be in any one language from the languages defined in `settings.LANGUAGES` and each quote doesn't necessarily have a translation:

```
# quotes/models.py
# -*- coding: UTF-8 -*-
from __future__ import unicode_literals
import os
from django.db import models
from django.utils.timezone import now as timezone_now
from django.utils.translation import ugettext_lazy as _
from django.utils.encoding import python_2_unicode_compatible
from django.conf import settings
from django.core.urlresolvers import reverse
from django.core.urlresolvers import NoReverseMatch

from utils.models import UrlMixin

def upload_to(instance, filename):
    now = timezone_now()
    filename_base, filename_ext = os.path.splitext(filename)
    return 'quotes/%s%s' % (
```

```
            now.strftime("%Y/%m/%Y%m%d%H%M%S"),
            filename_ext.lower(),
        )


@python_2_unicode_compatible
class InspirationalQuote(UrlMixin):
    author = models.CharField(_("Author"), max_length=200)
    quote = models.TextField(_("Quote"))
    picture = models.ImageField(_("Picture"), upload_to=upload_to,
        blank=True, null=True)
    language = models.CharField(_("Language"), max_length=2,
        blank=True, choices=settings.LANGUAGES)

    class Meta:
        verbose_name = _("Inspirational Quote")
        verbose_name_plural = _("Inspirational Quotes")

    def __str__(self):
        return self.quote

    def get_url_path(self):
        try:
            return reverse("quote_detail", kwargs={"id": self.pk})
        except NoReverseMatch:
            return ""
    # …
    def title(self):
        return self.quote
```

Put these two apps in `INSTALLED_APPS` in the settings, create and apply database migrations, and create the model administration for these models to add some data. Also, create list and detail views for these models and plug them in the URL rules. If you are having any difficulty with any of these tasks, familiarize yourself with the concepts in the official Django tutorial once again: `https://docs.djangoproject.com/en/1.8/intro/tutorial01/`.

Make sure you installed django-haystack, whoosh, and django-crispy-forms in your virtual environment:

```
(myproject_env)$ pip install django-crispy-forms
(myproject_env)$ pip install django-haystack
(myproject_env)$ pip install whoosh
```

How to do it...

Let's set up the multilingual search with Haystack and Whoosh by executing the following steps:

1. Create a `search` app that will contain the `MultilingualWhooshEngine` and search indexes for our ideas and quotes. The search engine will live in the `multilingual_whoosh_backend.py` file:

```python
# search/multilingual_whoosh_backend.py
# -*- coding: UTF-8 -*-
from __future__ import import unicode_literals
from django.conf import settings
from django.utils import translation
from haystack.backends.whoosh_backend import \
    WhooshSearchBackend, WhooshSearchQuery, WhooshEngine
from haystack import connections
from haystack.constants import DEFAULT_ALIAS


class MultilingualWhooshSearchBackend(WhooshSearchBackend):
    def update(self, index, iterable, commit=True,
        language_specific=False):
        if not language_specific and \
        self.connection_alias == "default":
            current_language = (translation.get_language()
                or settings.LANGUAGE_CODE)[:2]
            for lang_code, lang_name in settings.LANGUAGES:
                using = "default_%s" % lang_code
                translation.activate(lang_code)
                backend = connections[using].get_backend()
                backend.update(index, iterable, commit,
                    language_specific=True)
            translation.activate(current_language)
        elif language_specific:
            super(MultilingualWhooshSearchBackend, self).\
                update(index, iterable, commit)


class MultilingualWhooshSearchQuery(WhooshSearchQuery):
    def __init__(self, using=DEFAULT_ALIAS):
        lang_code = translation.get_language()[:2]
        using = "default_%s" % lang_code
        super(MultilingualWhooshSearchQuery, self).\
            __init__(using)


class MultilingualWhooshEngine(WhooshEngine):
    backend = MultilingualWhooshSearchBackend
    query = MultilingualWhooshSearchQuery
```

2. Then, let's create the search indexes, as follows:

```python
# search/search_indexes.py
# -*- coding: UTF-8 -*-
from __future__ import unicode_literals
from django.conf import settings
from django.utils.translation import get_language
from haystack import indexes
from ideas.models import Idea
from quotes.models import InspirationalQuote


class IdeaIndex(indexes.SearchIndex, indexes.Indexable):
    text = indexes.CharField(document=True)

    def get_model(self):
        return Idea

    def index_queryset(self, using=None):
        """Used when the entire index for model
            is updated."""
        return self.get_model().objects.all()

    def prepare_text(self, obj):
        # this will be called for each language / backend
        return "\n".join((
            obj.title,
            obj.subtitle,
            obj.description,
            "\n".join([cat.title
                for cat in obj.categories.all()
            ]),
        ))

class InspirationalQuoteIndex(indexes.SearchIndex,
        indexes.Indexable):
    text = indexes.CharField(document=True)

    def get_model(self):
        return InspirationalQuote

    def index_queryset(self, using=None):
        """Used when the entire index for model
            is updated."""
        if using and using != "default":
```

```
            lang_code = using.replace("default_", "")
        else:
            lang_code = settings.LANGUAGE_CODE[:2]
        return self.get_model().objects.filter(language=lang_code)

    def prepare_text(self, obj):
        # this will be called for each language / backend
        return "\n".join((
            obj.author,
            obj.quote,
        ))
```

3. Later, configure the settings to use our `MultilingualWhooshEngine`:

```python
INSTALLED_APPS = (
    # …
    # third party
    "crispy_forms",
    "haystack",
    # project-specific
    "quotes",
    "utils",
    "ideas",
    "search",
)
LANGUAGE_CODE = "en"
LANGUAGES = (
    ("en", "English"),
    ("de", "Deutsch"),
    ("fr", "Français"),
    ("lt", "Lietuvių kalba"),
)
CRISPY_TEMPLATE_PACK = "bootstrap3"
HAYSTACK_CONNECTIONS = {
    "default": {
        "ENGINE": "search.multilingual_whoosh_backend."\
            "MultilingualWhooshEngine",
        "PATH": os.path.join(PROJECT_PATH, "myproject",
            "tmp", "whoosh_index_en"),
    },
    "default_en": {
        "ENGINE": "search.multilingual_whoosh_backend."\
            "MultilingualWhooshEngine",
        "PATH": os.path.join(PROJECT_PATH, "myproject",
            "tmp", "whoosh_index_en"),
```

```
        },
        "default_de": {
            "ENGINE": "search.multilingual_whoosh_backend."\
                "MultilingualWhooshEngine",
            "PATH": os.path.join(PROJECT_PATH, "myproject",
                "tmp", "whoosh_index_de"),
        },
        "default_fr": {
            "ENGINE": "search.multilingual_whoosh_backend."\
                "MultilingualWhooshEngine",
            "PATH": os.path.join(PROJECT_PATH, "myproject",
                "tmp", "whoosh_index_fr"),
        },
        "default_lt": {
            "ENGINE": "search.multilingual_whoosh_backend."\
                "MultilingualWhooshEngine",
            "PATH": os.path.join(PROJECT_PATH, "myproject",
                "tmp", "whoosh_index_lt"),
        },
    }
```

4. Now, we need to define the URL rules for the search view:

```
# myproject/urls.py
# -*- coding: UTF-8 -*-
from django.conf.urls import patterns, include, url
from django.core.urlresolvers import reverse_lazy
from django.utils.translation import string_concat
from django.utils.translation import ugettext_lazy as _
from django.conf.urls.i18n import i18n_patterns

from crispy_forms.helper import FormHelper
from crispy_forms import layout, bootstrap
from haystack.views import SearchView

class CrispySearchView(SearchView):
    def extra_context(self):
        helper = FormHelper()
        helper.form_tag = False
        helper.disable_csrf = True
        return {"search_helper": helper}

urlpatterns = i18n_patterns('',
    # …
    url(r'^search/$', CrispySearchView(),
```

```
                    name='haystack_search'),
            # ...
    )
```

5. Then, here comes the template for the search form and search results, as shown in the following:

```
{# templates/search/search.html #}
{% extends "base.html" %}
{% load i18n crispy_forms_tags utility_tags %}

{% block content %}
    <h2>{% trans "Search" %}</h2>
    <form method="get" action="{{ request.path }}">
        <div class="well clearfix">
            {% crispy form search_helper %}
            <p class="pull-right">
                <input class="btn btn-primary" type="submit"
value="Search">
            </p>
        </div>
    </form>

    {% if query %}
        <h3>{% trans "Results" %}</h3>

        {% for result in page.object_list %}
            <p>
                <a href="{{ result.object.get_url_path }}">
                    {{ result.object.title }}
                </a>
            </p>
        {% empty %}
            <p>{% trans "No results found." %}</p>
        {% endfor %}

        {% if page.has_previous or page.has_next %}
            <nav>
                <ul class="pager">
                    <li class="previous">
                        {% if page.has_previous %}<a href="{%
modify_query page=page.previous_page_number %}">{% endif %}
```

```
                              <span aria-hidden="true">&laquo;</
span>
                            {% if page.has_previous %}</a>{% endif %}
                        </li>
                        <li class="next">
                            {% if page.has_next %}<a href="{% modify_
query page=page.next_page_number %}">{% endif %}
                              <span aria-hidden="true">&raquo;</
span>
                            {% if page.has_next %}</a>{% endif %}
                        </li>
                    </ul>
                </nav>
            {% endif %}
        {% endif %}
    {% endblock %}
```

6. Call the `rebuild_index` management command in order to index the database
    data and prepare the full-text search to be used:

    (myproject_env)$ python manage.py rebuild_index --noinput

How it works...

The `MultilingualWhooshEngine` specifies two custom properties: backend and
query. The custom `MultilingualWhooshSearchBackend` backend ensures that, for
each language, the items will be indexed just in that language and put under the specific
`Haystack` index location that is defined in the HAYSTACK_CONNECTIONS setting. The
`MultilingualWhooshSearchQuery` custom query ensures that when searching for
keywords, the specific Haystack connection of the current language will be used.

Each index has a field `text`, where full-text from a specific language of a model will be
stored. The model for the index is defined by the `get_model()` method, QuerySet to index
is defined by the `index_queryset()` method, and text to search in gets collected in the
`prepare_text()` method.

As we want to have a nice Bootstrap 3 form, we will be passing `FormHelper` from `django-crispy-forms` to the search view. We can do that by overriding the `extra_context()` method of `SearchView`. The final search form will look similar to the following:

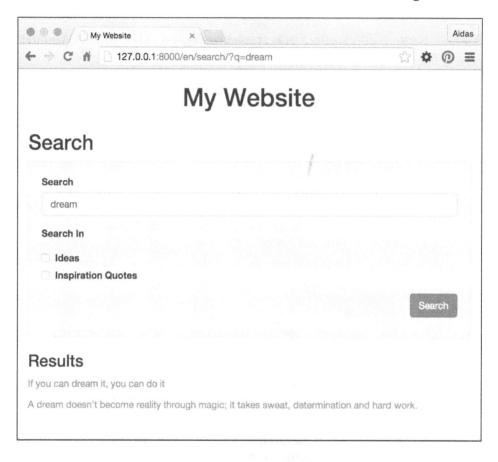

The easiest way to regularly update the search index is to call the `rebuild_index` management command by a cron job every night. To learn about it, check the *Setting up cron jobs for regular tasks* recipe in *Chapter 11, Testing and Deployment*.

See also

▸ The *Creating form layout with django-crispy-forms* recipe

▸ The *Downloading authorized file* recipe

▸ The *Setting up cron jobs for regular tasks* recipe in *Chapter 11, Testing and Deployment*

4
Templates and JavaScript

In this chapter, we will cover the following topics:

- ▸ Arranging the base.html template
- ▸ Including JavaScript settings
- ▸ Using HTML5 data attributes
- ▸ Opening object details in a modal dialog
- ▸ Implementing a continuous scroll
- ▸ Implementing the Like widget
- ▸ Uploading images by Ajax

Introduction

We are living in the Web2.0 world, where social web applications and smart websites communicate between servers and clients using Ajax, refreshing whole pages only when the context changes. In this chapter, you will learn best practices to deal with JavaScript in your templates in order to create a rich user experience. For responsive layouts, we will use the Bootstrap 3 frontend framework. For productive scripting, we will use the jQuery JavaScript framework.

Arranging the base.html template

When you start working on templates, one of the first actions is to create the `base.html` boilerplate, which will be extended by most of the page templates in your project. In this recipe, we will demonstrate how to create such template for multilingual HTML5 websites with responsiveness in mind.

 Responsive websites are the ones that adapt to the viewport of the device whether the visitor uses desktop browsers, tablets, or phones.

Getting ready

Create the `templates` directory in your project and set `TEMPLATE_DIRS` in the settings.

How to do it...

Perform the following steps:

1. In the root directory of your `templates`, create a `base.html` file with the following content:

```
{# templates/base.html #}
<!DOCTYPE html>
{% load i18n %}
<html lang="{{ LANGUAGE_CODE }}">
<head>
    <meta charset="utf-8" />
    <meta name="viewport" content="width=device-width, initial-
scale=1" />
    <title>{% block title %}{% endblock %}{% trans "My Website"
%}</title>
    <link rel="icon" href="{{ STATIC_URL }}site/img/favicon.ico"
type="image/png" />

    {% block meta_tags %}{% endblock %}

    {% block base_stylesheet %}
        <link rel="stylesheet" href="https://maxcdn.bootstrapcdn.
com/bootstrap/3.3.5/css/bootstrap.min.css" />
        <link href="{{ STATIC_URL }}site/css/style.css"
rel="stylesheet" media="screen" type="text/css" />
    {% endblock %}
```

```
    {% block stylesheet %}{% endblock %}

    {% block base_js %}
        <script src="//code.jquery.com/jquery-1.11.3.min.js"></
script>
        <script src="//code.jquery.com/jquery-migrate-1.2.1.min.
js"></script>
        <script src="https://maxcdn.bootstrapcdn.com/
bootstrap/3.3.5/js/bootstrap.min.js"></script>
        <script src="{% url "js_settings" %}"></script>
    {% endblock %}

    {% block js %}{% endblock %}
    {% block extrahead %}{% endblock %}
</head>
<body class="{% block bodyclass %}{% endblock %}">
    {% block page %}
        <section class="wrapper">
            <header class="clearfix container">
                <h1>{% trans "My Website" %}</h1>
                {% block header_navigation %}
                    {% include "utils/header_navigation.html" %}
                {% endblock %}
                {% block language_chooser %}
                    {% include "utils/language_chooser.html" %}
                {% endblock %}
            </header>
            <div id="content" class="clearfix container">
                {% block content %}
                {% endblock %}
            </div>
            <footer class="clearfix container">
                {% block footer_navigation %}
                    {% include "utils/footer_navigation.html" %}
                {% endblock %}
            </footer>
        </section>
    {% endblock %}
    {% block extrabody %}{% endblock %}
</body>
</html>
```

2. In the same directory, create another file named `base_simple.html` for specific cases, as follows:

```
{# templates/base_simple.html #}
{% extends "base.html" %}

{% block page %}
    <section class="wrapper">
        <div id="content" class="clearfix">
            {% block content %}
            {% endblock %}
        </div>
    </section>
{% endblock %}
```

How it works...

The base template contains the `<head>` and `<body>` sections of the HTML document with all the details that are reused on each page of the website. Depending on the web design requirements, you can have additional base templates for different layouts. For example, we added the `base_simple.html` file, which has the same HTML `<head>` section and a very minimalistic `<body>` section; and it can be used for the login screen, password reset, or other simple pages. You can have separate base templates for single-column, two-column, and three-column layouts, where each of them extends `base.html` and overwrites the content of the `<body>` section.

Let's look into the details of the `base.html` template that we defined earlier.

In the `<head>` section, we define UTF-8 as the default encoding to support multilingual content. Then, we have the viewport definition that will scale the website in the browser in order to use the full width. This is necessary for small-screen devices that will get specific screen layouts created with the Bootstrap frontend framework. Of course, there is a customizable website title and the favicon will be shown in the browser's tab. We have extendable blocks for meta tags, style sheets, JavaScript, and whatever else that might be necessary for the `<head>` section. Note that we load the Bootstrap CSS and JavaScript in the template as we want to have responsive layouts and basic solid predefined styles for all elements. Then, we load the JavaScript jQuery library that efficiently and flexibly allows us to create rich user experiences. We also load JavaScript settings that are rendered from a Django view. You will learn about this in the next recipe.

In the `<body>` section, we have the header with an overwritable navigation and a language chooser. We also have the content block and footer. At the very bottom, there is an extendable block for additional markup or JavaScript.

The base template that we created is, by no means, a static unchangeable template. You can add to it the elements that you need, for example, Google Analytics code, common JavaScript files, the Apple touch icon for iPhone bookmarks, Open Graph meta tags, Twitter Card tags, schema.org attributes, and so on.

See also

▸ The *Including JavaScript settings* recipe

Including JavaScript settings

Each Django project has its configuration set in the `conf/base.py` or `settings.py` settings file. Some of these configuration values also need to be set in JavaScript. As we want a single location to define our project settings, and we don't want to repeat the process when setting the configuration for the JavaScript values, it is a good practice to include a dynamically generated configuration file in the base template. In this recipe, we will see how to do that.

Getting ready

Make sure that you have the media, static, and request context processors set in the `TEMPLATE_CONTEXT_PROCESSORS` setting, as follows:

```
# conf/base.py or settings.py
TEMPLATE_CONTEXT_PROCESSORS = (
    "django.contrib.auth.context_processors.auth",
    "django.core.context_processors.debug",
    "django.core.context_processors.i18n",
    "django.core.context_processors.media",
    "django.core.context_processors.static",
    "django.core.context_processors.tz",
    "django.contrib.messages.context_processors.messages",
    "django.core.context_processors.request",
)
```

Also, create the `utils` app if you haven't done so already and place it under `INSTALLED_APPS` in the settings.

How to do it...

Follow these steps to create and include the JavaScript settings:

1. Create a URL rule to call a view that renders JavaScript settings, as follows:

```python
# urls.py
# -*- coding: UTF-8 -*-
from __future__ import unicode_literals
from django.conf.urls import patterns, include, url
from django.conf.urls.i18n import i18n_patterns

urlpatterns = i18n_patterns("",
    # …
    url(r"^js-settings/$", "utils.views.render_js",
        {"template_name": "settings.js"},
        name="js_settings",
    ),
)
```

2. In the views of your `utils` app, create the `render_js()` view that returns a response of the JavaScript content type, as shown in the following:

```python
# utils/views.py
# -*- coding: utf-8 -*-
from __future__ import unicode_literals
from datetime import datetime, timedelta
from django.shortcuts import render
from django.views.decorators.cache import cache_control

@cache_control(public=True)
def render_js(request, cache=True, *args, **kwargs):
    response = render(request, *args, **kwargs)
    response["Content-Type"] = \
        "application/javascript; charset=UTF-8"
    if cache:
        now = datetime.utcnow()
        response["Last-Modified"] = \
            now.strftime("%a, %d %b %Y %H:%M:%S GMT")
        # cache in the browser for 1 month
        expires = now + timedelta(days=31)

        response["Expires"] = \
            expires.strftime("%a, %d %b %Y %H:%M:%S GMT")
    else:
        response["Pragma"] = "No-Cache"
    return response
```

3. Create a `settings.js` template that returns JavaScript with the global settings variable, as follows:

```
# templates/settings.js
window.settings = {
    MEDIA_URL: '{{ MEDIA_URL|escapejs }}',
    STATIC_URL: '{{ STATIC_URL|escapejs }}',
    lang: '{{ LANGUAGE_CODE|escapejs }}',
    languages: { {% for lang_code, lang_name in LANGUAGES %}'{{
lang_code|escapejs }}': '{{ lang_name|escapejs }}'{% if not
forloop.last %},{% endif %} {% endfor %} }
};
```

4. Finally, if you haven't done it yet, include the rendered JavaScript settings file in the base template, as shown in the following:

```
# templates/base.html
<script src="{% url "js_settings" %}"></script>
```

How it works...

The Django template system is very flexible; you are not limited to using templates just for HTML. In this example, we will dynamically create the JavaScript file. You can access it in your development web server at `http://127.0.0.1:8000/en/js-settings/` and its content will be something similar to the following:

```
window.settings = {
    MEDIA_URL: '/media/',
    STATIC_URL: '/static/20140424140000/',
    lang: 'en',
    languages: { 'en': 'English', 'de': 'Deutsch', 'fr': 'Français',
'lt': 'Lietuvi kalba' }
};
```

The view will be cacheable in both server and browser.

If you want to pass more variables to the JavaScript settings, either create a custom view and pass all the values to the context or create a custom context processor and pass all the values there. In the latter case, the variables will also be accessed in all the templates of your project. For example, you might have indicators such as {{ is_mobile }}, {{ is_tablet }}, and {{ is_desktop }} in your templates, with the user agent string telling whether the visitor uses a mobile, tablet, or desktop browser.

See also

▸ The *Arranging the base.html template* recipe

▸ The *Using HTML5 data attributes* recipe

Using HTML5 data attributes

When you have dynamic data related to the DOM elements, you need a more efficient way to pass the values from Django to JavaScript. In this recipe, we will see a way to attach data from Django to custom HTML5 data attributes and then describe how to read the data from JavaScript with two practical examples. The first example will be an image that changes its source, depending on the viewport, so that the smallest version is shown on mobile devices, the medium-sized version is shown on tablets, and the biggest high-quality image is shown for the desktop version of the website. The second example will be a Google Map with a marker at a specified geographical position.

Getting ready

To get started, perform the following steps:

1. Create a `locations` app with a `Location` model, which will at least have the title character field, the slug field for URLs, the `small_image`, `medium_image`, and `large_image` image fields, and the latitude and longitude floating-point fields.

 The term *slug* comes from newspaper editing and it means a short string without any special characters; just letters, numbers, underscores, and hyphens. Slugs are generally used to create unique URLs.

2. Create an administration for this model and enter a sample location.

3. Lastly, create a detailed view for the location and set the URL rule for it.

How to do it...

Perform the following steps:

1. As we already have the app created, we will now need the template for the location detail:

```
{# templates/locations/location_detail.html #}
{% extends "base.html" %}

{% block content %}
```

```
<h2>{{ location.title }}</h2>

<img class="img-full-width"
  src="{{ location.small_image.url }}"
  data-small-src="{{ location.small_image.url }}"
  data-medium-src="{{ location.medium_image.url }}"
  data-large-src="{{ location.large_image.url }}"
  alt="{{ location.title|escape }}"
/>

<div id="map"
  data-latitude="{{ location.latitude|stringformat:"f" }}"
  data-longitude="{{ location.longitude|stringformat:"f" }}"
></div>
{% endblock %}

{% block extrabody %}
  <script src="https://maps-api-ssl.google.com/maps/api/js?v=3"></script>
  <script src="{{ STATIC_URL }}site/js/location_detail.js"></script>
{% endblock %}
```

2. Besides the template, we need the JavaScript file that will read out the HTML5 data attributes and use them accordingly, as follows:

```
//site_static/site/js/location_detail.js
jQuery(function($) {

function show_best_images() {
  $('img.img-full-width').each(function() {
    var $img = $(this);
    if ($img.width() > 1024) {
      $img.attr('src', $img.data('large-src'));
    } else if ($img.width() > 468) {
      $img.attr('src', $img.data('medium-src'));
    } else {
      $img.attr('src', $img.data('small-src'));
    }
  });
}

function show_map() {
```

```
    var $map = $('#map');
    var latitude = parseFloat($map.data('latitude'));
    var longitude = parseFloat($map.data('longitude'));
    var latlng = new google.maps.LatLng(latitude, longitude);

    var map = new google.maps.Map($map.get(0), {
      zoom: 15,
      center: latlng
    });
    var marker = new google.maps.Marker({
      position: latlng,
      map: map
    });
  }show_best_images();show_map();

  $(window).on('resize', show_best_images);

});
```

3. Finally, we need to set some CSS, as shown in the following:

```
/* site_static/site/css/style.css */
img.img-full-width {
    width: 100%;
}
#map {
    height: 300px;
}
```

How it works...

If you open your location detail view in a browser, you will see something similar to the following in the large window:

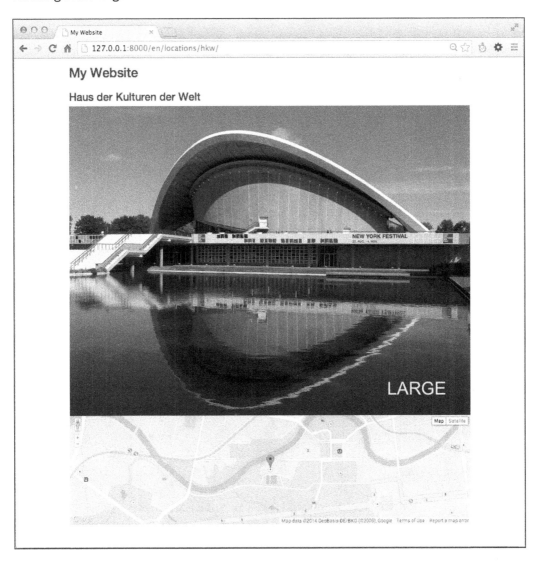

If you resize the browser window to 468 pixels or less, the image will change to its smallest version, as shown in the following:

Let's take a look at the code. In the template, we have an image tag with an `img-full-width` CSS class and its source is set to the smallest image by default. This `image` tag also has `data-small-src`, `data-medium-src`, and `data-large-src` custom attributes. In the JavaScript, the `show_best_images()` function is called when the page is loaded or the window is resized. The function goes through all images with the `img-full-width` CSS class and sets appropriate image sources from the custom data attributes, depending on the current image width.

Then, there is a `<div>` element with the map ID and the `data-latitude` and `data-longitude` custom attributes in the template. In the JavaScript, a `show_map()` function is called when the page is loaded. This function will create a Google Map in the `<div>` element. At first, the custom attributes are read and converted from strings to floating-point values. Then, the `LatLng` object is created that, in the next steps, becomes the center of the map and the geographical position of the marker shown on this map.

See also

▸ The *Including JavaScript settings* recipe

▸ The *Opening object details in a modal dialog* recipe

▸ The *Inserting a map into a change form* recipe in *Chapter 6, Model Administration*

Opening object details in a modal dialog

In this recipe, we will create a list of links to the locations, which when clicked, opens a Bootstrap 3 modal dialog (we will call it pop up in this recipe) with some information about the location and the *more...* link leading to the location detail page. The content for the dialog will be loaded by Ajax. For visitors without JavaScript, the detail page will open immediately, without this intermediate step.

Getting ready

Let's start with the `locations` app that we created in the previous recipe.

In the `urls.py` file, we will have three URL rules; one for the location list, other for the location detail, and the third one for the dialog, as follows:

```python
# locations/urls.py
# -*- coding: UTF-8 -*-
from __future__ import unicode_literals
from django.conf.urls import patterns, url

urlpatterns = patterns("locations.views",
    url(r"^$", "location_list", name="location_list"),
    url(r"^(?P<slug>[^/]+)/$", "location_detail",
        name="location_detail"),
    url(r"^(?P<slug>[^/]+)/popup/$", "location_detail_popup",
        name="location_detail_popup"),
)
```

Consequently, there will be three simple views, as shown in the following:

```
# locations/views.py
from __future__ import unicode_literals
# -*- coding: UTF-8 -*-
from django.shortcuts import render, get_object_or_404
from .models import Location

def location_list(request):
  location_list = Location.objects.all()
  return render(request, "locations/location_list.html",
    {"location_list": location_list})

def location_detail(request, slug):
  location = get_object_or_404(Location, slug=slug)
  return render(request, "locations/location_detail.html",
    {"location": location})

def location_detail_popup(request, slug):
  location = get_object_or_404(Location, slug=slug)
  return render(request, "locations/location_detail_popup.html",
    {"location": location})
```

How to do it...

Execute these steps one by one:

1. Create a template for the location's list view with a hidden empty modal dialog at the end. Each listed location will have custom HTML5 data attributes dealing with the pop-up information, as follows:

```
{# templates/locations/location_list.html #}
{% extends "base.html" %}
{% load i18n %}

{% block content %}
    <h2>{% trans "Locations" %}</h2>
    <ul>
        {% for location in location_list %}
            <li class="item">
                <a href="{% url "location_detail" slug=location.
slug %}"
                    data-popup-url="{% url "location_detail_popup"
slug=location.slug %}"
                        data-popup-title="{{ location.title|escape }}">
```

```
                        {{ location.title }}
                </a>
            </li>
        {% endfor %}
    </ul>
{% endblock %}

{% block extrabody %}
    <div id="popup" class="modal fade">
        <div class="modal-dialog">
            <div class="modal-content">
                <div class="modal-header">
                    <button type="button" class="close" data-
dismiss="modal" aria-hidden="true">&times;</button>
                    <h4 class="modal-title">Modal title</h4>
                </div>
                <div class="modal-body">
                </div>
            </div>
        </div>
    </div>
    <script src="{{ STATIC_URL }}site/js/location_list.js"></
script>
{% endblock %}
```

2. We need JavaScript to handle the opening of the dialog and loading the content dynamically:

```
// site_static/site/js/location_list.js
jQuery(function($) {
    var $popup = $('#popup');


    $('body').on('click', '.item a', function(e) {
        e.preventDefault();
        var $link = $(this);
        var popup_url = $link.data('popup-url');
        var popup_title = $link.data('popup-title');

        if (!popup_url) {
            return true;
        }
        $('.modal-title', $popup).html(popup_title);
        $('.modal-body', $popup).load(popup_url, function() {
            $popup.on('shown.bs.modal', function () {
```

```
                    // do something when dialog is shown
              }).modal("show");
          });

          $('.close', $popup).click(function() {
              // do something when dialog is closing
          });


      });
  });
```

3. Finally, we will create a template for the content that will be loaded in the modal dialog, as shown in the following:

```
{# templates/locations/location_detail_popup.html #}
{% load i18n %}
<p><img src="{{ location.small_image.url }}" alt="{{ location.
title|escape }}" /></p>

<p class="clearfix">
    <a href="{% url "location_detail" slug=location.slug %}"
    class="btn btn-default pull-right">
        {% trans "More" %}
        <span class="glyphicon glyphicon-chevron-right"></span>
    </a>
</p>
```

How it works...

If we go to the location's list view in a browser and click on one of the locations, we will see a modal dialog similar to the following:

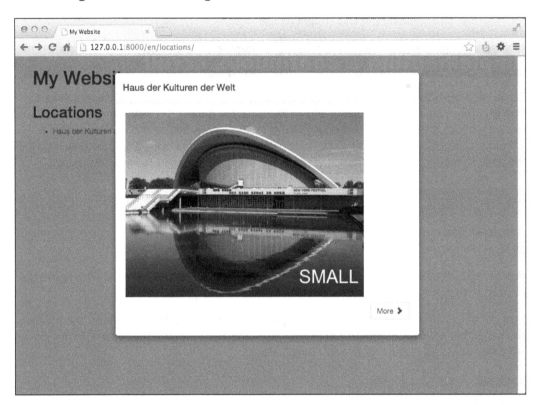

How does this work? In the template, there is a `<div>` element with the `item` CSS class and a link for each location. The links have the `data-popup-url` and `data-popup-title` custom attributes. In the JavaScript, when the page is loaded, we assign an `onclick` handler for the `<body>` tag. The handler checks if any link inside the tag with the `item` CSS class was clicked. For each such clicked link the custom attributes are read as `popup_url` and `popup_title`, the new title is set for the hidden dialog box, the content is loaded in the modal dialog using Ajax, and then it is shown to the visitor.

See also

> ▸ The *Using HTML5 data attributes* recipe
>
> ▸ The *Implementing a continuous scroll* recipe
>
> ▸ The *Implementing the Like widget* recipe

Implementing a continuous scroll

Social websites often have the feature of continuous scrolling, which is also known as infinite scrolling. There are long lists of items and as you scroll the page down, new items are loaded and attached to the bottom automatically. In this recipe, we will see how to achieve such an effect with Django and the jScroll jQuery plugin. We'll illustrate this using a sample view showing the top 250 movies of all time from Internet Movie Database (`http://www.imdb.com/`).

Getting ready

First, download the jScroll plugin from the following link: `https://github.com/pklauzinski/jscroll`.

Put the `jquery.jscroll.js` and `jquery.jscroll.min.js` files from the package in the `myproject/site_static/site/js/` directory.

Next, for this example, you will create a `movies` app with a paginated list view for the movies. You can either create a `Movie` model or a list of dictionaries with the movie data. Every movie will have rank, title, release year, and rating fields.

How to do it...

Perform the following steps to create an continuously scrolling page:

1. The first step is to create a template for the list view that will also show a link to the next page, as follows:

```
{# templates/movies/movie_list.html #}
{% extends "base.html" %}
{% load i18n utility_tags %}

{% block content %}
    <h2>{% trans "Top Movies" %}</h2>
    <div class="object_list">
        {% for movie in object_list %}
            <div class="item">
                <p>{{ movie.rank }}.
```

```
                <strong>{{ movie.title }}</strong>
                ({{ movie.year }})
                <span class="badge">{% trans "IMDB rating" %}:
{{ movie.rating }}</span>
                </p>
            </div>
        {% endfor %}
        {% if object_list.has_next %}
            <p class="pagination"><a class="next_page" href="{%
modify_query page=object_list.next_page_number %}">{% trans
"More..." %}</a></p>
        {% endif %}
    </div>
{% endblock %}

{% block extrabody %}
    <script src="{{ STATIC_URL }}site/js/jquery.jscroll.min.js"></
script>
    <script src="{{ STATIC_URL }}site/js/list.js"></script>
{% endblock %}
```

2. The second step is to add JavaScript, as shown in the following:

```
// site_static/site/js/list.js
jQuery(function($) {
    $('.object_list').jscroll({
        loadingHtml: '<img src="' + settings.STATIC_URL + 'site/
img/loading.gif" alt="Loading" />',
        padding: 100,
        pagingSelector: '.pagination',
        nextSelector: 'a.next_page:last',
        contentSelector: '.item,.pagination'
    });
});
```

How it works...

When you open the movie list view in a browser; a predefined number of items, for example, 25, is shown on the page. As you scroll down, an additional 25 items and the next pagination link are loaded and appended to the item container. Then, the third page of the items is loaded and attached at the bottom, and this continues until there are no more pages left to display.

Upon the page load, the `<div>` tag in JavaScript that has the `object_list` CSS class and contains the items and pagination links will become a jScroll object. The following parameters define its features:

- `loadingHtml`: This sets an animated loading indicator shown at the end of the list when a new page is loading

- `padding`: This will define that the new page has to be loaded, when there are 100 pixels between the scrolling position and the end of the scrolling area

- `pagingSelector`: This CSS selector finds the HTML elements that will be hidden in the browsers with JavaScript switched on

- `nextSelector`: This CSS selector finds the HTML elements that will be used to read the URL of the next page

- `contentSelector`: This CSS selector defines the HTML elements to be taken out of the loaded content and put in the container

See also

- The *Managing paginated lists* recipe in *Chapter 3, Forms and Views*
- The *Composing class-based views* recipe in *Chapter 3, Forms and Views*
- The *Including JavaScript settings* recipe

Implementing the Like widget

Nowadays, social websites usually have integrated Facebook, Twitter, and Google+ widgets to like and share pages. In this recipe, I will guide you through a similar internal liking Django app that saves all the likes in your database so that you can create specific views based on the things that are liked on your website. We will create a Like widget with a two-state button and badge showing the number of total likes. The following are the states:

- Inactive state, where you can click on a button to activate it:

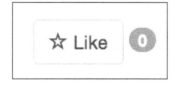

▶ Active state, where you can click on a button to deactivate it:

The state of the widget will be handled by Ajax calls.

Getting ready

First, create a `likes` app with a `Like` model, which has a foreign-key relation to the user that is liking something and a generic relationship to any object in the database. We will use `ObjectRelationMixin`, which we defined in the *Creating a model mixin to handle generic relations* recipe in *Chapter 2, Database Structure*. If you don't want to use the mixin, you can also define a generic relation in the following model yourself:

```python
# likes/models.py
# -*- coding: UTF-8 -*-
from __future__ import unicode_literals
from django.db import models
from django.utils.translation import ugettext_lazy as _
from django.conf import settings
from django.utils.encoding import python_2_unicode_compatible
from utils.models import CreationModificationDateMixin
from utils.models import object_relation_mixin_factory

@python_2_unicode_compatible
class Like(CreationModificationDateMixin,
object_relation_mixin_factory(is_required=True)):
    user = models.ForeignKey(settings.AUTH_USER_MODEL)

    class Meta:
        verbose_name = _("like")
        verbose_name_plural = _("likes")
        ordering = ("-created",)

    def __str__(self):
        return _(u"%(user)s likes %(obj)s") % {
            "user": self.user,
            "obj": self.content_object,
        }
```

Also, make sure that the request context processor is set in the settings. We also need an authentication middleware in the settings for the currently logged-in user attached to the request:

```
# conf/base.py or settings.py
TEMPLATE_CONTEXT_PROCESSORS = (
    # …
    "django.core.context_processors.request",
)
MIDDLEWARE_CLASSES = (
    # …
    "django.contrib.auth.middleware.AuthenticationMiddleware",
)
```

How to do it...

Execute these steps one by one:

1. In the `likes` app, create a `templatetags` directory with an empty `__init__.py` file in order to make it a Python module. Then, add the `likes_tags.py` file, where we'll define the `{% like_widget %}` template tag as follows:

```
# likes/templatetags/likes_tags.py
# -*- coding: UTF-8 -*-
from django import template
from django.contrib.contenttypes.models import ContentType
from django.template import loader

from likes.models import Like

register = template.Library()


### TAGS ###


@register.tag
def like_widget(parser, token):
    try:
        tag_name, for_str, obj = token.split_contents()
    except ValueError:
        raise template.TemplateSyntaxError, \
            "%r tag requires a following syntax: " \
            "{%% %r for <object> %%}" % (
                token.contents[0], token.contents[0])
    return ObjectLikeWidget(obj)


class ObjectLikeWidget(template.Node):
```

```
    def __init__(self, obj):
        self.obj = obj

    def render(self, context):
        obj = template.resolve_variable(self.obj, context)
        ct = ContentType.objects.get_for_model(obj)

        is_liked_by_user = bool(Like.objects.filter(
            user=context["request"].user,
            content_type=ct,
            object_id=obj.pk,
        ))

        context.push()
        context["object"] = obj
        context["content_type_id"] = ct.pk
        context["is_liked_by_user"] = is_liked_by_user
        context["count"] = get_likes_count(obj)

        output = loader.render_to_string(
            "likes/includes/like.html", context)
        context.pop()
        return output
```

2. Also, we'll add a filter in the same file to get the number of likes for a specified object:

```
### FILTERS ###

@register.filter
def get_likes_count(obj):
    ct = ContentType.objects.get_for_model(obj)
    return Like.objects.filter(
        content_type=ct,
        object_id=obj.pk,
    ).count()
```

3. In the URL rules, we need a rule for a view, which will handle the liking and unliking using Ajax:

   # likes/urls.py
```
# -*- coding: UTF-8 -*-
from django.conf.urls import patterns, url

urlpatterns = patterns("likes.views",

    url(r"^(?P<content_type_id>[^/]+)/(?P<object_id>[^/]+)/$",
```

```
                      "json_set_like", name="json_set_like"),
        )
```

4. Then, we need to define the view, as shown in the following:

```python
# likes/views.py
# -*- coding: UTF-8 -*-
import json
from django.http import HttpResponse
from django.views.decorators.cache import never_cache
from django.contrib.contenttypes.models import ContentType
from django.shortcuts import render
from django.views.decorators.csrf import csrf_exempt

from .models import Like
from .templatetags.likes_tags import get_likes_count


@never_cache
@csrf_exempt
def json_set_like(request, content_type_id, object_id):
    """
    Sets the object as a favorite for the current user
    """
    result = {
        "success": False,
    }
    if request.user.is_authenticated() and \
    request.method == "POST":
        content_type = ContentType.objects.get(id=content_type_id)
        obj = content_type.get_object_for_this_type(pk=object_id)
        like, is_created = Like.objects.get_or_create(
            content_type=ContentType.objects.get_for_model(obj),
            object_id=obj.pk,
            user=request.user,
        )
        if not is_created:
            like.delete()
        result = {
            "success": True,
            "obj": unicode(obj),
            "action": is_created and "added" or "removed",
            "count": get_likes_count(obj),
        }
    json_str = json.dumps(result, ensure_ascii=False,
            encoding="utf8")
```

```
    return HttpResponse(json_str,
    mimetype="application/json; charset=utf-8")
```

5. In the template for the list or detail view of any object, we can add the template tag for the widget. Let's add the widget to the location detail that we created in the previous recipes, as follows:

```
{# templates/locations/location_detail.html #}
{% extends "base.html" %}
{% load likes_tags %}

{% block content %}
    {% if request.user.is_authenticated %}
        {% like_widget for location %}
    {% endif %}
    {# the details of the object go here… #}
{% endblock %}

{% block extrabody %}
    <script src="{{ STATIC_URL }}site/js/likes.js"></script>
{% endblock %}
```

6. Then, we need a template for the widget, as shown in the following:

```
{# templates/likes/includes/like.html #}
{% load i18n %}
<div class="like-widget">
    <button type="button" class="like-button btn btn-default {% if
is_liked_by_user %} active{% endif %}"
        data-href="{% url "json_set_like" content_type_id=content_
type_id object_id=object.pk %}"
        data-like-text="{% trans "Like" %}"
        data-unlike-text="{% trans "Unlike" %}"
    >
        {% if is_liked_by_user %}
            <span class="glyphicon glyphicon-star"></span>
            {% trans "Unlike" %}
        {% else %}
            <span class="glyphicon glyphicon-star-empty"></span>
            {% trans "Like" %}
        {% endif %}
    </button>
    <span class="like-badge badge">{{ count }}</span>
</div>
```

7. Finally, we create JavaScript to handle the liking and unliking action in the browser, as follows:

```javascript
// site_static/site/js/likes.js
(function($) {
    $(document).on('click', '.like-button', function() {
        var $button = $(this);
        var $badge = $button.closest('.like-widget')
            .find('.like-badge');
        $.post($button.data('href'), function(data) {
            if (data['action'] == 'added') {
                $button.addClass('active').html(
'<span class="glyphicon glyphicon-star"></span> ' +
$button.data('unlike-text')
                );
            } else {
                $button.removeClass('active').html(
'<span class="glyphicon glyphicon-star-empty"></span> ' +
$button.data('like-text')
                );
            }
            $badge.html(data['count']);
        }, 'json');
    });
})(jQuery);
```

How it works...

For any object in your website, you can put the {% like_widget for object %} template tag that will check whether the object is already liked and will show an appropriate state. The data-href, data-like-text, and data-unlike-text custom HTML5 attributes are in the widget template. The first attribute holds a unique object-specific URL to change the current state of the widget. The other two attributes hold the translated texts for the widget. In the JavaScript, liking buttons are recognized by the like button CSS class. A click-event listener attached to the document watches for the onClick events from each such button and then posts an Ajax call to the URL that is specified by the data-href attribute. The specified view accepts two of the parameters, content type and object ID, of the liked object. The view checks whether Like for the specified object exists, and if it does, the view removes it; otherwise the Like object is added. As a result, the view returns a JSON response with the success status, liked object's text representation, the action whether the Like object was added or removed, and the total number of likes. Depending on the action that is returned, JavaScript will show an appropriate state for the button.

You can debug the Ajax responses in the Chrome Developer Tools or Firefox Firebug plugin. If any server errors occur while developing, you will see the error trace back in the preview of the response, otherwise you will see the returned JSON as shown in the following screenshot:

See also

▸ The *Opening object details in a modal dialog* recipe

▸ The *Implementing a continuous scroll* recipe

▸ The *Uploading images by Ajax* recipe

▸ The *Creating a model mixin to handle generic relations* recipe in *Chapter 2, Database Structure*

▸ *Chapter 5, Custom Template Filters and Tags*

Uploading images by Ajax

File uploads using Ajax has become the de facto standard on the web. People want to see what they have chosen right after selecting a file instead of seeing it after submitting a form. Also, if the form has validation errors, nobody wants to select the files again; the file should still be selected in the form with validation errors.

There is a third-party app, `django-ajax-uploader`, that can be used to upload images with Ajax. In this recipe, we will see how to do this.

Getting ready

Let's start with the `quotes` app that we created for the *Uploading images* recipe in *Chapter 3, Forms and Views*. We will reuse the model and view; however, we'll create a different form and template and add JavaScript too.

Install `django-crispy-forms` and `django-ajax-uploader` in your local environment using the following commands:

```
(myproject)$ pip install django-crispy-forms
(myproject)$ pip install ajaxuploader
```

Don't forget to put these apps in `INSTALLED_APPS`, as follows:

```python
# conf/base.py or settings.py
INSTALLED_APPS = (
    # …
    "quotes",
    "crispy_forms",
    "ajaxuploader",
)
```

How to do it...

Let's redefine the form for inspirational quotes using the following steps:

1. First, we create a layout for the Bootstrap 3 markup. Note that, instead of the `picture` image field, we have the hidden `picture_path` and `delete_picture` fields and some markup for the file upload widget:

```python
# quotes/forms.py
# -*- coding: UTF-8 -*-
import os
from django import forms
from django.utils.translation import ugettext_lazy as _
from django.core.files import File
from django.conf import settings
from crispy_forms.helper import FormHelper
from crispy_forms import layout, bootstrap
from .models import InspirationQuote

class InspirationQuoteForm(forms.ModelForm):
    picture_path = forms.CharField(
        max_length=255,
        widget=forms.HiddenInput(),
        required=False,
```

```
    )
    delete_picture = forms.BooleanField(
        widget=forms.HiddenInput(),
        required=False,
    )

    class Meta:
        model = InspirationQuote
        fields = ["author", "quote"]

    def __init__(self, *args, **kwargs):
            super(InspirationQuoteForm, self).\
            __init__(*args, **kwargs)

        self.helper = FormHelper()
        self.helper.form_action = ""
        self.helper.form_method = "POST"

        self.helper.layout = layout.Layout(
            layout.Fieldset(
                _("Quote"),
                layout.Field("author"),
                layout.Field("quote", rows=3),
                layout.HTML("""
{% include "quotes/includes/image_upload_widget.html" %}
                """),
                layout.Field("picture_path"), # hidden
                layout.Field("delete_picture"), # hidden
            ),
            bootstrap.FormActions(
                layout.Submit("submit", _("Save"),
                    css_class="btn btn-primary"),
            )
        )
```

2. Then, we will overwrite the save method in order to handle the saving of the inspirational quote, as follows:

```
    def save(self, commit=True):
        instance = super(InspirationQuoteForm, self).\
            save(commit=True)

        if self.cleaned_data['delete_picture'] and \
            instance.picture:
```

```
            instance.picture.delete()

        if self.cleaned_data['picture_path']:
            tmp_path = self.cleaned_data['picture_path']
            abs_tmp_path = os.path.join(
                settings.MEDIA_ROOT, tmp_path)

            filename = InspirationQuote._meta.\
                get_field('picture').upload_to(
                instance, tmp_path)
            instance.picture.save(
                filename,
                File(open(abs_tmp_path, "rb")),
                False
            )

            os.remove(abs_tmp_path)
        instance.save()
        return instance
```

3. In addition to the previously defined views in the quotes app, we add the `ajax_uploader` view that will handle uploads with Ajax, as shown in the following:

```python
# quotes/views.py
# …
from ajaxuploader.views import AjaxFileUploader
ajax_uploader = AjaxFileUploader()
```

4. Then, we set the URL rule for the view, as follows:

```python
# quotes/urls.py
# -*- coding: UTF-8 -*-
from django.conf.urls import patterns, url

urlpatterns = patterns("",
    # …
    url(r"^ajax-upload/$", "quotes.views.ajax_uploader",
        name="ajax_uploader"),
)
```

5. Next, create the `image_upload_widget.html` template that will be included in the crispy form:

```html
{# templates/quotes/includes/image_upload_widget.html #}
{% load i18n %}
<div id="image_upload_widget">
    <div class="preview">
```

```
        {% if instance.picture %}
            <img src="{{ instance.picture.url }}" alt="" />
        {% endif %}
    </div>
    <div class="uploader">
        <noscript>
            <p>{% trans "Please enable JavaScript to use file
uploader." %}</p>
        </noscript>
    </div>
    <p class="help_text" class="help-block">{% trans "Available
formats are JPG, GIF, and PNG." %}</p>
    <div class="messages"></div>
</div>
```

6. Then, it is time to create the template for the form page itself. In the extrabody block, we will set a `translatable_file_uploader_options` variable that will deal with all translatable options for the file uploader, such as the widget template markup, error messages, and notifications:

```
{# templates/quotes/change_quote.html #}
{% extends "base.html" %}
{% load i18n crispy_forms_tags %}

{% block stylesheet %}
    {{ block.super }}
    <link rel="stylesheet" href="{{ STATIC_URL }}ajaxuploader/css/
fileuploader.css" />
{% endblock %}

{% block content %}
    {% crispy form %}
{% endblock %}

{% block extrabody %}
    <script src="{{ STATIC_URL }}ajaxuploader/js/fileuploader.
js"></script>
    <script>
        var translatable_file_uploader_options = {
            template: '<div class="qq-upload-drop-area"><span>{%
trans "Drop image here" %}</span></div>' +
                '<div class="qq-uploader">' +
                '<div class="qq-upload-button btn"><span
class="glyphicon glyphicon-upload"></span>  {% trans "Upload
Image" %}</div>' +
```

```
                        ' <button class="btn btn-danger qq-delete-
button"><span class="glyphicon glyphicon-trash"></span> {% trans
"Delete" %}</button>' +
                    '<ul class="qq-upload-list"></ul>' +
                '</div>',
                // template for one item in file list
                fileTemplate: '<li>' +
                    '<span class="qq-upload-file"></span>' +
                    '<span class="qq-upload-spinner"></span>' +
                    '<span class="qq-upload-size"></span>' +
                    '<a class="qq-upload-cancel" href="#">{% trans
"Cancel" %}</a>' +
                    '<span class="qq-upload-failed-text">{% trans
"Failed" %}</span>' +
                '</li>',
                messages: {
                    typeError: '{% trans "{file} has invalid
extension. Only {extensions} are allowed." %}',
                    sizeError: '{% trans "{file} is too large, maximum
file size is {sizeLimit}." %}',
                    minSizeError: '{% trans "{file} is too small,
minimum file size is {minSizeLimit}." %}',
                    emptyError: '{% trans "{file} is empty, please
select files again without it." %}',
                    filesLimitError: '{% trans "No more than
{filesLimit} files are allowed to be uploaded." %}',
                    onLeave: '{% trans "The files are being uploaded,
if you leave now the upload will be cancelled." %}'
                }
            };
            var ajax_uploader_path = '{% url "ajax_uploader" %}';
        </script>
        <script src="{{ STATIC_URL }}site/js/change_quote.js"></
script>
{% endblock %}
```

7. Finally, we create the JavaScript file that will initialize the file upload widget and handle the image preview and deletion, as follows:

```
// site_static/site/js/change_quote.js
$(function() {
    var csrfmiddlewaretoken = $('input[name="csrfmiddlewaretok
en"]').val();
    var $image_upload_widget = $('#image_upload_widget');
    var current_image_path = $('#id_picture_path').val();
    if (current_image_path) {
```

```
        $('.preview', $image_upload_widget).html(
            '<img src="' + window.settings.MEDIA_URL + current_
image_path  + '" alt="" />'
        );
    }
    var options = $.extend(window.translatable_file_uploader_
options, {
        allowedExtensions: ['jpg', 'jpeg', 'gif', 'png'],
        action: window.ajax_uploader_path,
        element: $('.uploader', $image_upload_widget)[0],
        multiple: false,
        onComplete: function(id, fileName, responseJSON) {
            if(responseJSON.success) {
                $('.messages', $image_upload_widget).html("");
                // set the original to media_file_path
                $('#id_picture_path').val('uploads/' + fileName);
                // show preview link
                $('.preview', $image_upload_widget).html(
                    '<img src="' + window.settings.MEDIA_URL +
'uploads/' + fileName + '" alt="" />'
                );
            }
        },
        onAllComplete: function(uploads) {
            // uploads is an array of maps
            // the maps look like this: {file: FileObject,
response: JSONServerResponse}
            $('.qq-upload-success').fadeOut("slow", function() {
                $(this).remove();
            });
        },
        params: {
            'csrf_token': csrfmiddlewaretoken,
            'csrf_name': 'csrfmiddlewaretoken',
            'csrf_xname': 'X-CSRFToken'
        },
        showMessage: function(message) {
            $('.messages', $image_upload_widget).html(
                '<div class="alert alert-danger">' + message + '</
div>'
            );
        }
    });
    var uploader = new qq.FileUploader(options);
```

```
        $('.qq-delete-button', $image_upload_widget).click(function()
    {
            $('.messages', $image_upload_widget).html("");
            $('.preview', $image_upload_widget).html("");
            $('#id_delete_picture').val(1);
            return false;
        });
    });
```

How it works...

When an image is selected in the upload widget, the result in the browser will look similar to the following screenshot:

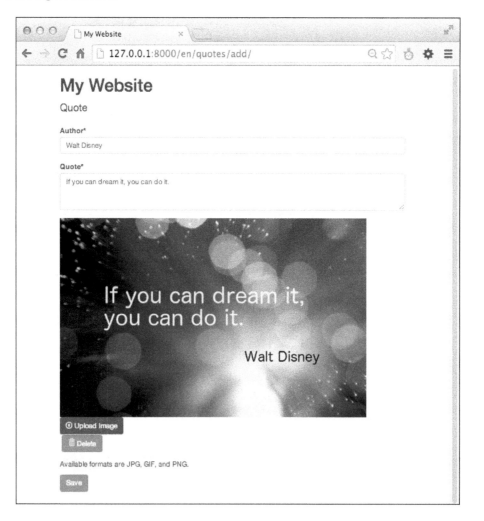

The same form can be used to create an inspirational quote and change an existing inspirational quote. Let's dig deeper into the process to see how it works. In the form, we have an uploading mechanism that consists of the following essential parts:

- ▸ The area for the preview of the image that is defined as a `<div>` tag with the preview CSS class. Initially, it might show an image if we are in an object change view and the `InspirationQuote` object is passed to the template as `{{ instance }}`.

- ▸ The area for the Ajax uploader widget that is defined as a `<div>` tag with the `uploader` CSS class. It will be filled with the dynamically-created uploading and deleting buttons as well as the uploading progress indicators.

- ▸ The help text for the upload.

- ▸ The area for error messages that is defined as a `<div>` tag with the `messages` CSS class.

- ▸ The hidden `picture_path` character field to set the path of the uploaded file.

- ▸ The hidden `delete_picture` Boolean field to mark the deletion of the file.

On page load, JavaScript will check whether `picture_path` is set; and if it is, it will show a picture preview. This will be the case only when the form is submitted with an image selected; however, there are validation errors.

Furthermore, we are defining the options for the upload widget in JavaScript. These options are combined of the global `translatable_file_uploader_options` variable with translatable strings set in the template and other configuration options set in the JavaScript file. The Ajax upload widget is initialized with these options. Some important settings to note are the `onComplete` callback that shows an image preview and fills in the `picture_path` field when an image is uploaded and the `showMessage` callback that defines how to show the error messages in the wanted area.

Lastly, there is a handler for the delete button in JavaScript, which when clicked, sets the hidden `delete_picture` field to `1` and removes the preview image.

The Ajax uploader widget dynamically creates a form with the file upload field and a hidden `<iframe>` tag to post the form data. When a file is selected, it is immediately uploaded to the `uploads` directory under `MEDIA_URL` and the path to the file is set to the `hidden picture_path` field. This directory is a temporary location for the uploaded files. When a user submits the inspirational quote form and the input is valid, the `save()` method is called. If `delete_picture` is set to `1`, the picture of the model instance will be deleted. If the `picture_path` field is defined, the image from the temporary location will be copied to its final destination and the original will be removed.

See also

▸ The *Uploading images* recipe in *Chapter 3, Forms and Views*

▸ The *Opening object details in a modal dialog* recipe

▸ The *Implementing a continuous scroll* recipe

▸ The *Implementing the Like widget* recipe

5
Custom Template Filters and Tags

In this chapter, we will cover the following topics:

- ▶ Following conventions for your own template filters and tags
- ▶ Creating a template filter to show how many days have passed since a post was published
- ▶ Creating a template filter to extract the first media object
- ▶ Creating a template filter to humanize URLs
- ▶ Creating a template tag to include a template if it exists
- ▶ Creating a template tag to load a QuerySet in a template
- ▶ Creating a template tag to parse content as a template
- ▶ Creating a template tag to modify request query parameters

Introduction

As you know, Django has an extensive template system with features such as template inheritance, filters to change the representation of values, and tags for presentational logic. Moreover, Django allows you to add your own template filters and tags to your apps. Custom filters or tags should be located in a template-tag library file under the `templatetags` Python package in your app. Then, your template-tag library can be loaded in any template with a `{% load %}` template tag. In this chapter, we will create several useful filters and tags that will give more control to template editors.

To see the template tags of this chapter in action, create a virtual environment, extract the code provided for this chapter there, run the development server, and visit `http://127.0.0.1:8000/en/` in a browser.

Following conventions for your own template filters and tags

Custom template filters and tags can become a total mess if you don't have persistent guidelines to follow. Template filters and tags should serve template editors as much as possible. They should be both handy and flexible. In this recipe, we will take a look at some conventions that should be used when enhancing the functionality of the Django template system.

How to do it...

Follow these conventions when extending the Django template system:

1. Don't create or use custom template filters or tags when the logic for the page fits better in the view, context processors, or model methods. When your content is context-specific, such as a list of objects or object-detail view, load the object in the view. If you need to show some content on every page, create a context processor. Use custom methods of the model instead of template filters when you need to get some properties of an object that are not related to the context of the template.

2. Name the template-tag library with the `_tags` suffix. When your app is named differently than your template-tag library, you can avoid ambiguous package importing problems.

3. In the newly created library, separate the filters from tags, for example, using comments as shown the following code:

```
# utils/templatetags/utility_tags.py
# -*- coding: UTF-8 -*-
from __future__ import unicode_literals
from django import template
register = template.Library()

### FILTERS ###
# .. your filters go here..

### TAGS ###
# .. your tags go here..
```

4. When creating advanced custom template tags, make sure that their syntax is easy to remember by including the following constructs:

   ❑ `for [app_name.model_name]`: Include this construct in order to use a specific model

- □ using [template_name]: Include this construct in order to use a template for the output of the template tag
- □ limit [count]: Include this construct in order to limit the results to a specific amount
- □ as [context_variable]: Include this construct in order to save the results to a context variable that can be reused multiple times

5. Try to avoid multiple values that are defined positionally in the template tags, unless they are self-explanatory. Otherwise, this will likely confuse the template developers.

6. Make as many resolvable arguments as possible. Strings without quotes should be treated as context variables that need to be resolved or short words that remind you of the structure of the template tag components.

Creating a template filter to show how many days have passed since a post was published

Not all people keep track of the date and when talking about creation or modification dates of cutting-edge information; for many of us, it is convenient to read the time difference. For example, the blog entry was posted *three days ago*, the news article was published *today*, and the user last logged in *yesterday*. In this recipe, we will create a template filter named days_since, which converts dates to humanized time differences.

Getting ready

Create the utils app and put it under INSTALLED_APPS in the settings, if you haven't done that yet. Then, create a templatetags Python package in this app (Python packages are directories with an empty __init__.py file).

How to do it...

Create a utility_tags.py file with the following content:

```
# utils/templatetags/utility_tags.py
# -*- coding: UTF-8 -*-
from __future__ import unicode_literals
from datetime import datetime
from django import template
from django.utils.translation import ugettext_lazy as _
from django.utils.timezone import now as tz_now
```

```
register = template.Library()

### FILTERS ###

@register.filter
def days_since(value):
    """ Returns number of days between today and value."""

    today = tz_now().date()
    if isinstance(value, datetime.datetime):
        value = value.date()
    diff = today - value
    if diff.days > 1:
        return _("%s days ago") % diff.days
    elif diff.days == 1:
        return _("yesterday")
    elif diff.days == 0:
        return _("today")
    else:
        # Date is in the future; return formatted date.
        return value.strftime("%B %d, %Y")
```

How it works...

If you use this filter in a template as shown in the following code, it will render something similar to *yesterday* or *5 days ago*:

```
{% load utility_tags %}
{{ object.published|days_since }}
```

You can apply this filter to values of the `date` and `datetime` types.

Each template-tag library has a register, where filters and tags are collected. Django filters are functions registered by the `@register.filter` decorator. By default, the filter in the template system will be named same as the function or other callable object. If you want, you can set a different name for the filter by passing the name to the decorator, as follows:

```
@register.filter(name="humanized_days_since")
def days_since(value):
    ...
```

The filter itself is quite self-explanatory. At first, the current date is read. If the given value of the filter is of the `datetime` type, `date` is extracted. Then, the difference between today and the extracted value is calculated. Depending on the number of days, different string results are returned.

There's more...

This filter is also easy to extend in order to show the difference in time, such as *just now*, *7 minutes ago*, and *3 hours ago*. Just operate on the datetime values instead of the date values.

See also

▸ The *Creating a template filter to extract the first media object* recipe

▸ The *Creating a template filter to humanize URLs* recipe

Creating a template filter to extract the first media object

Imagine that you are developing a blog overview page, and for each post, you want to show images, music, or videos in that page taken from the content. In such a case, you need to extract the `<figure>`, `<img>`, `<object>`, `<embed>`, `<video>`, `<audio>`, and `<iframe>` tags from the HTML content of the post. In this recipe, we will see how to perform this using regular expressions in the `first_media` filter.

Getting ready

We will start with the `utils` app that should be set in INSTALLED_APPS in the settings and the `templatetags` package in this app.

How to do it...

In the `utility_tags.py` file, add the following content:

```
# utils/templatetags/utility_tags.py
# -*- coding: UTF-8 -*-
from __future__ import unicode_literals
import re
from django import template
from django.utils.safestring import mark_safe
register = template.Library()

### FILTERS ###


media_tags_regex = re.compile(
```

```
        r"<figure[\S\s]+?</figure>|"
        r"<object[\S\s]+?</object>|"
        r"<video[\S\s]+?</video>|"
        r"<audio[\S\s]+?</audio>|"
        r"<iframe[\S\s]+?</iframe>|"
        r"<(img|embed)[^>]+>",
        re.MULTILINE
)


@register.filter
def first_media(content):
    """ Returns the first image or flash file from the html
     content """
    m = media_tags_regex.search(content)
    media_tag = ""
    if m:
        media_tag = m.group()
    return mark_safe(media_tag)
```

How it works...

If the HTML content in the database is valid, when you put the following code in the template, it will retrieve the media tags from the content field of the object; otherwise, an empty string will be returned if no media is found:

```
{% load utility_tags %}
{{ object.content|first_media }}
```

Regular expressions are powerful feature to search/replace patterns of text. At first, we will define the compiled regular expression as `media_file_regex`. In our case, we will search for all the possible media tags that can also occur in multiple lines.

 Python strings can be concatenated without a plus (+) symbol.

Let's see how this regular expression works, as follows:

- Alternating patterns are separated by the pipe (|) symbol.

- For possibly multiline tags, we will use the `[\S\s]+?` pattern that matches any symbol at least once; however, as little times as possible, until we find the the string that goes after it. Therefore, `<figure[\S\s]+?</figure>` searches for a `<figure>` tag and everything after it, until it finds the closing `</figure>` tag.

- Similarly, with the `[^>]+` pattern, we search for any symbol except the greater than (>) symbol at least once and as many times as possible.

The `re.MULTILINE` flag ensures that the search will happen in multiple lines. Then, in the filter, we will perform a search for this regular expression pattern. By default, the result of the filter will show the <, >, and & symbols escaped as the <, >, and & entities. However, we use the `mark_safe()` function that marks the result as safe and HTML-ready in order to be shown in the template without escaping.

There's more...

If you are interested in regular expressions, you can learn more about them in the official Python documentation at `https://docs.python.org/2/library/re.html`.

See also

- The *Creating a template filter to show how many days have passed since a post was published* recipe
- The *Creating a template filter to humanize URLs* recipe

Creating a template filter to humanize URLs

Usually, common web users enter URLs in address fields without protocol and trailing slashes. In this recipe, we will create a `humanize_url` filter that is used to present URLs to the user in a shorter format, truncating very long addresses, similar to what Twitter does with the links in the tweets.

Getting ready

Similar to the previous recipes, we will start with the `utils` app that should be set in `INSTALLED_APPS` in the settings and contain the `templatetags` package.

How to do it...

In the `FILTERS` section of the `utility_tags.py` template library in the `utils` app, let's add a `humanize_url` filter and register it, as shown in the following code:

```
# utils/templatetags/utility_tags.py
# -*- coding: UTF-8 -*-
from __future__ import unicode_literals
import re
from django import template
```

```
register = template.Library()

### FILTERS ###

@register.filter
def humanize_url(url, letter_count):
    """ Returns a shortened human-readable URL """
    letter_count = int(letter_count)
    re_start = re.compile(r"^https?://")
    re_end = re.compile(r"/$")
    url = re_end.sub("", re_start.sub("", url))
    if len(url) > letter_count:
        url = "%s…" % url[:letter_count - 1]
    return url
```

How it works...

We can use the `humanize_url` filter in any template, as follows:

```
{% load utility_tags %}
<a href="{{ object.website }}" target="_blank">
    {{ object.website|humanize_url:30 }}
</a>
```

The filter uses regular expressions to remove the leading protocol and trailing slash, shorten the URL to the given amount of letters, and add an ellipsis to the end if the URL doesn't fit in the specified letter count.

See also

▶ The *Creating a template filter to show how many days have passed since a post was published* recipe

▶ The *Creating a template filter to extract the first media object* recipe

▶ The *Creating a template tag to include a template if it exists* recipe

Creating a template tag to include a template if it exists

Django has the `{% include %}` template tag that renders and includes another template. However, there is a problem in some situations, where an error is raised if the template does not exist. In this recipe, we will see how to create a `{% try_to_include %}` template tag that includes another template and fails silently if there is no such template.

Getting ready

We will start again with the `utils` app that is installed and ready for custom template tags.

How to do it...

Advanced custom template tags consist of two things: the function that is parsing the arguments of the template tag and the `Node` class that is responsible for the logic of the template tag as well as the output. Perform the following steps to create the `{% try_to_ include %}` template tag:

1. First, let's create the function parsing the template-tag arguments, as follows:

    ```
    # utils/templatetags/utility_tags.py
    # -*- coding: UTF-8 -*-
    from __future__ import unicode_literals
    from django import template
    from django.template.loader import get_template
    register = template.Library()

    ### TAGS ###

    @register.tag
    def try_to_include(parser, token):
      """Usage: {% try_to_include "sometemplate.html" %}
      This will fail silently if the template doesn't exist.
      If it does exist, it will be rendered with the current
      context."""
      try:
        tag_name, template_name = token.split_contents()
      except ValueError:
        raise template.TemplateSyntaxError, \
          "%r tag requires a single argument" % \
          token.contents.split()[0]
      return IncludeNode(template_name)
    ```

2. Then, we need the `Node` class in the same file, as follows:

    ```
    class IncludeNode(template.Node):
      def __init__(self, template_name):
        self.template_name = template_name

      def render(self, context):
        try:
          # Loading the template and rendering it
          template_name = template.resolve_variable(
    ```

```
          self. template_name, context)
        included_template = get_template(
          template_name
        ).render(context)
      except template.TemplateDoesNotExist:
        included_template = ""
      return included_template
```

How it works...

The {% try_to_include %} template tag expects one argument, that is, template_ name. Therefore, in the try_to_include() function, we try to assign the split contents of the token only to the tag_name variable (which is try_to_include) and the template_ name variable. If this doesn't work, the template syntax error is raised. The function returns the IncludeNode object, which gets the template_name field for later use.

In the render() method of IncludeNode, we resolve the template_name variable. If a context variable was passed to the template tag, its value will be used here for template_ name. If a quoted string was passed to the template tag, then the content in the quotes will be used for template_name.

Lastly, we will try to load the template and render it with the current template context. If that doesn't work, an empty string is returned.

There are at least two situations where we could use this template tag:

- ▶ It is used when including a template whose path is defined in a model, as follows:

```
{% load utility_tags %}
{% try_to_include object.template_path %}
```

- ▶ It is used when including a template whose path is defined with the {% with %} template tag somewhere high in the template context variable's scope. This is especially useful when you need to create custom layouts for plugins in the placeholder of a template in Django CMS:

```
{# templates/cms/start_page.html #}
{% with editorial_content_template_path="cms/plugins/editorial_
content/start_page.html" %}
    {% placeholder "main_content" %}
{% endwith %}

{# templates/cms/plugins/editorial_content.html #}
{% load utility_tags %}

{% if editorial_content_template_path %}
    {% try_to_include editorial_content_template_path %}
```

```
{% else %}
    <div>
        <!-- Some default presentation of
             editorial content plugin -->
    </div>
{% endif %}
```

There's more...

You can use the `{% try_to_include %}` tag as well as the default `{% include %}` tag to include the templates that extend other templates. This is beneficial for large-scale portals, where you have different kinds of lists in which complex items share the same structure as widgets but have a different source of data.

For example, in the artist list template, you can include the artist item template, as follows:

```
{% load utility_tags %}
{% for object in object_list %}
    {% try_to_include "artists/includes/artist_item.html" %}
{% endfor %}
```

This template will extend from the item base, as follows:

```
{# templates/artists/includes/artist_item.html #}
{% extends "utils/includes/item_base.html" %}

{% block item_title %}
    {{ object.first_name }} {{ object.last_name }}
{% endblock %}
```

The item base defines the markup for any item and also includes a Like widget, as follows:

```
{# templates/utils/includes/item_base.html #}
{% load likes_tags %}

<h3>{% block item_title %}{% endblock %}</h3>
{% if request.user.is_authenticated %}
    {% like_widget for object %}
{% endif %}
```

See also

- ▶ The *Creating templates for Django CMS* recipe in *Chapter 7, Django CMS*
- ▶ The *Writing your own CMS plugin* recipe in *Chapter 7, Django CMS*
- ▶ The *Implementing the Like widget* recipe in *Chapter 4, Templates and JavaScript*

- ▶ The *Creating a template tag to load a QuerySet in a template* recipe
- ▶ The *Creating a template tag to parse content as a template* recipe
- ▶ The *Creating a template tag to modify request query parameters* recipe

Creating a template tag to load a QuerySet in a template

Most often, the content that should be shown on a webpage will have to be defined in the view. If this is the content to be shown on every page, it is logical to create a context processor. Another situation is where you need to show additional content such as the latest news or a random quote on some pages; for example, the starting page or the details page of an object. In this case, you can load the necessary content with the `{% get_objects %}` template tag, which we will implement in this recipe.

Getting ready

Once again, we will start with the `utils` app that should be installed and ready for custom template tags.

How to do it...

An advanced custom template tag consists of a function that parses arguments that are passed to the tag and a `Node` class that renders the output of the tag or modifies the template context. Perform the following steps to create the `{% get_objects %}` template tag:

1. First, let's create the function parsing the template-tag arguments, as follows:

```
# utils/templatetags/utility_tags.py
# -*- coding: UTF-8 -*-
from __future__ import unicode_literals
from django.db import models
from django import template
register = template.Library()

### TAGS ###

@register.tag
def get_objects(parser, token):
    """
    Gets a queryset of objects of the model specified
    by app and model names
    Usage:
        {% get_objects [<manager>.]<method> from
```

```
        <app_name>.<model_name> [limit <amount>] as
        <var_name> %}
    Example:
        {% get_objects latest_published from people.Person
         limit 3 as people %}
        {% get_objects site_objects.all from news.Article
         limit 3 as articles %}
        {% get_objects site_objects.all from news.Article
         as articles %}
    """
    amount = None
    try:
        tag_name, manager_method, str_from, appmodel, \
         str_limit, amount, str_as, var_name = \
            token.split_contents()
    except ValueError:
        try:
            tag_name, manager_method, str_from, appmodel, \
            str_as, var_name = token.split_contents()
        except ValueError:
            raise template.TemplateSyntaxError, \
                "get_objects tag requires a following "\
                "syntax: "\
                "{% get_objects [<manager>.]<method> "\
                "from <app_ name>.<model_name> "\
                "[limit <amount>] as <var_name> %}"
    try:
        app_name, model_name = appmodel.split(".")
    except ValueError:
        raise template.TemplateSyntaxError, \
            "get_objects tag requires application name "\
            "and model name separated by a dot"
    model = models.get_model(app_name, model_name)
    return ObjectsNode(
        model, manager_method, amount, var_name
    )
```

2. Then, we will create the Node class in the same file, as shown in the following code:

```
class ObjectsNode(template.Node):
    def __init__(
        self, model, manager_method, amount, var_name
    ):
        self.model = model
        self.manager_method = manager_method
```

```python
        self.amount = amount
        self.var_name = var_name

    def render(self, context):
        if "." in self.manager_method:
            manager, method = \
                self.manager_method.split(".")
        else:
            manager = "_default_manager"
            method = self.manager_method

        qs = getattr(
            getattr(self.model, manager),
            method,
            self.model._default_manager.none,
        )()
        if self.amount:
            amount = template.resolve_variable(
                self.amount, context
            )
            context[self.var_name] = qs[:amount]
        else:
            context[self.var_name] = qs
        return ""
```

How it works...

The `{% get_objects %}` template tag loads QuerySet defined by the method of the manager from a specified app and model, limits the result to the specified amount, and saves the result to a context variable.

The following code is the simplest example of how to use the template tag that we have just created. It will load all news articles in any template using the following snippet:

```
{% load utility_tags %}
{% get_objects all from news.Article as all_articles %}
{% for article in all_articles %}
    <a href="{{ article.get_url_path }}">{{ article.title }}</a>
{% endfor %}
```

This is using the `all()` method of the default `objects` manager of the `Article` model and it will sort the articles by the `ordering` attribute defined in the `Meta` class of the model.

A more advanced example would be required to create a custom manager with a custom method to query the objects from the database. A manager is an interface that provides the database query operations to models. Each model has at least one manager called `objects` by default. As an example, let's create an `Artist` model that has a draft or published status and a new `custom_manager` that allows you to select random published artists:

```
# artists/models.py
# -*- coding: UTF-8 -*-
from __future__ import unicode_literals
from django.db import models
from django.utils.translation import ugettext_lazy as _

STATUS_CHOICES = (
    ("draft", _("Draft")),
    ("published", _("Published")),
)
class ArtistManager(models.Manager):
    def random_published(self):
        return self.filter(status="published").order_by("?")

class Artist(models.Model):
    # ...
    status = models.CharField(_("Status"), max_length=20,
        choices=STATUS_CHOICES)
    custom_manager = ArtistManager()
```

To load a random published artist, you add the following snippet to any template:

```
{% load utility_tags %}
{% get_objects custom_manager.random_published from artists.Artist
limit 1 as random_artists %}
{% for artist in random_artists %}
    {{ artist.first_name }} {{ artist.last_name }}
{% endfor %}
```

Let's look at the code of the `{% get_objects %}` template tag. In the parsing function, there is one of the two formats expected; with the limit and without it. The string is parsed, the model is recognized, and then the components of the template tag are passed to the `ObjectNode` class.

In the `render()` method of the `Node` class, we will check the manager's name and its method's name. If this is not defined, `_default_manager` will be used, which is an automatic property of any model injected by Django and points to the first available `models.Manager()` instance. In most cases, `_default_manager` will be same as `objects`. After that, we will call the method of the manager and fall back to empty `QuerySet` if the method doesn't exist. If a limit is defined, we will resolve the value of it and limit `QuerySet`. Lastly, we will save the `QuerySet` to the context variable.

See also

> ▸ The *Creating a template tag to include a template if it exists* recipe
> ▸ The *Creating a template tag to parse content as a template* recipe
> ▸ The *Creating a template tag to modify request query parameters* recipe

Creating a template tag to parse content as a template

In this recipe, we will create a `{% parse %}` template tag, which will allow you to put template snippets in the database. This is valuable when you want to provide different content for authenticated and unauthenticated users, when you want to include a personalized salutation or you don't want to hardcode the media paths in the database.

Getting ready

As usual, we will start with the `utils` app that should be installed and ready for custom template tags.

How to do it...

An advanced custom template tag consists of a function that parses the arguments that are passed to the tag and a `Node` class that renders the output of the tag or modifies the template context. Perform the following steps to create them:

1. First, let's create the function parsing the arguments of the template tag, as follows:

```python
# utils/templatetags/utility_tags.py
# -*- coding: UTF-8 -*-
from __future__ import unicode_literals
from django import template
```

```
register = template.Library()

### TAGS ###

@register.tag
def parse(parser, token):
    """
    Parses the value as a template and prints it or
    saves to a variable
    Usage:
        {% parse <template_value> [as <variable>] %}
    Examples:
        {% parse object.description %}
        {% parse header as header %}
        {% parse "{{ MEDIA_URL }}js/" as js_url %}
    """
    bits = token.split_contents()
    tag_name = bits.pop(0)
    try:
        template_value = bits.pop(0)
        var_name = None
        if len(bits) == 2:
            bits.pop(0)  # remove the word "as"
            var_name = bits.pop(0)
    except ValueError:
        raise template.TemplateSyntaxError, \
            "parse tag requires a following syntax: "\
            "{% parse <template_value> [as <variable>] %}"

    return ParseNode(template_value, var_name)
```

2. Then, we will create the Node class in the same file, as follows:

```
class ParseNode(template.Node):
    def __init__(self, template_value, var_name):
        self.template_value = template_value
        self.var_name = var_name

    def render(self, context):
        template_value = template.resolve_variable(
            self.template_value, context)
        t = template.Template(template_value)
        context_vars = {}
        for d in list(context):
            for var, val in d.items():
```

```
                    context_vars[var] = val
        result = t.render(template.RequestContext(
            context["request"], context_vars))
        if self.var_name:
            context[self.var_name] = result
            return ""
        return result
```

How it works...

The `{% parse %}` template tag allows you to parse a value as a template and render it immediately or save it as a context variable.

If we have an object with a description field, which can contain template variables or logic, we can parse and render it using the following code:

```
{% load utility_tags %}
{% parse object.description %}
```

It is also possible to define a value in order to parse using a quoted string as shown in the following code:

```
{% load utility_tags %}
{% parse "{{ STATIC_URL }}site/img/" as img_path %}
<img src="{{ img_path }}someimage.png" alt="" />
```

Let's take a look at the code of the `{% parse %}` template tag. The parsing function checks the arguments of the template tag bit by bit. At first, we expect the `parse` name, then the template value, and at last we expect the optional `as` word followed by the context variable name. The template value and variable name are passed to the `ParseNode` class. The `render()` method of that class, at first, resolves the value of the template variable and creates a template object out of it. Then, it renders the template with all the context variables. If the variable name is defined, the result is saved to it; otherwise, the result is shown immediately.

See also

- ▸ The *Creating a template tag to include a template if it exists* recipe
- ▸ The *Creating a template tag to load a QuerySet in a template* recipe
- ▸ The *Creating a template tag to modify request query parameters* recipe

Creating a template tag to modify request query parameters

Django has a convenient and flexible system to create canonical and clean URLs just by adding regular expression rules to the URL configuration files. However, there is a lack of built-in mechanisms in order to manage query parameters. Views such as search or filterable object lists need to accept query parameters to drill down through the filtered results using another parameter or to go to another page. In this recipe, we will create the {% modify_query %}, {% add_to_query %}, and {% remove_from_query %} template tags, which let you add, change, or remove the parameters of the current query.

Getting ready

Once again, we start with the utils app that should be set in INSTALLED_APPS and contain the templatetags package.

Also, make sure that you have the request context processor set for the TEMPLATE_CONTEXT_PROCESSORS setting, as follows:

```python
# conf/base.py or settings.py
TEMPLATE_CONTEXT_PROCESSORS = (
    "django.contrib.auth.context_processors.auth",
    "django.core.context_processors.debug",
    "django.core.context_processors.i18n",
    "django.core.context_processors.media",
    "django.core.context_processors.static",
    "django.core.context_processors.tz",
    "django.contrib.messages.context_processors.messages",
    "django.core.context_processors.request",
)
```

How to do it...

For these template tags, we will be using the simple_tag decorator that parses the components and requires you to just define the rendering function, as follows:

1. At first, we will create the {% modify_query %} template tag:

    ```python
    # utils/templatetags/utility_tags.py
    # -*- coding: UTF-8 -*-
    from __future__ import unicode_literals
    import urllib
    from django import template
    ```

```
from django.utils.encoding import force_str
register = template.Library()


### TAGS ###


@register.simple_tag(takes_context=True)
def modify_query(
    context, *params_to_remove, **params_to_change
):
    """ Renders a link with modified current query
    parameters """
    query_params = []
    for key, value_list in \
        context["request"].GET._iterlists():
        if not key in params_to_remove:
            # don't add key-value pairs for
            # params_to_change
            if key in params_to_change:
                query_params.append(
                    (key, params_to_change[key])
                )
                params_to_change.pop(key)
            else:
                # leave existing parameters as they were
                # if not mentioned in the params_to_change
                for value in value_list:
                    query_params.append((key, value))
    # attach new params
    for key, value in params_to_change.items():
        query_params.append((key, value))
    query_string = context["request"].path
    if len(query_params):
        query_string += "?%s" % urllib.urlencode([
            (key, force_str(value))
            for (key, value) in query_params if value
        ]).replace("&", "&amp;")
    return query_string
```

2. Then, let's create the {% add_to_query %} template tag:

```
@register.simple_tag(takes_context=True)
def add_to_query(
    context, *params_to_remove, **params_to_add
):
    """ Renders a link with modified current query
```

```
    parameters """
    query_params = []
    # go through current query params..
    for key, value_list in \
        context["request"].GET._iterlists():
        if not key in params_to_remove:
            # don't add key-value pairs which already
            # exist in the query
            if key in params_to_add and \
            unicode(params_to_add[key]) in value_list:
                params_to_add.pop(key)
            for value in value_list:
                query_params.append((key, value))
    # add the rest key-value pairs
    for key, value in params_to_add.items():
        query_params.append((key, value))
    # empty values will be removed
    query_string = context["request"].path
    if len(query_params):
        query_string += "?%s" % urllib.urlencode([
            (key, force_str(value))
            for (key, value) in query_params if value
        ]).replace("&", "&amp;")
    return query_string
```

3. Lastly, let's create the {% remove_from_query %} template tag:

```
@register.simple_tag(takes_context=True)
def remove_from_query(context, *args, **kwargs):
    """ Renders a link with modified current query
    parameters """
    query_params = []
    # go through current query params..
    for key, value_list in \
        context["request"].GET._iterlists():
        # skip keys mentioned in the args
        if not key in args:
            for value in value_list:
                # skip key-value pairs mentioned in kwargs
                if not (key in kwargs and
                  unicode(value) == unicode(kwargs[key])):
                    query_params.append((key, value))
    # empty values will be removed
    query_string = context["request"].path
    if len(query_params):
```

```
query_string = "?%s" % urllib.urlencode([
    (key, force_str(value))
    for (key, value) in query_params if value
]).replace("&", "&amp;")
return query_string
```

How it works...

All the three created template tags behave similarly. At first, they read the current query parameters from the `request.GET` dictionary-like `QueryDict` object to a new list of key value `query_params` tuples. Then, the values are updated depending on the positional arguments and keyword arguments. Lastly, the new query string is formed, all spaces and special characters are URL-encoded, and the ampersands connecting the query parameters are escaped. This new query string is returned to the template.

 To read more about the `QueryDict` objects, refer to the official Django documentation at `https://docs.djangoproject.com/en/1.8/ref/request-response/#querydict-objects`.

Let's take a look at an example of how the `{% modify_query %}` template tag can be used. Positional arguments in the template tag define which query parameters are to be removed and the keyword arguments define which query parameters are to be modified at the current query. If the current URL is `http://127.0.0.1:8000/artists/?category=fine-art&page=5`, we can use the following template tag to render a link that goes to the next page:

```
{% load utility_tags %}
<a href="{% modify_query page=6 %}">6</a>
```

The following snippet is the output rendered using the preceding template tag:

```
<a href="/artists/?category=fine-art&amp;page=6">6</a>
```

We can also use the following example to render a link that resets pagination and goes to another category, *Sculpture*, as follows:

```
{% load utility_tags i18n %}
<a href="{% modify_query "page" category="sculpture" %}">{% trans
"Sculpture" %}</a>
```

The following snippet is the output rendered using the preceding template tag:

```
<a href="/artists/?category=sculpture">Sculpture</a>
```

With the {% add_to_query %} template tag, you can add the parameters step-by-step with the same name. For example, if the current URL is http://127.0.0.1:8000/artists/?category=fine-art, you can add another category, *Sculpture*, with the help of the following link:

```
{% load utility_tags i18n %}
<a href="{% add_to_query "page" category="sculpture" %}">{% trans
"Sculpture" %}</a>
```

This will be rendered in the template as shown in the following snippet:

```
<a href="/artists/?category=fine-art&amp;category=sculpture">Sculptu
re</a>
```

Lastly, with the help of the {% remove_from_query %} template tag, you can remove the parameters step-by-step with the same name. For example, if the current URL is http://127.0.0.1:8000/artists/?category=fine-art&category=sculpture, you can remove the *Sculpture* category with the help of the following link:

```
{% load utility_tags i18n %}
<a href="{% remove_from_query "page" category="sculpture" %}"><span
class="glyphicon glyphicon-remove"></span> {% trans "Sculpture" %}</a>
```

This will be rendered in the template as follows:

```
<a href="/artists/?category=fine-art"><span class="glyphicon
glyphicon-remove"></span> Sculpture</a>
```

See also

- ► The *Filtering object lists* recipe in *Chapter 3, Forms and Views*
- ► The *Creating a template tag to include a template if it exists* recipe
- ► The *Creating a template tag to load a QuerySet in a template* recipe
- ► The *Creating a template tag to parse content as a template* recipe

6
Model Administration

In this chapter, we will cover the following topics:

- ▶ Customizing columns on the change list page
- ▶ Creating admin actions
- ▶ Developing change list filters
- ▶ Customizing default admin settings
- ▶ Inserting a map on a change form

Introduction

The Django framework comes with a built-in administration system for your models. With very little effort, you can set up filterable, searchable, and sortable lists for browsing your models and configure forms to add and edit data. In this chapter, we will go through the advanced techniques to customize administration by developing some practical cases.

Customizing columns on the change list page

Change list views in the default Django administration system let you have an overview of all instances of the specific models. By default, the `list_display` model admin property controls the fields that are shown in different columns. Additionally, you can have custom functions set there that return the data from relations or display custom HTML. In this recipe, we will create a special function for the `list_display` property that shows an image in one of the columns of the list view. As a bonus, we will make one field directly editable in the list view by adding the `list_editable` setting.

Getting ready

To start with, make sure that `django.contrib.admin` is in `INSTALLED_APPS` in the settings and `AdminSite` is hooked in the URL configuration. Then, create a new `products` app and put it under `INSTALLED_APPS`. This app will have the `Product` and `ProductPhoto` models, where one product might have multiple photos. For this example, we will also be using `UrlMixin`, which was defined in the *Creating a model mixin with URL-related methods* recipe in *Chapter 2, Database Structure*.

Let's create the `Product` and `ProductPhoto` models in the `models.py` file, as follows:

```python
# products/models.py
# -*- coding: UTF-8 -*-
from __future__ import unicode_literals
import os
from django.db import models
from django.utils.timezone import now as timezone_now
from django.utils.translation import ugettext_lazy as _
from django.core.urlresolvers import reverse
from django.core.urlresolvers import NoReverseMatch
from django.utils.encoding import python_2_unicode_compatible
from utils.models import UrlMixin

def upload_to(instance, filename):
    now = timezone_now()
    filename_base, filename_ext = os.path.splitext(filename)
    return "products/%s/%s%s" % (
        instance.product.slug,
        now.strftime("%Y%m%d%H%M%S"),
        filename_ext.lower(),
    )

@python_2_unicode_compatible
class Product(UrlMixin):
    title = models.CharField(_("title"), max_length=200)
    slug = models.SlugField(_("slug"), max_length=200)
    description = models.TextField(_("description"), blank=True)
    price = models.DecimalField(_("price (€)"), max_digits=8,
        decimal_places=2, blank=True, null=True)

    class Meta:
        verbose_name = _("Product")
```

```
            verbose_name_plural = _("Products")

    def __str__(self):
        return self.title

    def get_url_path(self):
        try:
            return reverse("product_detail", kwargs={
                "slug": self.slug
            })
        except NoReverseMatch:
            return ""

@python_2_unicode_compatible
class ProductPhoto(models.Model):
    product = models.ForeignKey(Product)
    photo = models.ImageField(_("photo"), upload_to=upload_to)

    class Meta:
        verbose_name = _("Photo")
        verbose_name_plural = _("Photos")

    def __str__(self):
        return self.photo.name
```

How to do it...

We will create a simple administration for the `Product` model that will have instances of the `ProductPhoto` model attached to the product as inlines.

In the `list_display` property, we will list the `get_photo()` method of the model admin that will be used to show the first photo from many-to-one relationship.

Let's create an `admin.py` file with the following content:

```
# products/admin.py
# -*- coding: UTF-8 -*-
from __future__ import unicode_literals
from django.db import models
from django.contrib import admin
from django.utils.translation import ugettext_lazy as _
```

```python
from django.http import HttpResponse

from .models import Product, ProductPhoto

class ProductPhotoInline(admin.StackedInline):
    model = ProductPhoto
    extra = 0

class ProductAdmin(admin.ModelAdmin):
    list_display = ["title", "get_photo", "price"]
    list_editable = ["price"]

    fieldsets = (
        (_("Product"), {
            "fields": ("title", "slug", "description", "price"),
        }),
    )
    prepopulated_fields = {"slug": ("title",)}
    inlines = [ProductPhotoInline]

    def get_photo(self, obj):
        project_photos = obj.productphoto_set.all()[:1]
        if project_photos.count() > 0:
            return """<a href="%(product_url)s" target="_blank">
                <img src="%(photo_url)s" alt="" width="100" />
            </a>""" % {
                "product_url": obj.get_url_path(),
                "photo_url":  project_photos[0].photo.url,
            }
        return ""
    get_photo.short_description = _("Preview")
    get_photo.allow_tags = True

admin.site.register(Product, ProductAdmin)
```

How it works...

If you look at the product administration list in the browser, it will look similar to the following screenshot:

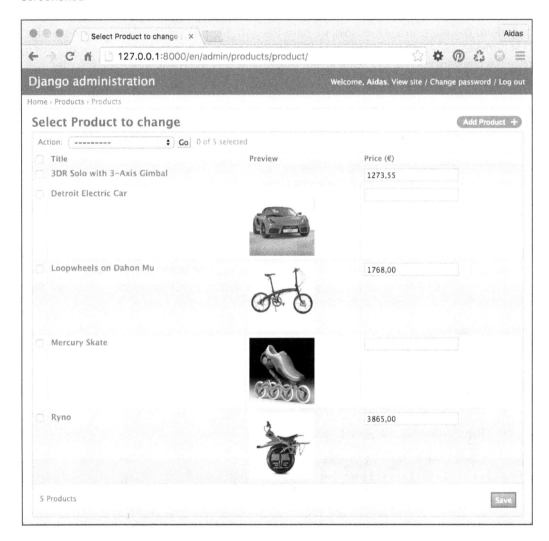

Usually, the `list_display` property defines the fields to list in the administration list view; for example, `title` and `price` are the fields of the `Product` model.

Besides the normal field names, the `list_display` property accepts a function or another callable, the name of an attribute of the admin model, or the name of the attribute of the model.

In Python, a callable is a function, method, or a class that implements the __call__() method. You can check whether a variable is callable using the callable() function.

Each callable that you use in list_display will get a model instance passed as the first argument. Therefore, in our example, we have the get_photo() method of the model admin that retrieves the Product instance as obj. The method tries to get the first ProductPhoto from the many-to-one relationship and, if it exists, it returns the HTML with the <img> tag linked to the detail page of Product.

You can set several attributes for the callables that you use in list_display. The short_description attribute of the callable defines the title shown for the column. The allow_tags attribute informs administration to not escape the HTML values.

In addition, the **Price** field is made editable by the list_editable setting and there is a **Save** button at the bottom to save the whole list of products.

There's more...

Ideally, the get_photo() method shouldn't have any hardcoded HTML in it; however, it should load and render a template from a file. For this, you can utilize the render_to_string() function from django.template.loader. Then, your presentation logic will be separated from the business logic. I am leaving this as an exercise for you.

See also

▶ The *Creating a model mixin with URL-related methods* recipe in *Chapter 2, Database Structure*

▶ The *Creating admin actions* recipe

▶ The *Developing change list filters* recipe

Creating admin actions

The Django administration system provides actions that we can execute for selected items in the list. There is one action given by default and it is used to delete selected instances. In this recipe, we will create an additional action for the list of the Product model that allows the administrators to export selected products to Excel spreadsheets.

Getting ready

We will start with the `products` app that we created in the previous recipe.

Make sure that you have the `xlwt` module installed in your virtual environment to create an Excel spreadsheet:

```
(myproject_env)$ pip install xlwt
```

How to do it...

Admin actions are functions that take three arguments: the current `ModelAdmin` value, the current `HttpRequest` value, and the `QuerySet` value containing the selected items. Perform the following steps to create a custom admin action:

1. Let's create an `export_xls()` function in the `admin.py` file of the products app, as follows:

    ```python
    # products/admin.py
    # -*- coding: UTF-8 -*-
    from __future__ import unicode_literals
    import xlwt
    # ... other imports ...

    def export_xls(modeladmin, request, queryset):
        response = HttpResponse(
            content_type="application/ms-excel"
        )
        response["Content-Disposition"] = "attachment; "\
            "filename=products.xls"
        wb = xlwt.Workbook(encoding="utf-8")
        ws = wb.add_sheet("Products")

        row_num = 0

        ### Print Title Row ###
        columns = [
            # column name, column width
            ("ID", 2000),
            ("Title", 6000),
            ("Description", 8000),
            ("Price (€)", 3000),
        ]

        header_style = xlwt.XFStyle()
    ```

```
        header_style.font.bold = True

        for col_num, (item, width) in enumerate(columns):
            ws.write(row_num, col_num, item, header_style)
            # set column width
            ws.col(col_num).width = width

        text_style = xlwt.XFStyle()
        text_style.alignment.wrap = 1

        price_style = xlwt.XFStyle()
        price_style.num_format_str = "0.00"

        styles = [
            text_style, text_style, text_style,
            price_style, text_style
        ]

        for obj in queryset.order_by("pk"):
            row_num += 1
            project_photos = obj.productphoto_set.all()[:1]
            url = ""
            if project_photos:
                url = "http://{0}{1}".format(
                    request.META['HTTP_HOST'],
                    project_photos[0].photo.url,
                )
            row = [
                obj.pk,
                obj.title,
                obj.description,
                obj.price,
                url,
            ]
            for col_num, item in enumerate(row):
                ws.write(
                    row_num, col_num, item, styles[col_num]
                )

    wb.save(response)
    return response

export_xls.short_description = _("Export XLS")
```

2. Then, add the `actions` setting to `ProductAdmin`, as follows:

```
class ProductAdmin(admin.ModelAdmin):
    # ...
    actions = [export_xls]
```

How it works...

If you take a look at the product administration list page in the browser, you will see a new action called **Export XLS**, along with the default **Delete selected Products** action, as shown in the following screenshot:

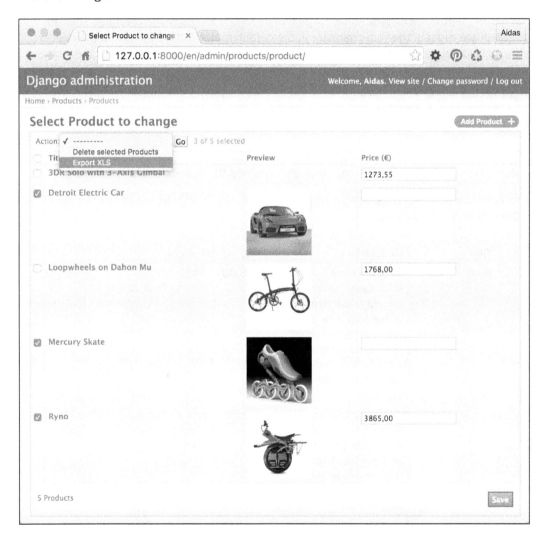

By default, admin actions do something with `QuerySet` and redirect the administrator back to the change list page. However, for more complex actions like these, `HttpResponse` can be returned. The `export_xls()` function returns `HttpResponse` with the content type of the Excel spreadsheet. Using the Content-Disposition header, we set the response to be downloadable with the `products.xls` file.

Then, we use the xlwt Python module to create the Excel file.

At first, a workbook with UTF-8 encoding is created. Then, we add a sheet named `Products` to it. We will be using the `write()` method of the sheet to set the content and style for each cell and the `col()` method to retrieve the column and set its width.

To get an overview of all the columns in the sheet, we will create a list of tuples with column names and widths. Excel uses some magical units for the widths of the columns. They are 1/256 of the width of the zero character in the default font. Next, we will define the header style as bold. As we have the columns defined, we will loop through them and fill the first row with the column names, also assigning the bold style to them.

Then, we will create a style for normal cells and prices. The text in normal cells will be wrapped in multiple lines. The prices will have a special number style with two numbers after the decimal point.

Lastly, we will go through `QuerySet` of the selected products ordered by ID and print the specified fields in the corresponding cells, also applying the specific styles.

The workbook is saved to the file-like `HttpResponse` object and the resulting Excel sheet looks similar to the following:

ID	Title	Description	Price (€)	Preview
1	Ryno	With the Ryno microcycle, you're not limited to the street or the bike lane. It's a transitional vehicle—it goes most places where a person can walk or ride a bike.	3865.00	`http://127.0.0.1:8000/media/products/ryno/20140523044813.jpg`
2	Mercury Skate	The main purpose of designing this Mercury Skate is to decrease the skater's fatigue and provide them with an easier and smoother ride on the pavement.		`http://127.0.0.1:8000/media/products/mercury-skate/20140521030128.png`

ID	Title	Description	Price (€)	Preview

4	Detroit Electric Car	The Detroit Electric SP:01 is a limited-edition, two-seat, pure-electric sports car that sets new standards for performance and handling in electric vehicles.		`http://127.0.0.1:8000/`
				`media/products/`
				`detroit-electric-`
				`car/20140521033122.jpg`

See also

▶ *Chapter 9, Data Import and Export*

▶ The *Customizing columns on the change list page* recipe

▶ The *Developing change list filters* recipe

Developing change list filters

If you want the administrators to be able to filter the change list by date, relation, or field choices, you need to use the `list_filter` property for the admin model. Additionally, there is a possibility of having custom-tailored filters. In this recipe, we will add a filter that allows you to select products by the number of photos attached to them.

Getting ready

Let's start with the `products` app that we created in the previous recipe.

How to do it...

Execute the following two steps:

1. In the `admin.py` file, create a `PhotoFilter` class extending from `SimpleListFilter`, as follows:

```
# products/admin.py
# -*- coding: UTF-8 -*-
# ... all previous imports go here ...
from django.db import models

class PhotoFilter(admin.SimpleListFilter):
    # Human-readable title which will be displayed in the
    # right admin sidebar just above the filter options.
```

```
        title = _("photos")

        # Parameter for the filter that will be used in the
        # URL query.
        parameter_name = "photos"

        def lookups(self, request, model_admin):
            """
            Returns a list of tuples. The first element in each
            tuple is the coded value for the option that will
            appear in the URL query. The second element is the
            human-readable name for the option that will appear
            in the right sidebar.
            """
            return (
                ("zero", _("Has no photos")),
                ("one", _("Has one photo")),
                ("many", _("Has more than one photo")),
            )

        def queryset(self, request, queryset):
            """
            Returns the filtered queryset based on the value
            provided in the query string and retrievable via
            `self.value()`.
            """
            qs = queryset.annotate(
                num_photos=models.Count("productphoto")
            )
            if self.value() == "zero":
                qs = qs.filter(num_photos=0)
            elif self.value() == "one":
                qs = qs.filter(num_photos=1)
            elif self.value() == "many":
                qs = qs.filter(num_photos__gte=2)
            return qs
```

2. Then, add a list filter to `ProductAdmin`, as shown in the following code:

```
class ProductAdmin(admin.ModelAdmin):
    # ...
    list_filter = [PhotoFilter]
```

How it works...

The list filter that we just created will be shown in the sidebar of the product list, as follows:

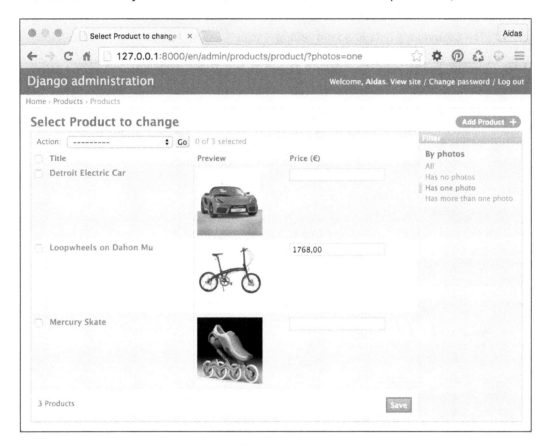

The `PhotoFilter` class has translatable title and query parameter names as properties. It also has two methods: the `lookups()` method that defines the choices of the filter and the `queryset()` method that defines how to filter `QuerySet` objects when a specific value is selected.

In the `lookups()` method, we define three choices: there are no photos, there is one photo, and there is more than one photo attached. In the `queryset()` method, we use the `annotate()` method of `QuerySet` to select the count of photos for each product. This count of the photos is then filtered according to the selected choice.

To learn more about the aggregation functions such as `annotate()`, refer to the official Django documentation at `https://docs.djangoproject.com/en/1.8/topics/db/aggregation/`.

See also

▸ The *Customizing columns on the change list page* recipe

▸ The *Creating admin actions* recipe

▸ The *Customizing default admin settings* recipe

Customizing default admin settings

Django apps as well as third-party apps come with their own administration settings; however, there is a mechanism to switch these settings off and use your own better administration settings. In this recipe, you will learn how to exchange the administration settings for the django.contrib.auth app with custom administration settings.

Getting ready

Create a custom_admin app and put this app under INSTALLED_APPS in the settings.

How to do it...

Insert the following content in the new admin.py file in the custom_admin app:

```python
# custom_admin/admin.py
# -*- coding: UTF-8 -*-
from __future__ import unicode_literals
from django.contrib import admin
from django.contrib.auth.admin import UserAdmin, GroupAdmin
from django.contrib.auth.admin import User, Group
from django.utils.translation import ugettext_lazy as _
from django.core.urlresolvers import reverse
from django.contrib.contenttypes.models import ContentType

class UserAdminExtended(UserAdmin):
    list_display = ("username", "email", "first_name",
        "last_name", "is_active", "is_staff", "date_joined",
        "last_login")
    list_filter = ("is_active", "is_staff", "is_superuser",
        "date_joined", "last_login")
    ordering = ("last_name", "first_name", "username")
```

```python
        save_on_top = True

class GroupAdminExtended(GroupAdmin):
    list_display = ("__unicode__", "display_users")
    save_on_top = True

    def display_users(self, obj):
        links = []
        for user in obj.user_set.all():
            ct = ContentType.objects.get_for_model(user)
            url = reverse(
                "admin:{}_{}_change".format(
                    ct.app_label, ct.model
                ),
                args=(user.id,)
            )
            links.append(
                """<a href="{}" target="_blank">{}</a>""".format(
                    url,
                    "{} {}".format(
                        user.first_name, user.last_name
                    ).strip() or user.username,
                )
            )
        return u"<br />".join(links)
    display_users.allow_tags = True
    display_users.short_description = _("Users")

admin.site.unregister(User)
admin.site.unregister(Group)
admin.site.register(User, UserAdminExtended)
admin.site.register(Group, GroupAdminExtended)
```

How it works...

The default user administration list looks similar to the following screenshot:

The default group administration list looks similar to the following screenshot:

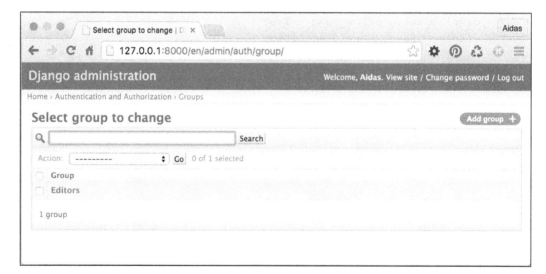

In this recipe, we created two model admin classes, `UserAdminExtended` and `GroupAdminExtended`, which extend the contributed `UserAdmin` and `GroupAdmin` classes, respectively, and overwrite some of the properties. Then, we unregistered the existing administration classes for the `User` and `Group` models and registered the new modified ones.

The following screenshot is how the user administration will look now:

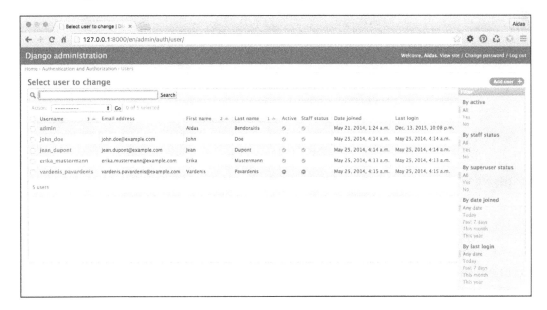

The modified user administration settings show more fields than the default settings in the list view, add additional filters and ordering options, and show **Submit** buttons at the top of the editing form.

In the change list of the new group administration settings, we will display the users who are assigned to the specific groups. This looks similar to the following screenshot in the browser:

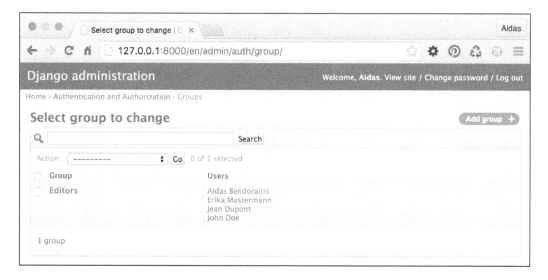

There's more...

In our Python code, we used a new way to format the strings. To learn more about the usage of the `format()` method of the string compared to the old style, refer to the following URL: `https://pyformat.info/`.

See also

- ▸ The *Customizing columns on the change list page* recipe
- ▸ The *Inserting a map into a change form* recipe

Inserting a map into a change form

Google Maps offer a JavaScript API to insert maps into your websites. In this recipe, we will create a `locations` app with the `Location` model and extend the template of the change form in order to add a map where an administrator can find and mark geographical coordinates of a location.

Getting ready

We will start with the `locations` app that should be put under `INSTALLED_APPS` in the settings. Create a `Location` model there with a title, description, address, and geographical coordinates, as follows:

```python
# locations/models.py
# -*- coding: UTF-8 -*-
from __future__ import unicode_literals
from django.db import models
from django.utils.translation import ugettext_lazy as _
from django.utils.encoding import python_2_unicode_compatible

COUNTRY_CHOICES = (
    ("UK", _("United Kingdom")),
    ("DE", _("Germany")),
    ("FR", _("France")),
    ("LT", _("Lithuania")),
)

@python_2_unicode_compatible
class Location(models.Model):
    title = models.CharField(_("title"), max_length=255,
        unique=True)
    description = models.TextField(_("description"), blank=True)
    street_address = models.CharField(_("street address"),
        max_length=255, blank=True)
    street_address2 = models.CharField(
        _("street address (2nd line)"), max_length=255,
        blank=True)
    postal_code = models.CharField(_("postal code"),
        max_length=10, blank=True)
    city = models.CharField(_("city"), max_length=255, blank=True)
    country = models.CharField(_("country"), max_length=2,
        blank=True, choices=COUNTRY_CHOICES)
    latitude = models.FloatField(_("latitude"), blank=True,
        null=True,
        help_text=_("Latitude (Lat.) is the angle between "
            "any point and the equator "
            "(north pole is at 90; south pole is at -90)."))
    longitude = models.FloatField(_("longitude"), blank=True,
        null=True,
        help_text=_("Longitude (Long.) is the angle "
            "east or west of "
```

```
        "an arbitrary point on Earth from Greenwich (UK), "
        "which is the international zero-longitude point "
        "(longitude=0 degrees). "
        "The anti-meridian of Greenwich is both 180 "
        "(direction to east) and -180 (direction to west).""))
class Meta:
    verbose_name = _("Location")
    verbose_name_plural = _("Locations")


def __str__(self):
    return self.title
```

How to do it...

The administration of the `Location` model is as simple as it can be. Perform the following steps:

1. Let's create the administration settings for the `Location` model. Note that we are using the `get_fieldsets()` method to define the field sets with a description rendered from a template, as follows:

```python
# locations/admin.py
# -*- coding: UTF-8 -*-
from __future__ import unicode_literals
from django.utils.translation import ugettext_lazy as _
from django.contrib import admin
from django.template.loader import render_to_string
from .models import Location

class LocationAdmin(admin.ModelAdmin):
    save_on_top = True
    list_display = ("title", "street_address",
        "description")
    search_fields = ("title", "street_address",
        "description")


    def get_fieldsets(self, request, obj=None):
        map_html = render_to_string(
            "admin/includes/map.html"
        )
        fieldsets = [
            (_("Main Data"), {"fields": ("title",
                "description")}),
            (_("Address"), {"fields": ("street_address",
                "street_address2", "postal_code", "city",
```

```
                       "country", "latitude", "longitude")}),
              (_("Map"), {"description": map_html,
                  "fields": []}),
          ]
          return fieldsets

  admin.site.register(Location, LocationAdmin)
```

2. To create a custom change form template, add a new `change_form.html` file under `admin/locations/location/` in your `templates` directory. This template will extend from the default `admin/change_form.html` template and will overwrite the `extrastyle` and `field_sets` blocks, as follows:

```
{# myproject/templates/admin/locations/location/change_form.html
#}
{% extends "admin/change_form.html" %}
{% load i18n admin_static admin_modify %}
{% load url from future %}
{% load admin_urls %}

{% block extrastyle %}
    {{ block.super }}
    <link rel="stylesheet" type="text/css" href="{{ STATIC_URL }}
site/css/locating.css" />
{% endblock %}

{% block field_sets %}
    {% for fieldset in adminform %}
        {% include "admin/includes/fieldset.html" %}
    {% endfor %}
    <script type="text/javascript" src="http://maps.google.com/
maps/api/js?language=en"></script>
    <script type="text/javascript" src="{{ STATIC_URL }}site/js/
locating.js"></script>
{% endblock %}
```

3. Then, we need to create the template for the map that will be inserted in the `Map` field set:

```
{# myproject/templates/admin/includes/map.html #}
{% load i18n %}
<div class="form-row">
    <div id="map_canvas">
        <!-- THE GMAPS WILL BE INSERTED HERE
        DYNAMICALLY -->
    </div>
    <ul id="map_locations"></ul>
    <div class="buttonHolder">
        <button id="locate_address" type="button"
```

```
            class="secondaryAction">
                {% trans "Locate address" %}
            </button>
            <button id="remove_geo" type="button"
            class="secondaryAction">
                {% trans "Remove from map" %}
            </button>
        </div>
    </div>
```

4. Of course, the map won't be styled by default. Therefore, we have to add some CSS, as shown in the following code:

```
/* site_static/site/css/locating.css */
#map_canvas {
    width:722px;
    height:300px;
    margin-bottom: 8px;
}
#map_locations {
    width:722px;
    margin: 0;
    padding: 0;
    margin-bottom: 8px;
}
#map_locations li {
    border-bottom: 1px solid #ccc;
    list-style: none;
}
#map_locations li:first-child {
    border-top: 1px solid #ccc;
}
.buttonHolder {
    width:722px;
}
#remove_geo {
    float: right;
}
```

5. Then, let's create a `locating.js` JavaScript file. We will be using jQuery in this file, as jQuery comes with the contributed administration system and makes the work easy and cross-browser. We don't want to pollute the environment with global variables, therefore, we will start with a closure to make a private scope for variables and functions (a closure is the local variables for a function kept alive after the function has returned), as follows:

```
// site_static/site/js/locating.js
(function ($, undefined) {
```

```
var gMap;
var gettext = window.gettext || function (val) {
    return val;
};
var gMarker;

// ... this is where all the further JavaScript
// functions go ...

} (django.jQuery));
```

6. We will create JavaScript functions one by one. The `getAddress4search()` function will collect the `address` string from the address fields that can later be used for geocoding, as follows:

```
function getAddress4search() {
    var address = [];
    var sStreetAddress2 = $('#id_street_address2').val();
    if (sStreetAddress2) {
        sStreetAddress2 = ' ' + sStreetAddress2;
    }
    address.push($('#id_street_address').val() + sStreetAddress2);
    address.push($('#id_city').val());
    address.push($('#id_country').val());
    address.push($('#id_postal_code').val());
    return address.join(', ');
}
```

7. The `updateMarker()` function will take the latitude and longitude arguments and draw or move a marker on the map. It also makes the marker draggable:

```
function updateMarker(lat, lng) {
    var point = new google.maps.LatLng(lat, lng);
    if (gMarker) {
        gMarker.setPosition(point);
    } else {
        gMarker = new google.maps.Marker({
            position: point,
            map: gMap
        });
    }
    gMap.panTo(point, 15);
    gMarker.setDraggable(true);
    google.maps.event.addListener(gMarker, 'dragend', function() {
        var point = gMarker.getPosition();
        updateLatitudeAndLongitude(point.lat(), point.lng());
    });
}
```

8. The `updateLatitudeAndLongitude()` function takes the latitude and longitude arguments and updates the values for the fields with the IDs `id_latitude` and `id_longitude`, as follows:

```
function updateLatitudeAndLongitude(lat, lng) {
    lat = Math.round(lat * 1000000) / 1000000;
    lng = Math.round(lng * 1000000) / 1000000;
    $('#id_latitude').val(lat);
    $('#id_longitude').val(lng);
}
```

9. The `autocompleteAddress()` function gets the results from Google Maps geocoding and lists them under the map in order to select the correct one, or if there is just one result, it updates the geographical position and address fields, as follows:

```
function autocompleteAddress(results) {
    var $foundLocations = $('#map_locations').html('');
    var i, len = results.length;

    // console.log(JSON.stringify(results, null, 4));

    if (results) {
        if (len > 1) {
            for (i=0; i<len; i++) {
                $('<a href="">' + results[i].formatted_address +
'</a>').data('gmap_index', i).click(function (e) {
                    e.preventDefault();
                    var result = results[$(this).data('gmap_
index')];
                    updateAddressFields(result.address_
components);
                    var point = result.geometry.location;
                    updateLatitudeAndLongitude(point.lat(), point.
lng());
                    updateMarker(point.lat(), point.lng());
                    $foundLocations.hide();
                }).appendTo($('<li>').appendTo($foundLocations));
            }
            $('<a href="">' + gettext('None of the listed') + '</
a>').click(function (e) {
                    e.preventDefault();
                    $foundLocations.hide();
                }).appendTo($('<li>').appendTo($foundLocations));
            $foundLocations.show();
        } else {
            $foundLocations.hide();
            var result = results[0];
            updateAddressFields(result.address_components);
```

```
            var point = result.geometry.location;
            updateLatitudeAndLongitude(point.lat(), point.lng());
            updateMarker(point.lat(), point.lng());
        }
    }
}
```

10. The `updateAddressFields()` function takes a nested dictionary with the address components as an argument and fills in all the address fields:

```
function updateAddressFields(addressComponents) {
    var i, len=addressComponents.length;
    var streetName, streetNumber;
    for (i=0; i<len; i++) {
        var obj = addressComponents[i];
        var obj_type = obj.types[0];
        if (obj_type == 'locality') {
            $('#id_city').val(obj.long_name);
        }
        if (obj_type == 'street_number') {
            streetNumber = obj.long_name;
        }
        if (obj_type == 'route') {
            streetName = obj.long_name;
        }
        if (obj_type == 'postal_code') {
            $('#id_postal_code').val(obj.long_name);
        }
        if (obj_type == 'country') {
            $('#id_country').val(obj.short_name);
        }
    }
    if (streetName) {
        var streetAddress = streetName;
        if (streetNumber) {
            streetAddress += ' ' + streetNumber;
        }
        $('#id_street_address').val(streetAddress);
    }
}
```

11. Finally, we have the initialization function that is called on the page load. It attaches the `onclick` event handlers to the buttons, creates a Google Map, and initially marks the geoposition that is defined in the `latitude` and `longitude` fields, as follows:

```
$(function (){
    $('#locate_address').click(function() {
```

```
            var oGeocoder = new google.maps.Geocoder();
            oGeocoder.geocode(
                {address: getAddress4search()},
                function (results, status) {
                    if (status === google.maps.GeocoderStatus.OK) {
                        autocompleteAddress(results);
                    } else {
                        autocompleteAddress(false);
                    }
                }
            );
        });

        $('#remove_geo').click(function() {
            $('#id_latitude').val('');
            $('#id_longitude').val('');
            gMarker.setMap(null);
            gMarker = null;
        });

        gMap = new google.maps.Map($('#map_canvas').get(0), {
            scrollwheel: false,
            zoom: 16,
            center: new google.maps.LatLng(51.511214, -0.119824),
            disableDoubleClickZoom: true
        });
        google.maps.event.addListener(gMap, 'dblclick',
function(event) {
            var lat = event.latLng.lat();
            var lng = event.latLng.lng();
            updateLatitudeAndLongitude(lat, lng);
            updateMarker(lat, lng);
        });
        $('#map_locations').hide();

        var $lat = $('#id_latitude');
        var $lng = $('#id_longitude');
        if ($lat.val() && $lng.val()) {
            updateMarker($lat.val(), $lng.val());
        }
    });
```

How it works...

If you look at the location change form in the browser, you will see a map shown in a field set followed by the field set containing the address fields, as shown in the following screenshot:

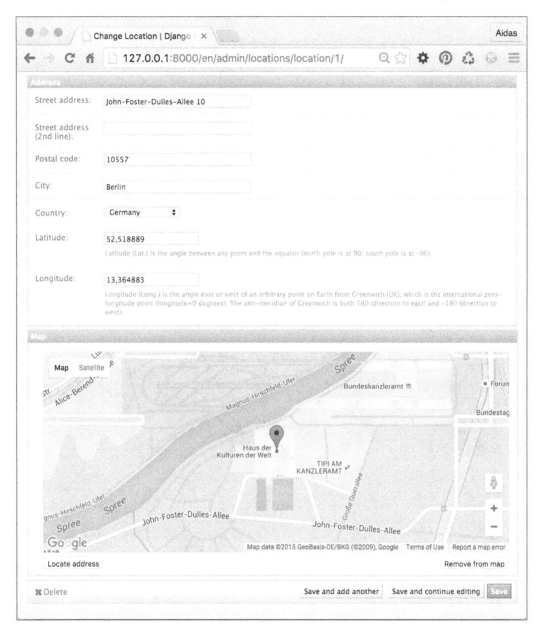

Under the map, there are two buttons: **Locate address** and **Remove from map**.

When you click on the **Locate address** button, the geocoding is called in order to search for the geographical coordinates of the entered address. The result of geocoding is either one or more addresses with latitudes and longitudes in a nested dictionary format. To see the structure of the nested dictionary in the console of the developer tools, put the following line in the beginning of the `autocompleteAddress()` function:

```
console.log(JSON.stringify(results, null, 4));
```

If there is just one result, the missing postal code or other missing address fields are populated, the latitude and longitude are filled in and a marker is put at a specific place on the map. If there are more results, the entire list is shown under the map with the option to select the correct one, as shown in the following screenshot:

Then, the administrator can move the marker on the map by dragging and dropping. Also, a double-click anywhere on the map will update the geographical coordinates and marker position.

Finally, if the **Remove from map** button is clicked, the geographical coordinates are cleaned and the marker is removed.

See also

▶ The *Using HTML5 data attributes* recipe in *Chapter 4, Templates and JavaScript*

7
Django CMS

In this chapter, we will cover the following recipes:

- ▸ Creating templates for Django CMS
- ▸ Structuring the page menu
- ▸ Converting an app to a CMS app
- ▸ Attaching your own navigation
- ▸ Writing your own CMS plugin
- ▸ Adding new fields to the CMS page

Introduction

Django CMS is an open source content management system that is based on Django and created by Divio AG, Switzerland. Django CMS takes care of a website's structure, provides navigation menus, makes it easy to edit page content in the frontend, and supports multiple languages in a website. You can also extend it according to your needs using the provided hooks. To create a website, you need to create a hierarchical structure of the pages, where each page has a template. Templates have placeholders that can be assigned different plugins with the content. Using special template tags, the menus can be generated out of the hierarchical page structure. The CMS takes care of URL mapping to specific pages.

In this chapter, we will look at Django CMS 3.1 from a developer's perspective. We will see what is necessary for the templates to function and take a look at the possible page structure for header and footer navigation. You will also learn how to attach the URL rules of an app to a CMS page tree node. Then, we will attach the custom navigation to the page menu and create our own CMS content plugins. Finally, you will learn how to add new fields to the CMS pages.

Although in this book, I won't guide you through all the bits and pieces of using Django CMS; by the end of this chapter, you will be aware of its purpose and use. The rest can be learned from the official documentation at `http://docs.django-cms.org/en/develop/` and by trying out the frontend user interface of the CMS.

Creating templates for Django CMS

For every page in your page structure, you need to choose a template from the list of templates that are defined in the settings. In this recipe, we will look at the minimum requirements for these templates.

Getting ready

If you want to start a new Django CMS project, execute the following commands in a virtual environment and answer all the prompted questions:

```
(myproject_env)$ pip install djangocms-installer
(myproject_env)$ djangocms -p project/myproject myproject
```

Here, `project/myproject` is the path where the project will be created and `myproject` is the project name.

On the other hand, if you want to integrate Django CMS in an existing project, check the official documentation at `http://docs.django-cms.org/en/latest/how_to/install.html`.

How to do it...

We will update the Bootstrap-powered `base.html` template so that it contains everything that Django CMS needs. Then, we will create and register two templates, `default.html` and `start.html`, to choose from for CMS pages:

1. First of all, we will update the base template that we created in the *Arranging the base.html template* recipe in *Chapter 4, Templates and JavaScript*, as follows:

```
{# templates/base.html #}
<!DOCTYPE html>
{% load i18n cms_tags sekizai_tags menu_tags %}
<html lang="{{ LANGUAGE_CODE }}">
<head>
    <meta charset="utf-8" />
    <meta name="viewport" content="width=device-width, initial-scale=1" />
    <title>{% block title %}{% endblock %}{% trans "My Website" %}</title>
```

```
    <link rel="icon" href="{{ STATIC_URL }}site/img/favicon.ico"
type="image/png" />

    {% block meta_tags %}{% endblock %}

    {% render_block "css" %}
    {% block base_stylesheet %}
        <link rel="stylesheet" href="//maxcdn.bootstrapcdn.com/
bootstrap/3.3.5/css/bootstrap.min.css" />
        <link href="{{ STATIC_URL }}site/css/style.css"
rel="stylesheet" media="screen" type="text/css" />
    {% endblock %}
    {% block stylesheet %}{% endblock %}

    {% block base_js %}
        <script src="//code.jquery.com/jquery-1.11.3.min.js"></
script>
        <script src="//code.jquery.com/jquery-migrate-1.2.1.min.
js"></script>
        <script src="//maxcdn.bootstrapcdn.com/bootstrap/3.3.5/js/
bootstrap.min.js"></script>
    {% endblock %}
    {% block js %}{% endblock %}
    {% block extrahead %}{% endblock %}
</head>
<body class="{% block bodyclass %}{% endblock %} {{ request.
current_page.cssextension.body_css_class }}">
    {% cms_toolbar %}
    {% block page %}
        <div class="wrapper">
            <div id="header" class="clearfix container">
                <h1>{% trans "My Website" %}</h1>
                <nav class="navbar navbar-default"
role="navigation">
                    {% block header_navigation %}
                        <ul class="nav navbar-nav">
                            {% show_menu_below_id "start_page" 0 1
1 1 %}
                        </ul>
                    {% endblock %}
                    {% block language_chooser %}
                        <ul class="nav navbar-nav pull-right">
                            {% language_chooser %}
                        </ul>
                    {% endblock %}
```

```
            </nav>
        </div>
        <div id="content" class="clearfix container">
            {% block content %}
            {% endblock %}
        </div>
        <div id="footer" class="clearfix container">
            {% block footer_navigation %}
                <nav class="navbar navbar-default"
    role="navigation">
                    <ul class="nav navbar-nav">
                        {% show_menu_below_id "footer_
navigation" 0 1 1 1 %}
                    </ul>
                </nav>
            {% endblock %}
        </div>
    </div>
    {% endblock %}
    {% block extrabody %}{% endblock %}
    {% render_block "js" %}
</body>
</html>
```

2. Then, we will create a `cms` directory under `templates` and add two templates for CMS pages: `default.html` for normal pages and `start.html` for the home page, as follows:

```
{# templates/cms/default.html #}
{% extends "base.html" %}
{% load cms_tags %}

{% block title %}{% page_attribute "page_title" %} - {% endblock %}

{% block meta_tags %}
    <meta name="description" content="{% page_attribute meta_
description %}"/>
{% endblock %}

{% block content %}
    <h1>{% page_attribute "page_title" %}</h1>
    <div class="row">
        <div class="col-md-8">
            {% placeholder main_content %}
        </div>
```

```
        <div class="col-md-4">
            {% placeholder sidebar %}
        </div>
    </div>
{% endblock %}

{# templates/cms/start.html #}
{% extends "base.html" %}
{% load cms_tags %}

{% block meta_tags %}
    <meta name="description" content="{% page_attribute meta_
description %}"/>
{% endblock %}

{% block content %}
    <!--
    Here goes very customized website-specific content like
slideshows, latest tweets, latest news, latest profiles, etc.
    -->
{% endblock %}
```

3. Lastly, we will set the paths of these two templates in the settings, as shown in the following:

```
# conf/base.py or settings.py
CMS_TEMPLATES = (
    ("cms/default.html", gettext("Default")),
    ("cms/start.html", gettext("Homepage")),
)
```

How it works...

As usual, the base.html template is the main template that is extended by all the other templates. In this template, Django CMS uses the {% render_block %} template tag from the django-sekizai module to inject CSS and JavaScript in the templates that create a toolbar and other administration widgets in the frontend. We will insert the {% cms_toolbar %} template tag at the beginning of the <body> section—that's where the toolbar will be placed. We will use the {% show_menu_below_id %} template tag to render the header and footer menus from the specific page menu trees. Also, we will use the {% language_chooser %} template tag to render the language chooser that switches to the same page in different languages.

The `default.html` and `start.html` templates that are defined in the `CMS_TEMPLATES` setting will be available as a choice when creating a CMS page. In these templates, for each area that needs to have dynamically entered content, add a `{% placeholder %}` template tag when you need page-specific content or `{% static_placeholder %}` when you need the content that is shared among different pages. Logged-in administrators can add content plugins to the placeholders when they switch from the **Live** mode to the **Draft** mode in the CMS toolbar and switch to the **Structure** section.

See also

▶ The *Arranging the base.html template* recipe in *Chapter 4, Templates and JavaScript*

▶ The *Structuring the page menu* recipe

Structuring the page menu

In this recipe, we will discuss some guidelines about defining the tree structures for the pages of your website.

Getting ready

It is good practice to set the available languages for your website before creating the structure of your pages (although the Django CMS database structure also allows you to add new languages later). Besides `LANGUAGES`, make sure that you have `CMS_LANGUAGES` set in your settings. The `CMS_LANGUAGES` setting defines which languages should be active for each Django site, as follows:

```python
# conf/base.py or settings.py
# ...
from __future__ import unicode_literals
gettext = lambda s: s

LANGUAGES = (
    ("en", "English"),
    ("de", "Deutsch"),
    ("fr", "Français"),
    ("lt", "Lietuvių kalba"),
)

CMS_LANGUAGES = {
    "default": {
        "public": True,
        "hide_untranslated": False,
```

```
            "redirect_on_fallback": True,
        },
        1: [
            {
                "public": True,
                "code": "en",
                "hide_untranslated": False,
                "name": gettext("en"),
                "redirect_on_fallback": True,
            },
            {
                "public": True,
                "code": "de",
                "hide_untranslated": False,
                "name": gettext("de"),
                "redirect_on_fallback": True,
            },
            {
                "public": True,
                "code": "fr",
                "hide_untranslated": False,
                "name": gettext("fr"),
                "redirect_on_fallback": True,
            },
            {
                "public": True,
                "code": "lt",
                "hide_untranslated": False,
                "name": gettext("lt"),
                "redirect_on_fallback": True,
            },
        ],
    }
```

How to do it...

The page navigation is set in tree structures. The first tree is the main tree and, contrary to the other trees, the root node of the main tree is not reflected in the URL structure. The root node of this tree is the home page of the website. Usually, this page has a specific template, where you add the content aggregated from different apps; for example, a slideshow, actual news, newly registered users, latest tweets, or other latest or featured objects. For a convenient way to render items from different apps, check the *Creating a template tag to a QuerySet in a template* recipe in *Chapter 5, Custom Template Filters and Tags*.

If your website has multiple navigations such as a top, meta, and footer navigation, give an ID to the root node of each tree in the **Advanced** settings of the page. This ID will be used in the base template by the `{% show_menu_below_id %}` template tag. You can read more about this and other menu-related template tags in the official documentation at `http://docs.django-cms.org/en/latest/reference/navigation.html`.

The first tree defines the main structure of the website. If you want a page under the root-level URL, for example, `/en/search/` but not `/en/meta/search/`, put this page under the home page. If you don't want a page to be shown in the menu as it will be linked from an icon or widget, just hide it from the menu.

The footer navigation usually shows different items than the top navigation with some of the items being repeated, for example, the page for developers will be shown only in the footer; whereas, the page for news will be shown in both header and footer. For all the repeated items, just create a page with the **Redirect** setting in the advanced settings of the page and set it to the original page in the main tree. By default, when you create a secondary tree structure, all pages under the root of that tree will include the slug of the root page in their URL paths. If you want to skip the slug of the root in the URL path, you will need to set the **Overwrite URL** setting in the advanced settings of the page. For example, the developers page should be under `/en/developers/` and not `/en/secondary/developers/`.

How it works...

Finally, your page structure will look similar to the following image (of course, the page structure can be much more complex too):

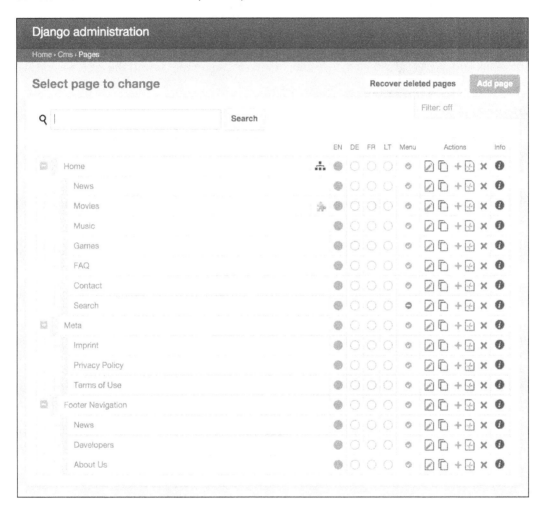

See also

▸ The *Creating a template tag to load a QuerySet in a template* recipe in *Chapter 5, Custom Template Filters and Tags*

▸ The *Creating templates for Django CMS* recipe

▸ The *Attaching your own navigation* recipe

Converting an app to a CMS app

The simplest Django CMS website will have the whole page tree created using administration interface. However, for real-world cases, you will probably need to show forms or lists of objects under some page nodes. If you have created an app that is responsible for some type of objects in your website, such as `movies`, you can easily convert it to a Django CMS app and attach it to one of the pages. This will ensure that the root URL of the app is translatable and the menu item is highlighted when selected. In this recipe, we will convert the `movies` app to a CMS app.

Getting ready

Let's start with the `movies` app that we created in the *Filtering object lists* recipe in *Chapter 3*, *Forms and Views*.

How to do it...

Follow these steps to convert a usual `movies` Django app to a Django CMS app:

1. First of all, remove or comment out the inclusion of the URL configuration of the app as it will be included by an apphook in Django CMS, as follows:

```
# myproject/urls.py
# -*- coding: UTF-8 -*-
from __future__ import unicode_literals
from django.conf.urls import patterns, include, url
from django.conf import settings
from django.conf.urls.static import static
from django.contrib.staticfiles.urls import \
    staticfiles_urlpatterns
from django.conf.urls.i18n import i18n_patterns
from django.contrib import admin
admin.autodiscover()

urlpatterns = i18n_patterns("",
    # remove or comment out the inclusion of app's urls
    # url(r"^movies/", include("movies.urls")),

    url(r"^admin/", include(admin.site.urls)),
    url(r"^", include("cms.urls")),
)
urlpatterns += staticfiles_urlpatterns()
urlpatterns += static(settings.MEDIA_URL,
    document_root=settings.MEDIA_ROOT)
```

2. Create a `cms_app.py` file in the `movies` directory and create `MoviesApphook` there, as follows:

```
# movies/cms_app.py
# -*- coding: UTF-8 -*-
from __future__ import unicode_literals
from django.utils.translation import ugettext_lazy as _
from cms.app_base import CMSApp
from cms.apphook_pool import apphook_pool


class MoviesApphook(CMSApp):
    name = _("Movies")
    urls = ["movies.urls"]


apphook_pool.register(MoviesApphook)
```

3. Set the newly created apphook in the settings, as shown in the following:

```
# settings.py
CMS_APPHOOKS = (
    # ...
    "movies.cms_app.MoviesApphook",
)
```

4. Finally, in all the movie templates, change the first line to extend from the template of the current CMS page instead of `base.html`, as follows:

```
{# templates/movies/movies_list.html #}

Change
{% extends "base.html" %}

to
{% extends CMS_TEMPLATE %}
```

How it works...

Apphooks are the interfaces that join the URL configuration of apps to the CMS pages. Apphooks need to extend from `CMSApp`. To define the name, which will be shown in the **Application** selection list under the **Advanced** settings of a page, put the path of the apphook in the `CMS_APPHOOKS` project setting and restart the web server; the apphook will appear as one of the applications in the advanced page settings. After selecting an application for a page, you need to restart the server for the URLs to take effect.

The templates of the app should extend the page template if you want them to contain the placeholders or attributes of the page, for example, the `title` or the `description` meta tag.

> ▸ The *Filtering object lists* recipe in *Chapter 3, Forms and Views*
> ▸ The *Attaching your own navigation* recipe

Attaching your own navigation

Once you have an app hooked in the CMS pages, all the URL paths under the page node will be controlled by the urls.py file of the app. To add some menu items under this page, you need to add a dynamical branch of navigation to the page tree. In this recipe, we will improve the movies app and add new navigation items under the **Movies** page.

Getting ready

Let's say that we have a URL configuration for different lists of movies: editor's picks, commercial movies, and independent movies, as shown in the following code:

```python
# movies/urls.py
# -*- coding: UTF-8 -*-
from __future__ import unicode_literals
from django.conf.urls import url, patterns
from django.shortcuts import redirect

urlpatterns = patterns("movies.views",
    url(r"^$", lambda request: redirect("featured_movie_list")),
    url(r"^editors-picks/$", "movie_list", {"featured": True},
        name='featured_movie_list'),
    url(r"^commercial/$", "movie_list", {"commercial": True},
        name="commercial_movie_list"),
    url(r"^independent/$", "movie_list", {"independent": True},
        name="independent_movie_list"),
    url(r"^(?P<slug>[^/]+)/$", "movie_detail",
        name="movie_detail"),
)
```

How to do it...

Follow these two steps to attach the **Editor's Picks**, **Commercial Movies**, and **Independent Movies** menu choices to the navigational menu under the **Movies** page:

1. Create the `menu.py` file in the `movies` app and add the following `MoviesMenu` class, as follows:

```python
# movies/menu.py
# -*- coding: UTF-8 -*-
from __future__ import unicode_literals
from django.utils.translation import ugettext_lazy as _
from django.core.urlresolvers import reverse
from menus.base import NavigationNode
from menus.menu_pool import menu_pool
from cms.menu_bases import CMSAttachMenu


class MoviesMenu(CMSAttachMenu):
    name = _("Movies Menu")

    def get_nodes(self, request):
        nodes = [
            NavigationNode(
                _("Editor's Picks"),
                reverse("featured_movie_list"),
                1,
            ),
            NavigationNode(
                _("Commercial Movies"),
                reverse("commercial_movie_list"),
                2,
            ),
            NavigationNode(
                _("Independent Movies"),
                reverse("independent_movie_list"),
                3,
            ),
        ]
        return nodes

menu_pool.register_menu(MoviesMenu)
```

2. Restart the web server and then edit the **Advanced** settings of the **Movies** page and select **Movies Menu** for the **Attached** menu setting.

How it works...

In the frontend, you will see the new menu items attached to the **Movies** page, as shown in the following image:

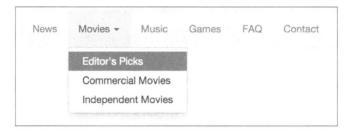

Dynamic menus that are attachable to pages need to extend CMSAttachMenu, define the name by which they will be selected, and define the get_nodes() method that returns a list of NavigationNode objects. The NavigationNode class takes at least three parameters: the title of the menu item, the URL path of the menu item, and the ID of the node. The IDs can be chosen freely with the only requirement being that they have to be unique among this attached menu. The other optional parameters are as follows:

- ▶ parent_id: This is the ID of the parent node if you want to create a hierarchical dynamical menu

- ▶ parent_namespace: This is the name of another menu if this node is to be attached to a different menu tree, for example, the name of this menu is "MoviesMenu"

- ▶ attr: This is a dictionary of the additional attributes that can be used in a template or menu modifier

- ▶ visible: This sets whether or not the menu item should be visible

For other examples of attachable menus, refer to the official documentation at https://django-cms.readthedocs.org/en/latest/how_to/menus.html.

See also

- ▶ The *Structuring the page menu* recipe
- ▶ The *Converting an app to a CMS app* recipe

Writing your own CMS plugin

Django CMS comes with a lot of content plugins that can be used in template placeholders, such as the text, flash, picture, and Google map plugins. However, for more structured and better styled content, you will need your own custom plugins, which are not too difficult to implement. In this recipe, we will see how to create a new plugin and have a custom layout for its data, depending on the chosen template of the page.

Getting ready

Let's create an `editorial` app and mention it in the `INSTALLED_APPS` setting. Also, we will need the `cms/magazine.html` template that was created and mentioned in the `CMS_TEMPLATES` setting; you can simply duplicate the `cms/default.html` template for this.

How to do it...

To create the `EditorialContent` plugin, follow these steps:

1. In the `models.py` file of the newly created app, add the `EditorialContent` model extending from `CMSPlugin`. The `EditorialContent` model will have the following fields: title, subtitle, description, website, image, image caption, and a CSS class:

```python
# editorial/models.py
# -*- coding: UTF-8 -*-
from __future__ import unicode_literals
import os
from django.db import models
from django.utils.translation import ugettext_lazy as _
from django.utils.timezone import now as tz_now
from cms.models import CMSPlugin
from cms.utils.compat.dj import python_2_unicode_compatible

def upload_to(instance, filename):
    now = tz_now()
    filename_base, filename_ext = \
        os.path.splitext(filename)
    return "editorial/%s%s" % (
        now.strftime("%Y/%m/%Y%m%d%H%M%S"),
        filename_ext.lower(),
    )

@python_2_unicode_compatible
class EditorialContent(CMSPlugin):
```

```python
title = models.CharField(_("Title"), max_length=255)
subtitle = models.CharField(_("Subtitle"),
    max_length=255, blank=True)
description = models.TextField(_("Description"),
    blank=True)
website = models.CharField(_("Website"),
    max_length=255, blank=True)

image = models.ImageField(_("Image"), max_length=255,
    upload_to=upload_to, blank=True)
image_caption = models.TextField(_("Image Caption"),
    blank=True)

css_class = models.CharField(_("CSS Class"),
    max_length=255, blank=True)

def __str__(self):
    return self.title

class Meta:
    ordering = ["title"]
    verbose_name = _("Editorial content")
    verbose_name_plural = _("Editorial contents")
```

2. In the same app, create a `cms_plugins.py` file and add a `EditorialContentPlugin` class extending `CMSPluginBase`. This class is a little bit like `ModelAdmin`—it defines the appearance of administration settings for the plugin:

```python
# editorial/cms_plugins.py
# -*- coding: utf-8 -*-
from __future__ import unicode_literals
from django.utils.translation import ugettext as _
from cms.plugin_base import CMSPluginBase
from cms.plugin_pool import plugin_pool
from .models import EditorialContent

class EditorialContentPlugin(CMSPluginBase):
    model = EditorialContent
    name = _("Editorial Content")
    render_template = "cms/plugins/editorial_content.html"

    fieldsets = (
        (_("Main Content"), {
            "fields": (
```

```
                "title", "subtitle", "description",
                "website"),
            "classes": ["collapse open"]
        }),
        (_("Image"), {
            "fields": ("image", "image_caption"),
            "classes": ["collapse open"]
        }),
        (_("Presentation"), {
            "fields": ("css_class",),
            "classes": ["collapse closed"]
        }),
    )

    def render(self, context, instance, placeholder):
        context.update({
            "object": instance,
            "placeholder": placeholder,
        })
        return context

plugin_pool.register_plugin(EditorialContentPlugin)
```

3. To specify which plugins go to which placeholders, you have to define the
   CMS_PLACEHOLDER_CONF setting. You can also define the extra context for the
   templates of the plugins that are rendered in a specific placeholder. Let's allow
   EditorialContentPlugin for the main_content placeholder and set the
   editorial_content_template context variable for the main_content
   placeholder in the cms/magazine.html template, as follows:

```
# settings.py
CMS_PLACEHOLDER_CONF = {
    "main_content": {
        "name": gettext("Main Content"),
        "plugins": (
            "EditorialContentPlugin",
            "TextPlugin",
        ),
    },
    "cms/magazine.html main_content": {
        "name": gettext("Magazine Main Content"),
        "plugins": (
            "EditorialContentPlugin",
            "TextPlugin"
        ),
```

```
            "extra_context": {
                "editorial_content_template": \
                "cms/plugins/editorial_content/magazine.html",
            }
        },
    }
```

4. Then, we will create two templates. One of them will be the `editorial_content.html` template. It checks whether the `editorial_content_template` context variable exists. If the variable exists, it is included. Otherwise, it shows the default layout for editorial content:

```
{# templates/cms/plugins/editorial_content.html #}
{% load i18n %}

{% if editorial_content_template %}
    {% include editorial_content_template %}
{% else %}
    <div class="item{% if object.css_class %} {{ object.css_class }}{% endif %}">
        <!-- editorial content for non-specific placeholders -->
        <div class="img">
            {% if object.image %}
                <img class="img-responsive" alt="{{ object.image_caption|striptags }}" src="{{ object.image.url }}" />
            {% endif %}
            {% if object.image_caption %}<p class="caption">{{ object.image_caption|removetags:"p" }}</p>
            {% endif %}
        </div>
        <h3><a href="{{ object.website }}">{{ object.title }}</a></h3>
        <h4>{{ object.subtitle }}</h4>
        <div class="description">{{ object.description|safe }}</div>
    </div>
{% endif %}
```

5. The second template is a specific template for the `EditorialContent` plugin in the `cms/magazine.html` template. There's nothing too fancy here, just an additional Bootstrap-specific `well` CSS class for the container to make the plugin stand out:

```
{# templates/cms/plugins/editorial_content/magazine.html #}
{% load i18n %}
<div class="well item{% if object.css_class %} {{ object.css_class }}{% endif %}">
    <!-- editorial content for non-specific placeholders -->
```

```
<div class="img">
    {% if object.image %}
        <img class="img-responsive" alt="{{ object.image_
caption|striptags }}" src="{{ object.image.url }}" />
    {% endif %}
    {% if object.image_caption %}<p class="caption">{{ object.
image_caption|removetags:"p" }}</p>
    {% endif %}
</div>
<h3><a href="{{ object.website }}">{{ object.title }}</a></h3>
<h4>{{ object.subtitle }}</h4>
<div class="description">{{ object.description|safe }}</div>
</div>
```

How it works...

If you go to the **Draft** mode of any CMS page and switch to the **Structure** section, you can add the **Editorial Content** plugin to a placeholder. The content of this plugin will be rendered with a specified template and it can also be customized, depending on the template of the page where the plugin is chosen. For example, choose the `cms/magazine.html` template for the **News** page and then add the **Editorial Content** plugin. The **News** page will look similar to the following screenshot:

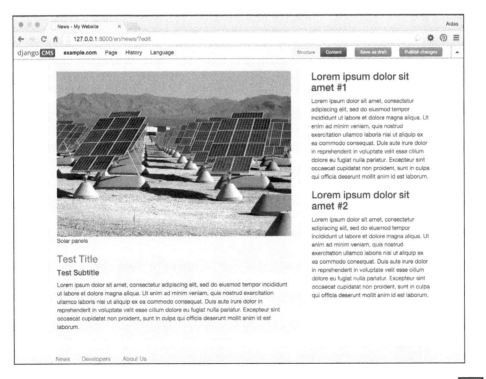

Here, the **Test Title** with an image and description is the custom plugin inserted in the `main_content` placeholder in the `magazine.html` page template. If the page template was different, the plugin would be rendered without the Bootstrap-specific `well` CSS class; therefore, it would not have a gray background.

See also

▸ The *Creating templates for Django CMS* recipe

▸ The *Structuring the page menu* recipe

Adding new fields to the CMS page

CMS pages have several multilingual fields such as title, slug, menu title, page title, description meta tag, and overwrite URL. They also have several common nonlanguage-specific fields such as template, ID used in template tags, attached application, and attached menu. However, that might not be enough for more complex websites. Thankfully, Django CMS features a manageable mechanism to add new database fields for CMS pages. In this recipe, you will see how to add fields for the CSS classes for the navigational menu items and page body.

Getting ready

Let's create the `cms_extensions` app and put it under `INSTALLED_APPS` in the settings.

How to do it...

To create a CMS page extension with the CSS class fields for the navigational menu items and page body, follow these steps:

1. In the `models.py` file, create a `CSSExtension` class extending `PageExtension` and put fields for the menu item's CSS class and `<body>` CSS class, as follows:

```python
# cms_extensions/models.py
# -*- coding: UTF-8 -*-
from __future__ import unicode_literals
from django.db import models
from django.utils.translation import ugettext_lazy as _
from cms.extensions import PageExtension
from cms.extensions.extension_pool import extension_pool

MENU_ITEM_CSS_CLASS_CHOICES = (
```

```
        ("featured", ".featured"),
    )


    BODY_CSS_CLASS_CHOICES = (
        ("serious", ".serious"),
        ("playful", ".playful"),
    )


    class CSSExtension(PageExtension):
        menu_item_css_class = models.CharField(
            _("Menu Item CSS Class"),
            max_length=200,
            blank=True,
            choices=MENU_ITEM_CSS_CLASS_CHOICES,
        )
        body_css_class = models.CharField(
            _("Body CSS Class"),
            max_length=200,
            blank=True,
            choices=BODY_CSS_CLASS_CHOICES,
        )


    extension_pool.register(CSSExtension)
```

2. In the `admin.py` file, let's add administration options for the `CSSExtension` model that we just created:

```
# cms_extensions/admin.py
# -*- coding: UTF-8 -*-
from __future__ import unicode_literals
from django.contrib import admin
from cms.extensions import PageExtensionAdmin
from .models import CSSExtension


class CSSExtensionAdmin(PageExtensionAdmin):
    pass


admin.site.register(CSSExtension, CSSExtensionAdmin)
```

3. Then, we need to show the CSS extension in the toolbar for each page. This can be done by putting the following code in the `cms_toolbar.py` file of the app:

```
# cms_extensions/cms_toolbar.py
# -*- coding: UTF-8 -*-
from __future__ import unicode_literals
from cms.api import get_page_draft
```

```
from cms.toolbar_pool import toolbar_pool
from cms.toolbar_base import CMSToolbar
from cms.utils import get_cms_setting
from cms.utils.permissions import has_page_change_permission
from django.core.urlresolvers import reverse, NoReverseMatch
from django.utils.translation import ugettext_lazy as _
from .models import CSSExtension


@toolbar_pool.register
class CSSExtensionToolbar(CMSToolbar):
    def populate(self):
        # always use draft if we have a page
        self.page = get_page_draft(
            self.request.current_page)

        if not self.page:
            # Nothing to do
            return

        # check global permissions
        # if CMS_PERMISSIONS is active
        if get_cms_setting("PERMISSION"):
            has_global_current_page_change_permission = \
                has_page_change_permission(self.request)
        else:
            has_global_current_page_change_permission = \
                False
            # check if user has page edit permission
        can_change = self.request.current_page and \
                    self.request.current_page.\
                        has_change_permission(self.request)
        if has_global_current_page_change_permission or \
            can_change:
            try:
                extension = CSSExtension.objects.get(
                    extended_object_id=self.page.id)
            except CSSExtension.DoesNotExist:
                extension = None
            try:
                if extension:
                    url = reverse(
                "admin:cms_extensions_cssextension_change",
                        args=(extension.pk,)
                    )
```

```
                        else:
                            url = reverse(
                        "admin:cms_extensions_cssextension_add") + \
                            "?extended_object=%s" % self.page.pk
                    except NoReverseMatch:
                        # not in urls
                        pass
                    else:
                        not_edit_mode = not self.toolbar.edit_mode
                        current_page_menu = self.toolbar.\
                            get_or_create_menu("page")
                        current_page_menu.add_modal_item(
                            _("CSS"),
                            url=url,
                            disabled=not_edit_mode
                        )
```

This code checks whether the user has the permission to change the current page, and if so, it loads the page menu from the current toolbar and adds a new menu item, CSS, with the link to create or edit `CSSExtension`.

4. As we want to access the CSS extension in the navigation menu in order to attach a CSS class, we need to create a menu modifier in the `menu.py` file of the same app:

```
# cms_extensions/menu.py
# -*- coding: UTF-8 -*-
from __future__ import unicode_literals
from cms.models import Page
from menus.base import Modifier
from menus.menu_pool import menu_pool


class CSSModifier(Modifier):
    def modify(self, request, nodes, namespace, root_id,
        post_cut, breadcrumb):
        if post_cut:
            return nodes
        for node in nodes:
            try:
                page = Page.objects.get(pk=node.id)
            except:
                continue
            try:
                page.cssextension
            except:
                pass
            else:
```

```
                node.cssextension = page.cssextension
            return nodes


    menu_pool.register_modifier(CSSModifier)
```

5. Then, we will add the body CSS class to the `<body>` element in the `base.html` template, as follows:

   {# templates/base.html #}

   ```
   <body class="{% block bodyclass %}{% endblock %}{% if request.
   current_page.cssextension %}{{ request.current_page.cssextension.
   body_css_class }}{% endif %}">
   ```

6. Lastly, we will modify the `menu.html` file, which is the default template for the navigation menu, and add the menu item's CSS class as follows:

   {# templates/menu/menu.html #}

   ```
   {% load i18n menu_tags cache %}


   {% for child in children %}
       <li class="{% if child.ancestor %}ancestor{% endif %}
   {% if child.selected %} active{% endif %}{% if child.children
   %} dropdown{% endif %}{% if child.cssextension %} {{ child.
   cssextension.menu_item_css_class }}{% endif %}">
           {% if child.children %}<a class="dropdown-toggle" data-
   toggle="dropdown" href="#">{{ child.get_menu_title }} <span
   class="caret"></span></a>
               <ul class="dropdown-menu">
                   {% show_menu from_level to_level extra_inactive
   extra_active template "" "" child %}
               </ul>
           {% else %}
               <a href="{{ child.get_absolute_url }}"><span>{{ child.
   get_menu_title }}</span></a>
           {% endif %}
       </li>
   {% endfor %}
   ```

How it works...

The `PageExtension` class is a model mixin with a one-to-one relationship with the `Page` model. To be able to administrate the custom extension model in Django CMS, there is a specific `PageExtensionAdmin` class to extend. Then, in the `cms_toolbar.py` file, we will create the `CSSExtensionToolbar` class, inheriting from the `CMSToolbar` class, to create an item in the Django CMS toolbar. In the `populate()` method, we will perform the general routine to check the page permissions and then we will add a CSS menu item to the toolbar.

If the administrator has the permission to edit the page, then they will see a **CSS** option in the toolbar under the **Page** menu item, as shown in the following screenshot:

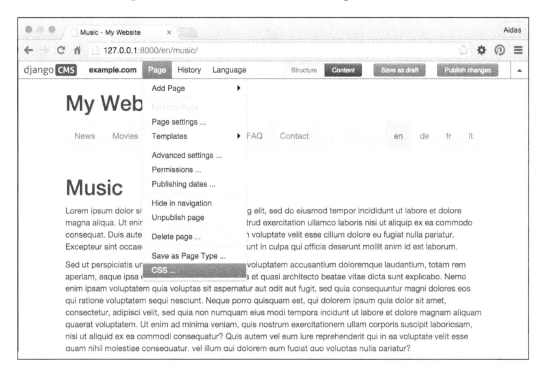

When the administrator clicks on the new **CSS** menu item, a pop-up window opens and they can select the **CSS** classes for the navigation menu item and body, as shown in the following screenshot:

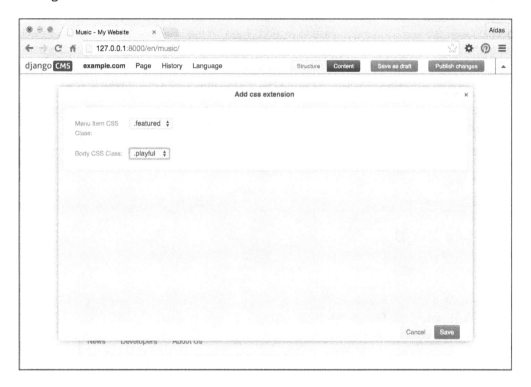

To show a specific CSS class from the `Page` extension in the navigation menu, we need to attach the `CSSExtension` object to the navigation items accordingly. Then, these objects can be accessed in the `menu.html` template as `{{ child.cssextension }}`. In the end, you will have some navigation menu items highlighted, such as the **Music** item shown here (depending on your CSS):

To show a specific CSS class for `<body>` of the current page is much simpler. We can use `{{ request.current_page.cssextension.body_css_class }}` right away.

See also

 ▸ The *Creating templates for Django CMS* recipe

Hierarchical Structures

8

In this chapter, we will cover the following recipes:

- Creating hierarchical categories
- Creating a category administration interface with django-mptt-admin
- Creating a category administration interface with django-mptt-tree-editor
- Rendering categories in a template
- Using a single selection field to choose a category in forms
- Using a checkbox list to choose multiple categories in forms

Introduction

Whether you build your own forum, threaded comments, or categorization system, there will be a moment when you need to save hierarchical structures in the database. Although the tables of relational databases (such as MySQL and PostgreSQL) are of a flat manner, there is a fast and effective way to store hierarchical structures. It is called **Modified Preorder Tree Traversal** (**MPTT**). MPTT allows you to read the tree structures without recursive calls to the database.

At first, let's get familiar with the terminology of the tree structures. A tree data structure is a recursive collection of nodes, starting at the root node and having references to child nodes. There is a restriction that no node references back to create a loop and no reference is duplicated. The following are some other terms to learn:

- **Parent** is any node that is referencing to the child nodes.
- **Descendants** are the nodes that can be reached by recursively traversing from a parent to its children. Therefore, the node's descendants will be its child, the child's children, and so on.

- ▸ **Ancestors** are the nodes that can be reached by recursively traversing from a child to its parent. Therefore, the node's ancestors will be its parent, the parent's parent, and so on up to the root.
- ▸ **Siblings** are the nodes with the same parent.
- ▸ **Leaf** is a node without children.

Now, I'll explain how MPTT works. Imagine that you lay out your tree horizontally with the root node at the top. Each node in the tree has left and right values. Imagine them as small left and right handles on the left and right-hand side of the node. Then, you walk (traverse) around the tree counter-clockwise, starting from the root node and mark each left or right value that you find with a number: 1, 2, 3, and so on. It will look similar to the following diagram:

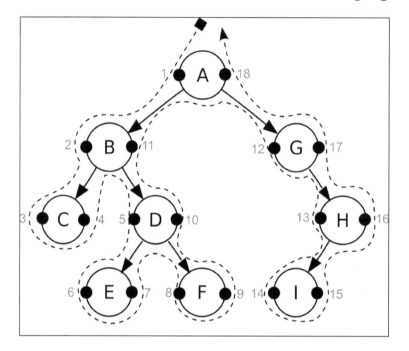

In the database table of this hierarchical structure, you will have a title, left value, and right value for each node.

Now, if you want to get the subtree of the **B** node with **2** as the left value and **11** as the right value, you will have to select all the nodes that have a left value between **2** and **11**. They are **C**, **D**, **E**, and **F**.

To get all the ancestors of the **D** node with **5** as the left value and **10** as the right value, you have to select all the nodes that have a left value that is less than **5** and a right value that is more than **10**. These would be **B** and **A**.

To get the number of the descendants for a node, you can use the following formula: *descendants = (right - left - 1) / 2*

Therefore, the number of descendants for the **B** node can be calculated as shown in the following: *(11 - 2 - 1) / 2 = 4*

If we want to attach the **E** node to the **C** node, we will have to update the left and right values only for the nodes of their first common ancestor, the **B** node. Then, the **C** node will still have **3** as the left value; the **E** node will get **4** as the left value and **5** as the right value; the right value of the **C** node will become **6**; the left value of the **D** node will become **7**; the left value of the **F** node will stay **8**; and the others will also remain the same.

Similarly, there are other tree-related operations with nodes in MPTT. It might be too complicated to manage all this by yourself for every hierarchical structure in your project. Luckily, there is a Django app called **django-mptt** that handles these algorithms and provides an easy API to handle the tree structures. In this chapter, you will learn how to use this helper app.

Creating hierarchical categories

To illustrate how to deal with MPTT, we will create a `movies` app that will have a hierarchical `Category` model and a `Movie` model with a many-to-many relationship with the categories.

Getting ready

To get started, perform the following steps:

1. Install `django-mptt` in your virtual environment using the following command:

   ```
   (myproject_env)$ pip install django-mptt
   ```

2. Then, create a `movies` app. Add the `movies` app as well as `mptt` to `INSTALLED_APPS` in the settings, as follows:

   ```
   # conf/base.py or settings.py
   INSTALLED_APPS = (
       # ...
       "mptt",
       "movies",
   )
   ```

How to do it...

We will create a hierarchical `Category` model and a `Movie` model, which will have a many-to-many relationship with the categories, as follows:

1. Open the `models.py` file and add a `Category` model that extends `mptt.models.MPTTModel` and `CreationModificationDateMixin`, which we defined in *Chapter 2, Database Structure*. In addition to the fields coming from the mixins, the `Category` model will need to have a `parent` field of the `TreeForeignKey` type and a `title` field:

```python
# movies/models.py
# -*- coding: UTF-8 -*-
from __future__ import unicode_literals
from django.db import models
from django.utils.translation import ugettext_lazy as _
from django.utils.encoding import \
    python_2_unicode_compatible
from utils.models import CreationModificationDateMixin
from mptt.models import MPTTModel
from mptt.fields import TreeForeignKey, TreeManyToManyField


@python_2_unicode_compatible
class Category(MPTTModel, CreationModificationDateMixin):
    parent = TreeForeignKey("self", blank=True, null=True)
    title = models.CharField(_("Title"), max_length=200)

    def __str__(self):
        return self.title

    class Meta:
        ordering = ["tree_id", "lft"]
        verbose_name = _("Category")
        verbose_name_plural = _("Categories")
```

2. Then, create the `Movie` model that extends `CreationModificationDateMixin`. Also, include a `title` field and a `categories` field of the `TreeManyToManyField` type:

```python
@python_2_unicode_compatible
class Movie(CreationModificationDateMixin):
    title = models.CharField(_("Title"), max_length=255)
    categories = TreeManyToManyField(Category,
        verbose_name=_("Categories"))

    def __str__(self):
```

```
        return self.title

    class Meta:
        verbose_name = _("Movie")
        verbose_name_plural = _("Movies")
```

How it works...

The `MPTTModel` mixin will add the `tree_id`, `lft`, `rght`, and `level` fields to the `Category` model. The `tree_id` field is used as you can have multiple trees in the database table. In fact, each root category is saved in a separate tree. The `lft` and `rght` fields store the left and right values used in the MPTT algorithms. The `level` field stores the node's depth in the tree. The root node will be level `0`.

Besides new fields, the `MPTTModel` mixin adds methods to navigate through the tree structure similar to how you would navigate through DOM elements using JavaScript. These methods are listed as follows:

- ▶ If you want to get the ancestors of a category, use the following code:

  ```
  ancestor_categories = category.get_ancestors(
      ascending=False,
      include_self=False,
  )
  ```

  The ascending parameter defines from which direction to read the nodes (the default is `False`). The `include_self` parameter defines whether to include the category itself in `QuerySet` (the default is `False`).

- ▶ To just get the root category, use the following code:

  ```
  root = category.get_root()
  ```

- ▶ If you want to get the direct children of a category, use the following code:

  ```
  children = category.get_children()
  ```

- ▶ To get all the descendants of a category, use the following code:

  ```
  descendants = category.get_descendants(include_self=False)
  ```

  Here, the `include_self` parameter again defines whether or not to include the category itself in `QuerySet`.

- ▶ If you want to get the descendant count without querying the database, use the following code:

  ```
  descendants_count = category.get_descendant_count()
  ```

> ▸ To get all the siblings, call the following method:

```
siblings = category.get_siblings(include_self=False)
```

> Root categories are considered to be siblings of other root categories.

> ▸ To just get the previous and next siblings, call the following methods:

```
previous_sibling = category.get_previous_sibling()
next_sibling = category.get_next_sibling()
```

> ▸ Also, there are methods to check whether the category is a root, child, or leaf, as follows:

```
category.is_root_node()
category.is_child_node()
category.is_leaf_node()
```

All these methods can be used either in the views, templates, or management commands. If you want to manipulate the tree structure, you can also use the `insert_at()` and `move_to()` methods. In this case, you can read about them and the tree manager methods at `http://django-mptt.github.io/django-mptt/models.html`.

In the preceding models, we used `TreeForeignKey` and `TreeManyToManyField`. These are similar to `ForeignKey` and `ManyToManyField`, except that they show the choices indented in hierarchies in the administration interface.

Also, note that in the `Meta` class of the `Category` model, we order the categories by `tree_id` and then by the `lft` value in order to show the categories naturally in the tree structure.

See also

> ▸ The *Creating a model mixin to handle creation and modification dates* recipe in *Chapter 2, Database Structure*

> ▸ The *Structuring the page menu* recipe in *Chapter 7, Django CMS*

> ▸ The *Creating a category administration interface with django-mptt-admin* recipe

Creating a category administration interface with django-mptt-admin

The `django-mptt` app comes with a simple model administration mixin that allows you to create the tree structure and list it with indentation. To reorder trees, you need to either create this functionality yourself or use a third-party solution. Currently, there are two apps that can help you to create a draggable administration interface for hierarchical models. One of them is `django-mptt-admin`. Let's take a look at it in this recipe.

Getting ready

First, we need to have the `django-mptt-admin` app installed by performing the following steps:

1. To start, install the app in your virtual environment using the following command:

   (myproject_env)$ pip install django-mptt-admin

2. Then, put it in `INSTALLED_APPS` in the settings, as follows:

```python
# conf/base.py or settings.py
INSTALLED_APPS = (
    # ...
    "django_mptt_admin"
)
```

How to do it...

Create an administration interface for the `Category` model that extends `DjangoMpttAdmin` instead of `admin.ModelAdmin`, as follows:

```python
# movies/admin.py
# -*- coding: UTF-8 -*-
from __future__ import unicode_literals
from django.contrib import admin
from django_mptt_admin.admin import DjangoMpttAdmin
from .models import Category

class CategoryAdmin(DjangoMpttAdmin):
    list_display = ["title", "created", "modified"]
    list_filter = ["created"]

admin.site.register(Category, CategoryAdmin)
```

How it works...

The administration interface for the categories will have two modes: Tree view and Grid view. The Tree view looks similar to the following screenshot:

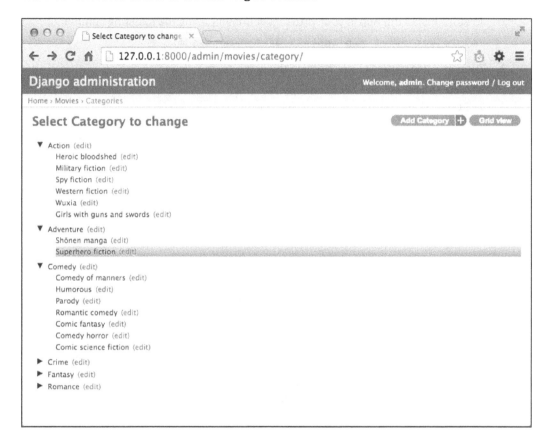

The Tree view uses the jqTree jQuery library for node manipulation. You can expand and collapse categories for a better overview. To reorder them or change the dependencies, you can drag and drop the titles in this list view. During reordering, the user interface looks similar to the following screenshot:

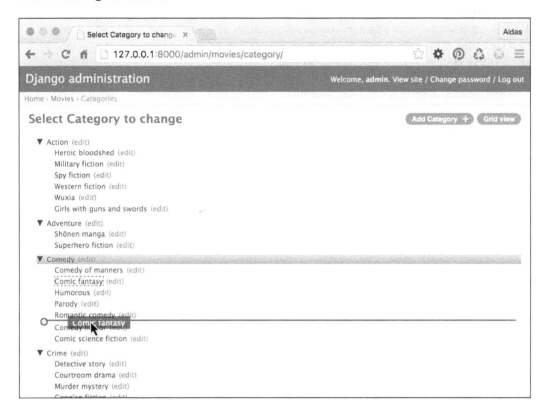

 Note that any usual list-related settings such as `list_display` or `list_filter` will be ignored.

If you want to filter categories, sort or filter them by a specific field, or apply admin actions, you can switch to the Grid view, which shows the default category change list.

See also

▶ The *Creating hierarchical categories* recipe

▶ The *Creating a category administration interface with django-mptt-tree-editor* recipe

Creating a category administration interface with django-mptt-tree-editor

If you want to use the common functionality of the change list, such as columns, admin actions, editable fields, or filters, in your administration interface as well as manipulate the tree structure in the same view, you need to use another third-party app called `django-mptt-tree-editor`. Let's see how to do that.

Getting ready

First, we need to have the `django-mptt-tree-editor` app installed. Perform the following steps:

1. To start, install the app in your virtual environment using the following command:

   ```
   (myproject_env)$ pip install django-mptt-tree-editor
   ```

2. Then, put it in `INSTALLED_APPS` in the settings, as follows:

   ```
   # conf/base.py or settings.py
   INSTALLED_APPS = (
       # ...
       "mptt_tree_editor"
   )
   ```

How to do it...

Create an administration interface for the `Category` model that extends `TreeEditor` instead of `admin.ModelAdmin`. Make sure that you add `indented_short_title` and `actions_column` at the beginning of the `list_display` setting, as follows:

```
# movies/admin.py
# -*- coding: UTF-8 -*-
from __future__ import unicode_literals
from django.contrib import admin
from mptt_tree_editor.admin import TreeEditor
from .models import Category

class CategoryAdmin(TreeEditor):
    list_display = ["indented_short_title", "actions_column",
        "created", "modified"]
    list_filter = ["created"]

admin.site.register(Category, CategoryAdmin)
```

How it works...

The administration interface for your categories now looks similar to the following screenshot:

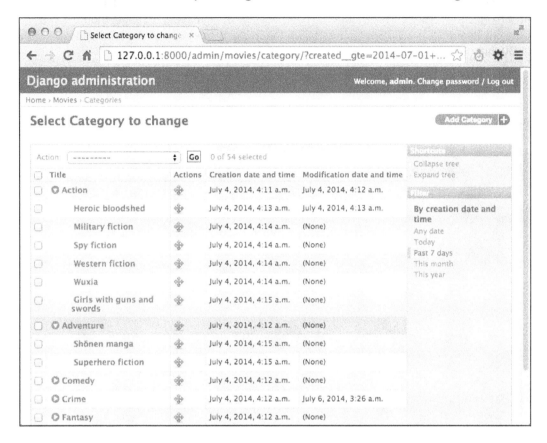

The category administration interface allows you to expand or collapse the categories. The `indented_short_title` column will either return the indented short title from the `short_title()` method of the category (if there is one) or the indented Unicode representation of the category. The column defined as `actions_column` will be rendered as a handle to reorder or restructure the categories by dragging and dropping them. As the dragging handle is in a different column than the category title, it might feel weird to work with it. During reordering, the user interface looks similar to the following screenshot:

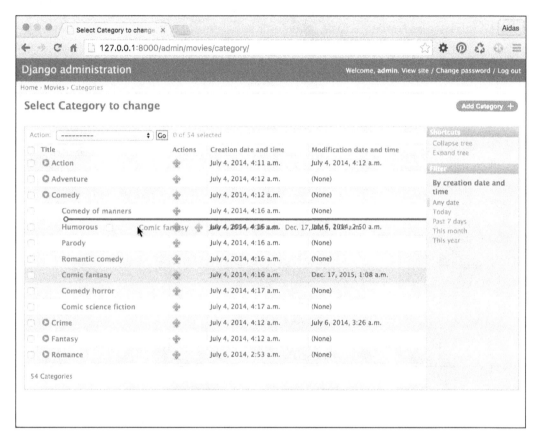

As you can see, it is possible to use all the list-related features of the default Django administration interface in the same view.

In `django-mptt-tree-editor`, the tree-editing functionality is ported from FeinCMS, another content management system made with Django.

- ▸ The *Creating hierarchical categories* recipe
- ▸ The *Creating a category administration interface with django-mptt-admin* recipe

Rendering categories in a template

Once you have created categories in your app, you need to display them hierarchically in a template. The easiest way to do this is to use the `{% recursetree %}` template tag from the `django-mptt` app. I will show you how to do that in this recipe.

Getting ready

Make sure that you have the `Category` model created and some categories entered in the database.

How to do it...

Pass `QuerySet` of your hierarchical categories to the template and then use the `{% recursetree %}` template tag as follows:

1. Create a view that loads all the categories and passes them to a template:

```python
# movies/views.py
# -*- coding: UTF-8 -*-
from __future__ import unicode_literals
from django.shortcuts import render
from .models import Category

def movie_category_list(request):
    context = {
        "categories": Category.objects.all(),
    }
    return render(
        request,
        "movies/movie_category_list.html",
        context
    )
```

2. Create a template with the following content:

```
{# templates/movies/movie_category_list.html #}
{% extends "base_single_column.html" %}
```

```
{% load i18n utility_tags mptt_tags %}

{% block sidebar %}
{% endblock %}

{% block content %}
<ul class="root">
    {% recursetree categories %}
        <li>
            {{ node.title }}
            {% if not node.is_leaf_node %}
                <ul class="children">
                    {{ children }}
                </ul>
            {% endif %}
        </li>
    {% endrecursetree %}
</ul>
{% endblock %}
```

3. Create a URL rule to show the view.

How it works...

The template will be rendered as nested lists, as shown in the following screenshot:

- Action
    - Heroic bloodshed
    - Military fiction
    - Spy fiction
    - Western fiction
    - Wuxia
    - Girls with guns and swords
- Adventure
    - Shōnen manga
    - Superhero fiction
- Comedy
    - Comedy of manners
    - Humorous
    - Parody
    - Romantic comedy
    - Comic fantasy
    - Comedy horror
    - Comic science fiction

The {% recursetree %} block template tag takes QuerySet of the categories and renders the list using the template content in the tag. There are two special variables used here: node and children. The node variable is an instance of the Category model. You can use its fields or methods such as {{ node.get_descendant_count }}, {{ node.level }}, or {{ node.is_root }} to add specific CSS classes or HTML5 data-* attributes for JavaScript. The second variable, children, defines where to place the children of the current category.

There's more...

If your hierarchical structure is very complex, with more than 20 depth levels, it is recommended to use the non-recursive template filter, tree_info. For more information on how to do this, refer to the official documentation at http://django-mptt.github.io/django-mptt/templates.html#tree-info-filter.

See also

▸   The *Using HTML5 data attributes* recipe in *Chapter 4, Templates and JavaScript*

▸   The *Creating hierarchical categories* recipe

▸   The *Using a single selection field to choose a category in forms* recipe

Using a single selection field to choose a category in forms

What happens if you want to show category selection in a form? How will the hierarchy be presented? In django-mptt, there is a special TreeNodeChoiceField form field that you can use to show the hierarchical structures in a selected field. Let's take a look at how to do this.

Getting ready

We will start with the movies app that we defined in the previous recipes.

How to do it...

Let's create a form with the category field and then show it in a view:

1.   In the forms.py file of the app, create a form with a category field as follows:

```
# movies/forms.py
# -*- coding: UTF-8 -*-
from __future__ import unicode_literals
```

```
from django import forms
from django.utils.translation import ugettext_lazy as _
from django.utils.html import mark_safe
from mptt.forms import TreeNodeChoiceField
from .models import Category

class MovieFilterForm(forms.Form):
    category = TreeNodeChoiceField(
        label=_("Category"),
        queryset=Category.objects.all(),
        required=False,
        level_indicator=mark_safe(
            "    "
        ),
    )
```

2. Then, create a URL rule, view, and template to show this form.

How it works...

The category selection will look similar to the following:

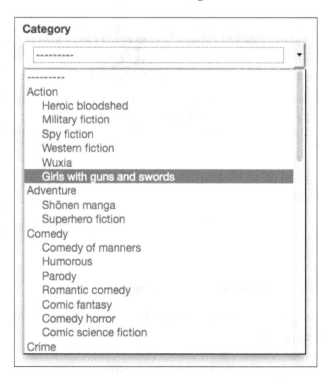

The `TreeNodeChoiceField` acts like `ModelChoiceField`; however, it shows hierarchical choices as indented. By default, `TreeNodeChoiceField` represents each deeper level prefixed by three dashes, `---`. In our example, we will change the level indicator to be four nonbreakable spaces (the ` ` HTML entities) by passing the `level_indicator` parameter to the field. To ensure that the nonbreakable spaces aren't escaped, we use the `mark_safe()` function.

See also

▸ The *Using a checkbox list to choose multiple categories in forms* recipe

Using a checkbox list to choose multiple categories in forms

When more than one category needs to be selected in a form, you can use the `TreeNodeMultipleChoiceField` multiple selection field that is provided by `django-mptt`. However, multiple selection fields are not very user-friendly from GUI point of view as the user needs to scroll and hold the control keys while clicking in order to make multiple choices. That's really awful. A much better way will be to provide a checkbox list to choose the categories. In this recipe, we will create a field that allows you to show the indented checkboxes in the form.

Getting ready

We will start with the `movies` app that we defined in the previous recipes and also the `utils` app that you should have in your project.

How to do it...

To render an indented list of categories with checkboxes, create and use a new `MultipleChoiceTreeField` form field and also create an HTML template for this field. The specific template will be passed to the crispy forms layout in the form. To do this, perform the following steps:

1. In the `utils` app, add a `fields.py` file and create a `MultipleChoiceTreeField` form field that extends `ModelMultipleChoiceField`, as follows:

```
# utils/fields.py
# -*- coding: utf-8 -*-
from __future__ import unicode_literals
from django import forms

class MultipleChoiceTreeField(
```

```
        forms.ModelMultipleChoiceField
):
    widget = forms.CheckboxSelectMultiple

    def label_from_instance(self, obj):
        return obj
```

2. Use the new field with the categories to choose from in the form for movie creation. Also, in the form layout, pass a custom template to the categories field, as shown in the following:

```python
# movies/forms.py
# -*- coding: UTF-8 -*-
from __future__ import unicode_literals
from django import forms
from django.utils.translation import ugettext_lazy as _
from crispy_forms.helper import FormHelper
from crispy_forms import layout, bootstrap
from utils.fields import MultipleChoiceTreeField
from .models import Movie, Category

class MovieForm(forms.ModelForm):
    categories = MultipleChoiceTreeField(
        label=_("Categories"),
        required=False,
        queryset=Category.objects.all(),
    )
    class Meta:
        model = Movie

    def __init__(self, *args, **kwargs):
        super(MovieForm, self).__init__(*args, **kwargs)
        self.helper = FormHelper()
        self.helper.form_action = ""
        self.helper.form_method = "POST"
        self.helper.layout = layout.Layout(
            layout.Field("title"),
            layout.Field(
                "categories",
                template="utils/"\
                    "checkbox_select_multiple_tree.html"
            ),
            bootstrap.FormActions(
                layout.Submit("submit", _("Save")),
            )
        )
```

3. Create a template for a Bootstrap-style checkbox list, as shown in the following:

```
{# templates/utils/checkbox_select_multiple_tree.html #}
{% load crispy_forms_filters %}
{% load l10n %}

<div id="div_{{ field.auto_id }}" class="form-group{% if wrapper_
class %} {{ wrapper_class }}{% endif %}{% if form_show_errors%}
{% if field.errors %} has-error{% endif %}{% endif %}{% if field.
css_classes %} {{ field.css_classes }}{% endif %}">
    {% if field.label and form_show_labels %}
        <label for="{{ field.id_for_label }}" class="control-label
{{ label_class }}{% if field.field.required %} requiredField{%
endif %}">
            {{ field.label|safe }}{% if field.field.required
%}<span class="asteriskField">*</span>{% endif %}
        </label>
    {% endif %}
    <div class="controls {{ field_class }}"{% if flat_attrs %} {{
flat_attrs|safe }}{% endif %}>
        {% include 'bootstrap3/layout/field_errors_block.html' %}

        {% for choice_value, choice_instance in field.field.
choices %}
            <label class="checkbox{% if inline_class %}-{{ inline_
class }}{% endif %} level-{{ choice_instance.level }}">
                <input type="checkbox"{% if choice_value in
field.value or choice_value|stringformat:"s" in field.value or
choice_value|stringformat:"s" == field.value|stringformat:"s" %}
checked="checked"{% endif %}

name="{{ field.html_name }}"id="id_{{ field.html_name }}_{{
forloop.counter }}"value="{{ choice_value|unlocalize }}"{{ field.
field.widget.attrs|flatatt }}>
                {{ choice_instance }}
            </label>
        {% endfor %}
        {% include "bootstrap3/layout/help_text.html" %}
    </div>
</div>
```

4. Create a URL rule, view, and template to show the form with the {% crispy %} template tag. To see how to use this template tag, refer to the *Creating a form layout with django-crispy-forms* recipe in *Chapter 3, Forms and Views*.

5. Lastly, add a rule to your CSS file to indent the labels with classes, such as `.level-0`, `.level-1`, `.level-2`, and so on, by setting the margin-left parameter. Make sure that you have a reasonable amount of these CSS classes for a possible maximal depth of the tree in your context, as follows:

```css
/* style.css */
.level-0 {
    margin-left: 0;
}
.level-1 {
    margin-left: 20px;
}
.level-2 {
    margin-left: 40px;
}
```

How it works...

As a result, we get the following form:

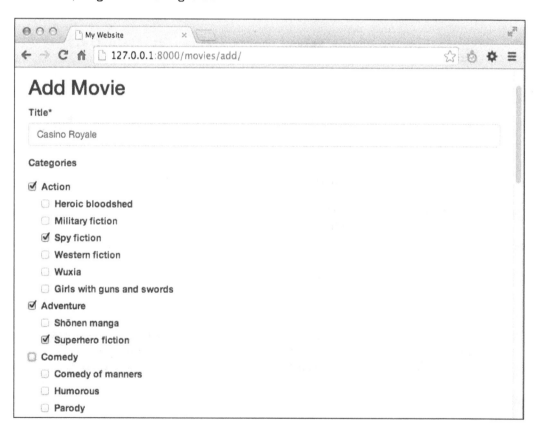

Contrary to the default behavior of Django, which hardcodes field generation in the Python code, the `django-crispy-forms` app uses templates to render the fields. You can browse them under `crispy_forms/templates/bootstrap3` and copy some of them to an analogous path in your project's template directory and overwrite them when necessary.

In our movie creation form, we pass a custom template for the categories field that will add the `.level-*` CSS classes to the `<label>` tag, wrapping the checkboxes. One problem with the normal `CheckboxSelectMultiple` widget is that when rendered, it only uses choice values and choice texts, and in our case, we need other properties of the category such as the depth level. To solve this, we will created a custom `MultipleChoiceTreeField` form field, which extends `ModelMultipleChoiceField` and overrides the `label_from_instance` method to return the category itself instead of its Unicode representation. The template for the field looks complicated; however, it is just a combination of a common field template (`crispy_forms/templates/bootstrap3/field.html`) and multiple checkbox field template (`crispy_forms/templates/bootstrap3/layout/checkboxselectmultiple.html`), with all the necessary Bootstrap 3 markup. We just made a slight modification to add the `.level-*` CSS classes.

See also

- The *Creating a form layout with django-crispy-forms* recipe in *Chapter 3*, *Forms and Views*
- The *Using a single selection field to choose a category in forms* recipe

Data Import and Export

9

In this chapter, we will cover the following recipes:

- ▶ Importing data from a local CSV file
- ▶ Importing data from a local Excel file
- ▶ Importing data from an external JSON file
- ▶ Importing data from an external XML file
- ▶ Creating filterable RSS feeds
- ▶ Using Tastypie to create API
- ▶ Using Django REST framework to create API

Introduction

There are times when your data needs to be transported from a local format to the database, imported from external resources, or provided to third parties. In this chapter, we will take a look at some practical examples of how to write management commands and APIs to do this.

Importing data from a local CSV file

The **comma-separated values** (**CSV**) format is probably the simplest way to store tabular data in a text file. In this recipe, we will create a management command that imports data from CSV to a Django database. We will need a CSV list of movies with a title, URL, and release year. You can easily create such files with Excel, Calc, or another spreadsheet application.

Getting ready

Create a movies app with the Movie model containing the following fields: title, url, and release_year. Place the app under INSTALLED_APPS in the settings.

How to do it...

Follow these steps to create and use a management command that imports movies from a local CSV file:

1. In the movies app, create a management directory and then a commands directory in the new management directory. Put the empty __init__.py files in both new directories to make them Python packages.

2. Add an import_movies_from_csv.py file there with the following content:

```
# movies/management/commands/import_movies_from_csv.py
# -*- coding: UTF-8 -*-
from __future__ import unicode_literals
import csv
from django.core.management.base import BaseCommand
from movies.models import Movie

SILENT, NORMAL, VERBOSE, VERY_VERBOSE = 0, 1, 2, 3

class Command(BaseCommand):
    help = (
        "Imports movies from a local CSV file. "
        "Expects title, URL, and release year."
    )

    def add_arguments(self, parser):
        # Positional arguments
        parser.add_argument(
            "file_path",
            nargs=1,
            type=unicode,
        )

    def handle(self, *args, **options):
        verbosity = options.get("verbosity", NORMAL)
        file_path = options["file_path"][0]

        if verbosity >= NORMAL:
```

```
        self.stdout.write("=== Movies imported ===")

with open(file_path) as f:
    reader = csv.reader(f)
    for rownum, (title, url, release_year) in \
    enumerate(reader):
        if rownum == 0:
            # let's skip the column captions
            continue
        movie, created = \
        Movie.objects.get_or_create(
            title=title,
            url=url,
            release_year=release_year,
        )
        if verbosity >= NORMAL:
            self.stdout.write("{}. {}".format(
                rownum, movie.title
            ))
```

3. To run the import, call the following in the command line:

```
(myproject_env)$ python manage.py import_movies_from_csv \
data/movies.csv
```

How it works...

For a management command, we need to create a `Command` class deriving from `BaseCommand` and overwriting the `add_arguments()` and `handle()` method. The `help` attribute defines the help text for the management command. It can be seen when you type the following in the command line:

```
(myproject_env)$ python manage.py help import_movies_from_csv
```

Django management commands use the built-in argparse module to parse the passed arguments. The `add_arguments()` method defines what positional or named arguments should be passed to the management command. In our case, we will add a positional `file_path` argument of Unicode type. By `nargs` set to the `1` attribute, we allow only one value. To learn about the other arguments that you can define and how to do this, refer to the official argparse documentation at `https://docs.python.org/2/library/argparse.html#the-add-argument-method`.

At the beginning of the `handle()` method, the `verbosity` argument is checked. Verbosity defines how verbose the command is, from `0` not giving any output to the command-line tool to `3` being very verbose. You can pass this argument to the command as follows:

```
(myproject_env)$ python manage.py import_movies_from_csv \
data/movies.csv --verbosity=0
```

Then, we also expect the filename as the first positional argument. The `options["file_path"]` returns a list of the values defined in the nargs, therefore, it is one value in this case.

We open the given file and pass its pointer to `csv.reader`. Then, for each line in the file, we will create a new `Movie` object if a matching movie doesn't exist yet. The management command will print out the imported movie titles to the console, unless you set the verbosity to `0`.

 If you want to debug the errors of a management command while developing it, pass the `--traceback` parameter for it. If an error occurs, you will see the full stack trace of the problem.

There's more...

You can learn more about the CSV library from the official documentation at `https://docs.python.org/2/library/csv.html`.

See also

- ▸ The *Importing data from a local Excel file* recipe

Importing data from a local Excel file

Another popular format to store tabular data is an Excel spread sheet. In this recipe, we will import movies from a file of this format.

Getting ready

Let's start with the `movies` app that we created in the previous recipe. Install the `xlrd` package to read Excel files, as follows:

```
(project_env)$ pip install xlrd
```

How to do it...

Follow these steps to create and use a management command that imports movies from a local XLS file:

1. If you haven't done that, in the `movies` app, create a `management` directory and then a `commands` directory in the new `management` directory. Put the empty `__init__.py` files in both the new directories to make them Python packages.

2. Add the `import_movies_from_xls.py` file with the following content:

```python
# movies/management/commands/import_movies_from_xls.py
# -*- coding: UTF-8 -*-
from __future__ import unicode_literals
import xlrd
from django.utils.six.moves import range
from django.core.management.base import BaseCommand
from movies.models import Movie

SILENT, NORMAL, VERBOSE, VERY_VERBOSE = 0, 1, 2, 3

class Command(BaseCommand):
    help = (
        "Imports movies from a local XLS file. "
        "Expects title, URL, and release year."
    )

    def add_arguments(self, parser):
        # Positional arguments
        parser.add_argument(
            "file_path",
            nargs=1,
            type=unicode,
        )

    def handle(self, *args, **options):
        verbosity = options.get("verbosity", NORMAL)
        file_path = options["file_path"][0]

        wb = xlrd.open_workbook(file_path)
        sh = wb.sheet_by_index(0)

        if verbosity >= NORMAL:
            self.stdout.write("=== Movies imported ===")
        for rownum in range(sh.nrows):
```

```
if rownum == 0:
    # let's skip the column captions
    continue
(title, url, release_year) = \
    sh.row_values(rownum)
movie, created = Movie.objects.get_or_create(
    title=title,
    url=url,
    release_year=release_year,
)
if verbosity >= NORMAL:
    self.stdout.write("{}. {}".format(
        rownum, movie.title
    ))
```

3. To run the import, call the following in the command line:

```
(myproject_env)$ python manage.py import_movies_from_xls \
data/movies.xls
```

How it works...

The principle of importing from an XLS file is the same as with CSV. We open the file, read it row by row, and create the Movie objects from the provided data. A detailed explanation is as follows.

- Excel files are workbooks containing sheets as different tabs.

- We are using the xlrd library to open a file passed as a positional argument to the command. Then, we will read the first sheet from the workbook.

- Afterwards, we will read the rows one by one (except the first row with the column titles) and create the Movie objects from them. Once again, the management command will print out the imported movie titles to the console, unless you set the verbosity to 0.

There's more...

You can learn more about how to work with Excel files at http://www.python-excel.org/.

See also

- The *Importing data from a local CSV file* recipe

Importing data from an external JSON file

The `Last.fm` music website has an API under the `http://ws.audioscrobbler.com/` domain that you can use to read the albums, artists, tracks, events, and more. The API allows you to either use the JSON or XML format. In this recipe, we will import the top tracks tagged disco using the JSON format.

Getting ready

Follow these steps in order to import data in the JSON format from `Last.fm`:

1. To use `Last.fm`, you need to register and get an API key. The API key can be created at `http://www.last.fm/api/account/create`.

2. The API key has to be set in the settings as `LAST_FM_API_KEY`.

3. Also, install the `requests` library in your virtual environment using the following command:

   ```
   (myproject_env)$ pip install requests
   ```

4. Let's check the structure of the JSON endpoint (`http://ws.audioscrobbler.com/2.0/?method=tag.gettoptracks&tag=disco&api_key=xxx&format=json`):

   ```
   {
     "tracks":{
       "track":[
         {
           "name":"Billie Jean",
           "duration":"293",
           "mbid":"f980fc14-e29b-481d-ad3a-5ed9b4ab6340",
           "url":"http://www.last.fm/music/Michael+Jackson/_/Billie+Jean",
           "streamable":{
             "#text":"0",
             "fulltrack":"0"
           },
           "artist":{
             "name":"Michael Jackson",
             "mbid":"f27ec8db-af05-4f36-916e-3d57f91ecf5e",
             "url":"http://www.last.fm/music/Michael+Jackson"
           },
           "image":[
             {
   ```

```
                    "#text":"http://img2-ak.lst.fm/i/u/34s/114a4599f3bd451
        ca915f482345bc70f.png",
                    "size":"small"
                },
                {
                    "#text":"http://img2-ak.lst.fm/i/u/64s/114a4599f3bd451
        ca915f482345bc70f.png",
                    "size":"medium"
                },
                {
                    "#text":"http://img2-ak.lst.fm/i/u/174s/114a4599f3bd45
        1ca915f482345bc70f.png",
                    "size":"large"
                },
                {
                    "#text":"http://img2-ak.lst.fm/i/u/300x300/114a4599f3b
        d451ca915f482345bc70f.png",
                    "size":"extralarge"
                }
            ],
            "@attr":{
                "rank":"1"
            }
        },
        ...
    ],
    "@attr":{
        "tag":"disco",
        "page":"1",
        "perPage":"50",
        "totalPages":"26205",
        "total":"1310249"
    }
  }
}
```

We want to read the track name, artist, URL, and medium-sized images.

How to do it...

Follow these steps to create a `Track` model and management command, which imports top tracks from `Last.fm` to the database:

1. Let's create a `music` app with a simple `Track` model, as follows:

```python
# music/models.py
# -*- coding: UTF-8 -*-
from __future__ import unicode_literals
import os
from django.utils.translation import ugettext_lazy as _
from django.db import models
from django.utils.text import slugify
from django.utils.encoding import \
    python_2_unicode_compatible


def upload_to(instance, filename):
    filename_base, filename_ext = \
        os.path.splitext(filename)
    return "tracks/%s--%s%s" % (
        slugify(instance.artist),
        slugify(instance.name),
        filename_ext.lower(),
    )


@python_2_unicode_compatible
class Track(models.Model):
    name = models.CharField(_("Name"), max_length=250)
    artist = models.CharField(_("Artist"), max_length=250)
    url = models.URLField(_("URL"))
    image = models.ImageField(_("Image"),
        upload_to=upload_to, blank=True, null=True)

    class Meta:
        verbose_name = _("Track")
        verbose_name_plural = _("Tracks")

    def __str__(self):
        return "%s - %s" % (self.artist, self.name)
```

2. Then, create the management command as shown in the following:

```python
# music/management/commands/import_music_from_lastfm_as_json.py
# -*- coding: UTF-8 -*-
from __future__ import unicode_literals
```

```python
import os
import requests
from StringIO import StringIO
from django.utils.six.moves import range
from django.core.management.base import BaseCommand
from django.utils.encoding import force_text
from django.conf import settings
from django.core.files import File
from music.models import Track

SILENT, NORMAL, VERBOSE, VERY_VERBOSE = 0, 1, 2, 3

class Command(BaseCommand):
    help = "Imports top tracks from last.fm as XML."

    def add_arguments(self, parser):
        # Named (optional) arguments
        parser.add_argument(
            "--max_pages",
            type=int,
            default=0,
        )

    def handle(self, *args, **options):
        self.verbosity = options.get("verbosity", NORMAL)
        max_pages = options["max_pages"]

        params = {
            "method": "tag.gettoptracks",
            "tag": "disco",
            "api_key": settings.LAST_FM_API_KEY,
            "format": "json",
        }

        r = requests.get(
            "http://ws.audioscrobbler.com/2.0/",
            params=params
        )

        response_dict = r.json()
        total_pages = int(
            response_dict["tracks"]["@attr"]["totalPages"]
        )
        if max_pages > 0:
```

```
                    total_pages = max_pages

              if self.verbosity >= NORMAL:
                  self.stdout.write("=== Tracks imported ===")

          self.save_page(response_dict)
          for page_number in range(2, total_pages + 1):
              params["page"] = page_number
              r = requests.get(
                  "http://ws.audioscrobbler.com/2.0/",
                  params=params
              )
              response_dict = r.json()
              self.save_page(response_dict)
```

3. As the list is paginated, we will add the `save_page()` method to the `Command` class to save a single page of tracks. This method takes the dictionary with the top tracks from a single page as a parameter, as follows:

```python
def save_page(self, d):
    for track_dict in d["tracks"]["track"]:
        track, created = Track.objects.get_or_create(
            name=force_text(track_dict["name"]),
            artist=force_text(
                track_dict["artist"]["name"]
            ),
            url=force_text(track_dict["url"]),
        )
        image_dict = track_dict.get("image", None)
        if created and image_dict:
            image_url = image_dict[1]["#text"]
            image_response = requests.get(image_url)
            track.image.save(
                os.path.basename(image_url),
                File(StringIO(image_response.content))
            )
        if self.verbosity >= NORMAL:
            self.stdout.write(" - {} - {}".format(
                track.artist, track.name
            ))
```

4. To run the import, call the following in the command line:

```
(myproject_env)$ python manage.py \
import_music_from_lastfm_as_json --max_pages=3
```

How it works...

The optional named `max_pages` argument limits the imported data to three pages. Just skip it if you want to download all the available top tracks; however, beware that there are above 26,000 pages as detailed in the `totalPages` value and this will take a while.

Using the `requests.get()` method, we read the data from `Last.fm`, passing the `params` query parameters. The response object has a built-in method called `json()`, which converts a JSON string and returns a parsed dictionary.

We read the total pages value from this dictionary and then save the first page of results. Then, we get the second and later pages one by one and save them. One interesting part in the import is downloading and saving the image. Here, we also use `request.get()` to retrieve the image data and then we pass it to `File` through `StringIO`, which is accordingly used in the `image.save()` method. The first parameter of `image.save()` is a filename that will be overwritten anyway by the value from the `upload_to` function and is necessary only for the file extension.

See also

> ▸ The *Importing data from an external XML file* recipe

Importing data from an external XML file

The `Last.fm` file also allows you to take data from their services in XML format. In this recipe, I will show you how to do this.

Getting ready

To prepare importing top tracks from `Last.fm` in the XML format, follow these steps:

1. Start with the first three steps from the *Getting ready* section in the *Importing data from an external JSON file* recipe.

2. Then, let's check the structure of the XML endpoint (`http://ws.audioscrobbler.com/2.0/?method=tag.gettoptracks&tag=disco&api_key=xxx&format=xml`), as follows:

```
<?xml version="1.0" encoding="UTF-8"?>
<lfm status="ok">
  <tracks tag="disco" page="1" perPage="50" totalPages="26205"
total="1310249">
    <track rank="1">
      <name>Billie Jean</name>
      <duration>293</duration>
```

```
      <mbid>f980fc14-e29b-481d-ad3a-5ed9b4ab6340</mbid>
      <url>http://www.last.fm/music/Michael+Jackson/_/
Billie+Jean</url>
      <streamable fulltrack="0">0</streamable>
      <artist>
        <name>Michael Jackson</name>
        <mbid>f27ec8db-af05-4f36-916e-3d57f91ecf5e</mbid>
        <url>http://www.last.fm/music/Michael+Jackson</url>
      </artist>
      <image size="small">http://img2-ak.lst.fm/i/u/34s/114a4599f3
bd451ca915f482345bc70f.png</image>
      <image size="medium">http://img2-ak.lst.fm/i/u/64s/114a4599f
3bd451ca915f482345bc70f.png</image>
      <image size="large">http://img2-ak.lst.fm/i/u/174s/114a4599f
3bd451ca915f482345bc70f.png</image>
      <image size="extralarge">http://img2-ak.lst.fm/i/u/300x300/1
14a4599f3bd451ca915f482345bc70f.png</image>
    </track>
    ...
  </tracks>
</lfm>
```

How to do it...

Execute the following steps one by one to import the top tracks from Last.fm in the XML format:

1. Create a music app with a Track model similar to the previous recipe, if you've not already done this.

2. Then, create an import_music_from_lastfm_as_xml.py management command. We will be using the ElementTree XML API that comes with Python to parse the XML nodes, as follows:

```python
# music/management/commands/import_music_from_lastfm_as_xml.py
# -*- coding: UTF-8 -*-
from __future__ import unicode_literals
import os
import requests
from xml.etree import ElementTree
from StringIO import StringIO
from django.utils.six.moves import range
from django.core.management.base import BaseCommand
from django.utils.encoding import force_text
from django.conf import settings
from django.core.files import File
```

```
from music.models import Track

SILENT, NORMAL, VERBOSE, VERY_VERBOSE = 0, 1, 2, 3

class Command(BaseCommand):
    help = "Imports top tracks from last.fm as XML."

    def add_arguments(self, parser):
        # Named (optional) arguments
        parser.add_argument(
            "--max_pages",
            type=int,
            default=0,
        )

    def handle(self, *args, **options):
        self.verbosity = options.get("verbosity", NORMAL)
        max_pages = options["max_pages"]

        params = {
            "method": "tag.gettoptracks",
            "tag": "disco",
            "api_key": settings.LAST_FM_API_KEY,
            "format": "xml",
        }

        r = requests.get(
            "http://ws.audioscrobbler.com/2.0/",
            params=params
        )

        root = ElementTree.fromstring(r.content)
        total_pages = int(
            root.find("tracks").attrib["totalPages"]
        )
        if max_pages > 0:
            total_pages = max_pages

        if self.verbosity >= NORMAL:
            self.stdout.write("=== Tracks imported ===")

        self.save_page(root)
        for page_number in range(2, total_pages + 1):
            params["page"] = page_number
```

```
r = requests.get(
    "http://ws.audioscrobbler.com/2.0/",
    params=params
)
root = ElementTree.fromstring(r.content)
self.save_page(root)
```

3. As the list is paginated, we will add a `save_page()` method to the `Command` class to save a single page of tracks. This method takes the root node of the XML as a parameter, as shown in the following:

```
def save_page(self, root):
    for track_node in root.findall("tracks/track"):
        track, created = Track.objects.get_or_create(
            name=force_text(
                track_node.find("name").text
            ),
            artist=force_text(
                track_node.find("artist/name").text
            ),
            url=force_text(
                track_node.find("url").text
            ),
        )
        image_node = track_node.find(
            "image[@size='medium']"
        )
        if created and image_node is not None:
            image_response = \
                requests.get(image_node.text)
            track.image.save(
                os.path.basename(image_node.text),
                File(StringIO(image_response.content))
            )
        if self.verbosity >= NORMAL:
            self.stdout.write(" - {} - {}".format(
                track.artist, track.name
            ))
```

4. To run the import, call the following in the command line:

```
(myproject_env)$ python manage.py \
import_music_from_lastfm_as_xml --max_pages=3
```

How it works...

The process is analogous to the JSON approach. Using the `requests.get()` method, we read the data from `Last.fm`, passing the query parameters as `params`. The XML content of the response is passed to the `ElementTree` parser and the root node is returned.

The `ElementTree` nodes have the `find()` and `findall()` methods, where you can pass XPath queries to filter out specific subnodes.

The following is a table of the available XPath syntax supported by `ElementTree`:

XPath Syntax Component	Meaning
`tag`	This selects all the child elements with the given tag.
`*`	This selects all the child elements.
`.`	This selects the current node.
`//`	This selects all the subelements on all the levels beneath the current element.
`..`	This selects the parent element.
`[@attrib]`	This selects all the elements that have the given attribute.
`[@attrib='value']`	This selects all the elements for which the given attribute has the given value.
`[tag]`	This selects all the elements that have a child named tag. Only immediate children are supported.
`[position]`	This selects all the elements that are located at the given position. The position can either be an integer (`1` is the first position), the `last()` expression (for the last position), or a position relative to the last position (for example, `last()-1`).

Therefore, using `root.find("tracks").attrib["totalPages"]`, we read the total amount of pages. We will save the first page and then go through the other pages one by one and save them too.

In the `save_page()` method, `root.findall("tracks/track")` returns an iterator through the `<track>` nodes under the `<tracks>` node. With `track_node.find("image[@size='medium']")`, we get the medium-sized image.

There's more...

You can learn more about XPath at `https://en.wikipedia.org/wiki/XPath`.

The full documentation of `ElementTree` can be found at `https://docs.python.org/2/library/xml.etree.elementtree.html`.

See also

► The *Importing data from an external JSON file* recipe

Creating filterable RSS feeds

Django comes with a syndication feed framework that allows you to create RSS and Atom feeds easily. RSS and Atom feeds are XML documents with specific semantics. They can be subscribed in an RSS reader such as Feedly or they can be aggregated in other websites, mobile applications, or desktop applications. In this recipe, we will create `BulletinFeed`, which provides a bulletin board with images. Moreover, the results will be filterable by URL query parameters.

Getting ready

Create a new `bulletin_board` app and put it under `INSTALLED_APPS` in the settings.

How to do it...

We will create a `Bulletin` model and an RSS feed for it. We will be able to filter the RSS feed by type or category so that it is possible to only subscribe to the bulletins that are, for example, offering used books:

1. In the `models.py` file of this app, add the `Category` and `Bulletin` models with a foreign key relationship between them, as follows:

```python
# bulletin_board/models.py
# -*- coding: UTF-8 -*-
from __future__ import unicode_literals
from django.db import models
from django.utils.translation import ugettext_lazy as _
from django.core.urlresolvers import reverse
from django.utils.encoding import \
    python_2_unicode_compatible
from utils.models import CreationModificationDateMixin
from utils.models import UrlMixin

TYPE_CHOICES = (
    ("searching", _("Searching")),
    ("offering", _("Offering")),
)


@python_2_unicode_compatible
```

```python
class Category(models.Model):
    title = models.CharField(_("Title"), max_length=200)

    def __str__(self):
        return self.title

    class Meta:
        verbose_name = _("Category")
        verbose_name_plural = _("Categories")

@python_2_unicode_compatible
class Bulletin(CreationModificationDateMixin, UrlMixin):
    bulletin_type = models.CharField(_("Type"),
        max_length=20, choices=TYPE_CHOICES)
    category = models.ForeignKey(Category,
        verbose_name=_("Category"))

    title = models.CharField(_("Title"), max_length=255)
    description = models.TextField(_("Description"),
        max_length=300)

    contact_person = models.CharField(_("Contact person"),
        max_length=255)
    phone = models.CharField(_("Phone"), max_length=50,
        blank=True)
    email = models.CharField(_("Email"), max_length=254,
        blank=True)

    image = models.ImageField(_("Image"), max_length=255,
        upload_to="bulletin_board/", blank=True)

    class Meta:
        verbose_name = _("Bulletin")
        verbose_name_plural = _("Bulletins")
        ordering = ("-created",)

    def __str__(self):
        return self.title

    def get_url_path(self):
        try:
            path = reverse(
                "bulletin_detail",
                kwargs={"pk": self.pk}
```

```
        )
    except:
        # the apphook is not attached yet
        return ""
    else:
        return path
```

2. Then, create `BulletinFilterForm` that allows the visitor to filter the bulletins by type and category, as follows:

 # bulletin_board/forms.py
```
# -*- coding: UTF-8 -*-
from django import forms
from django.utils.translation import ugettext_lazy as _
from models import Category, TYPE_CHOICES


class BulletinFilterForm(forms.Form):
    bulletin_type = forms.ChoiceField(
        label=_("Bulletin Type"),
        required=False,
        choices=(("", "---------"),) + TYPE_CHOICES,
    )
    category = forms.ModelChoiceField(
        label=_("Category"),
        required=False,
        queryset=Category.objects.all(),
    )
```

3. Add a `feeds.py` file with the `BulletinFeed` class, as shown in the following:

 # bulletin_board/feeds.py
```
# -*- coding: UTF-8 -*-
from __future__ import unicode_literals
from django.contrib.syndication.views import Feed
from django.core.urlresolvers import reverse
from .models import Bulletin, TYPE_CHOICES
from .forms import BulletinFilterForm


class BulletinFeed(Feed):
    description_template = \
        "bulletin_board/feeds/bulletin_description.html"

    def get_object(self, request, *args, **kwargs):
        form = BulletinFilterForm(data=request.REQUEST)
        obj = {}
        if form.is_valid():
```

```python
        obj = {
            "bulletin_type": \
                form.cleaned_data["bulletin_type"],
            "category": form.cleaned_data["category"],
            "query_string": \
                request.META["QUERY_STRING"],
        }
        return obj

    def title(self, obj):
        t = "My Website - Bulletin Board"
        # add type "Searching" or "Offering"
        if obj.get("bulletin_type", False):
            tp = obj["bulletin_type"]
            t += " - %s" % dict(TYPE_CHOICES)[tp]
        # add category
        if obj.get("category", False):
            t += " - %s" % obj["category"].title
        return t

    def link(self, obj):
        if obj.get("query_string", False):
            return reverse("bulletin_list") + "?" + \
                obj["query_string"]
        return reverse("bulletin_list")

    def feed_url(self, obj):
        if obj.get("query_string", False):
            return reverse("bulletin_rss") + "?" + \
                obj["query_string"]
        return reverse("bulletin_rss")

    def item_pubdate(self, item):
        return item.created

    def items(self, obj):
        qs = Bulletin.objects.order_by("-created")
        if obj.get("bulletin_type", False):
            qs = qs.filter(
                bulletin_type=obj["bulletin_type"],
            ).distinct()
        if obj.get("category", False):
            qs = qs.filter(
```

```
                    category=obj["category"],
                ).distinct()
        return qs[:30]
```

4. Create a template for the bulletin description that will be provided in the feed, as shown in the following:

```
{# templates/bulletin_board/feeds/bulletin_description.html #}
{% if obj.image %}
    <p><a href="{{ obj.get_url }}"><img src="http://{{ request.
META.HTTP_HOST }}{{ obj.image.url }}" alt="" /></a></p>
{% endif %}
<p>{{ obj.description }}</p>
```

5. Create a URL configuration for the bulletin board app and include it in the root URL configuration, as follows:

```
# templates/bulletin_board/urls.py
# -*- coding: UTF-8 -*-
from __future__ import unicode_literals
from django.conf.urls import *
from .feeds import BulletinFeed

urlpatterns = patterns("bulletin_board.views",
    url(r"^$", "bulletin_list", name="bulletin_list"),
    url(r"^(?P<bulletin_id>[0-9]+)/$", "bulletin_detail",
        name="bulletin_detail"),
    url(r"^rss/$", BulletinFeed(), name="bulletin_rss"),
)
```

6. You will also need the views and templates for the filterable list and details of the bulletins. In the `Bulletin` list page template, add the following link:

```
<a href="{% url "bulletin_rss" %}?{{ request.META.QUERY_STRING
}}">RSS Feed</a>
```

How it works...

Therefore, if you have some data in the database and you open `http://127.0.0.1:8000/bulletin-board/rss/?bulletin_type=offering&category=4` in your browser, you will get an RSS feed of bulletins with the `Offering` type and the `4` category ID.

The `BulletinFeed` class has the `get_objects()` method that takes the current `HttpRequest` and defines the `obj` dictionary used in other methods of the same class. The `obj` dictionary contains the bulletin type, category, and current query string.

The `title()` method returns the title of the feed. It can either be generic or related to the selected bulletin type or category. The `link()` method returns the link to the original bulletin list with the filtering done. The `feed_url()` method returns the URL of the current feed. The `items()` method does the filtering itself and returns a filtered `QuerySet` of bulletins. Finally, the `item_pubdate()` method returns the creation date of the bulletin.

To see all the available methods and properties of the `Feed` class that we are extending, refer to the following documentation at `https://docs.djangoproject.com/en/1.8/ref/contrib/syndication/#feed-class-reference`.

The other parts of the code are self-explanatory.

See also

▶ The *Creating a model mixin with URL-related methods* recipe in *Chapter 2, Database Structure*

▶ The *Creating a model mixin to handle creation and modification dates* recipe in *Chapter 2, Database Structure*

▶ The *Using Tastypie to create API* recipe

Using Tastypie to create API

Tastypie is a framework for Django to create web service **Application Program Interface** (**API**). It supports full `GET/POST/PUT/DELETE/PATCH HTTP` methods to deal with online resources. It also supports different types of authentication and authorization, serialization, caching, throttling, and so on. In this recipe, you will learn how to provide bulletins to third parties for reading, that is, we will implement only the `GET HTTP` method.

Getting ready

First of all, install `Tastypie` in your virtual environment using the following command:

```
(myproject_env)$ pip install django-tastypie
```

Add Tastypie to `INSTALLED_APPS` in the settings. Then, enhance the `bulletin_board` app that we defined in the *Creating filterable RSS feeds* recipe.

How to do it...

We will create an API for bulletins and inject it in the URL configuration as follows:

1. In the `bulletin_board` app, create an `api.py` file with two resources, `CategoryResource` and `BulletinResource`, as follows:

```
# bulletin_board/api.py
# -*- coding: UTF-8 -*-
from __future__ import unicode_literals
from tastypie.resources import ModelResource
from tastypie.resources import ALL, ALL_WITH_RELATIONS
from tastypie.authentication import ApiKeyAuthentication
from tastypie.authorization import DjangoAuthorization
from tastypie import fields
from .models import Category, Bulletin


class CategoryResource(ModelResource):
    class Meta:
        queryset = Category.objects.all()
        resource_name = "categories"
        fields = ["title"]
        allowed_methods = ["get"]
        authentication = ApiKeyAuthentication()
        authorization = DjangoAuthorization()
        filtering = {
            "title": ALL,
        }


class BulletinResource(ModelResource):
    category = fields.ForeignKey(CategoryResource,
        "category", full=True)

    class Meta:
        queryset = Bulletin.objects.all()
        resource_name = "bulletins"
        fields = [
            "bulletin_type", "category", "title",
            "description", "contact_person", "phone",
            "email", "image"
        ]
        allowed_methods = ["get"]
        authentication = ApiKeyAuthentication()
        authorization = DjangoAuthorization()
        filtering = {
```

```
                    "bulletin_type": ALL,
                    "title": ALL,
                    "category": ALL_WITH_RELATIONS,
            }
```

2. In the main URL configuration, include the API URLs, as follows:

```python
# myproject/urls.py
# -*- coding: UTF-8 -*-
from __future__ import unicode_literals
from django.conf.urls import patterns, include, url
from django.conf import settings
from django.conf.urls.static import static
from django.contrib.staticfiles.urls import \
    staticfiles_urlpatterns

from django.contrib import admin
admin.autodiscover()

from tastypie.api import Api
from bulletin_board.api import CategoryResource
from bulletin_board.api import BulletinResource

v1_api = Api(api_name="v1")
v1_api.register(CategoryResource())
v1_api.register(BulletinResource())

urlpatterns = patterns('',
    url(r"^admin/", include(admin.site.urls)),
    url(r"^api/", include(v1_api.urls)),
)

urlpatterns += staticfiles_urlpatterns()
urlpatterns += static(settings.MEDIA_URL,
    document_root=settings.MEDIA_ROOT)
```

3. Create a Tastypie API key for the admin user in the model administration. To do this, navigate to **Tastypie | Api key | Add Api key**, select the admin user, and save the entry. This will generate a random API key, as shown in the following screenshot:

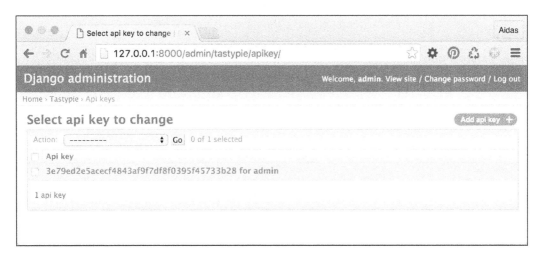

4. Then, you can open this URL to see the JSON response in action (simply replace xxx with your API key): `http://127.0.0.1:8000/api/v1/bulletins/?format=js on&username=admin&api_key=xxx`.

How it works...

Each endpoint of `Tastypie` should have a class extending `ModelResource` defined. Similar to the Django models, the configuration of the resource is set in the `Meta` class:

▶ The `queryset` parameter defines the `QuerySet` of objects to list.

▶ The `resource_name` parameter defines the name of the URL endpoint.

▶ The `fields` parameter lists out the fields of the model that should be shown in the API.

▶ The `allowed_methods` parameter lists out the request methods, such as `get`, `post`, `put`, `delete`, and `patch`.

▶ The `authentication` parameter defines how third parties can authenticate themselves when connecting to the API. The available options are `Authentication`, `BasicAuthentication`, `ApiKeyAuthentication`, `SessionAuthentication`, `DigestAuthentication`, `OAuthAuthentication`, `MultiAuthentication`, or your own custom authentication. In our case, we are using `ApiKeyAuthentication` as we want each user to use `username` and `api_key`.

- ▸ The `authorization` parameter answers the authorization question: is permission granted to this user to take the stated action? The possible choices are `Authorization`, `ReadOnlyAuthorization`, `DjangoAuthorization`, or your own custom authorization. In our case, we are using `ReadOnlyAuthorization` as we only want to allow read access to the users.

- ▸ The `filtering` parameter defines by which fields one can filter the lists in the URL query parameters. For example, with the current configuration, you can filter the items by titles that contain the word "movie": `http://127.0.0.1:8000/api/v1/bulletins/?format=json&username=admin&api_key=xxx&title__contains=movie`.

Also, there is a `category` foreign key that is defined in `BulletinResource` with the `full=True` argument, meaning that the full list of category fields will be shown in the bulletin resource instead of an endpoint link.

Besides JSON, `Tastypie` allows you to use other formats such as XML, YAML, and bplist.

There is a lot more that you can do with APIs using Tastypie. To find out more details, check the official documentation at `http://django-tastypie.readthedocs.org/en/latest/`.

See also

- ▸ The *Creating filterable RSS feeds* recipe
- ▸ The *Using Django REST framework to create API* recipe

Using Django REST framework to create API

Besides Tastypie, there is a newer and fresher framework to create API for your data transfers to and from third parties. That's Django REST Framework. This framework has more extensive documentation and Django-ish implementation, it is also more maintainable. Therefore, if you have to choose between Tastypie or Django REST Framework, I would recommend the latter one. In this recipe, you will learn how to use Django REST Framework in order to allow your project partners, mobile clients, or Ajax-based website to access data on your site to create, read, update, and delete.

Getting ready

First of all, install Django REST Framework and its optional dependencies in your virtual environment using the following commands:

```
(myproject_env)$ pip install djangorestframework
(myproject_env)$ pip install markdown
(myproject_env)$ pip install django-filter
```

Add `rest_framework` to `INSTALLED_APPS` in the settings. Then, enhance the `bulletin_board` app that we defined in the *Creating filterable RSS feeds* recipe.

How to do it...

To integrate a new REST API in our `bulletin_board` app, execute the following steps:

1. Add the specific configurations to the settings:

```python
# conf/base.py or settings.py
REST_FRAMEWORK = {
    "DEFAULT_PERMISSION_CLASSES": [
        "rest_framework.permissions."
            "DjangoModelPermissionsOrAnonReadOnly"
    ],
    "DEFAULT_PAGINATION_CLASS": \
        "rest_framework.pagination.LimitOffsetPagination",
    "PAGE_SIZE": 100,
}
```

2. In the `bulletin_board` app, create the `serializers.py` file with the following content:

```python
# bulletin_board/serializers.py
# -*- coding: UTF-8 -*-
from __future__ import unicode_literals
from rest_framework import serializers
from .models import Category, Bulletin

class CategorySerializer(serializers.ModelSerializer):
    class Meta:
        model = Category
        fields = ["id", "title"]

class BulletinSerializer(serializers.ModelSerializer):
    category = CategorySerializer()

    class Meta:
        model = Bulletin
        fields = [
            "id", "bulletin_type", "category", "title",
            "description", "contact_person", "phone",
            "email", "image"
        ]

    def create(self, validated_data):
```

```
            category_data = validated_data.pop('category')
            category, created = Category.objects.\
                get_or_create(title=category_data['title'])
            bulletin = Bulletin.objects.create(
                category=category, **validated_data
            )
            return bulletin

        def update(self, instance, validated_data):
            category_data = validated_data.pop('category')
            category, created = Category.objects.get_or_create(
                title=category_data['title'],
            )
            for fname, fvalue in validated_data.items():
                setattr(instance, fname, fvalue)
            instance.category = category
            instance.save()
            return instance
```

3. Add two new class-based views to the `views.py` file in the `bulletin_board` app:

```
# bulletin_board/views.py
# -*- coding: UTF-8 -*-
from __future__ import unicode_literals
from rest_framework import generics

from .models import Bulletin
from .serializers import BulletinSerializer

class RESTBulletinList(generics.ListCreateAPIView):
    queryset = Bulletin.objects.all()
    serializer_class = BulletinSerializer


class RESTBulletinDetail(
    generics.RetrieveUpdateDestroyAPIView
):
    queryset = Bulletin.objects.all()
    serializer_class = BulletinSerializer
```

4. Finally, plug in the new views to the URL configuration:

```
# myproject/urls.py
# -*- coding: UTF-8 -*-
from __future__ import unicode_literals
from django.conf.urls import patterns, include, url
```

```
from bulletin_board.views import RESTBulletinList
from bulletin_board.views import RESTBulletinDetail

urlpatterns = [
    # ...
    url(
        r"^api-auth/",
        include("rest_framework.urls",
        namespace="rest_framework")
    ),
    url(
        r"^rest-api/bulletin-board/$",
        RESTBulletinList.as_view(),
        name="rest_bulletin_list"
    ),
    url(
        r"^rest-api/bulletin-board/(?P<pk>[0-9]+)/$",
        RESTBulletinDetail.as_view(),
        name="rest_bulletin_detail"
    ),
]
```

How it works...

What we created here is an API for the bulletin board, where one can read a paginated bulletin list; create a new bulletin; and read, change, or delete a single bulletin by ID. Reading is allowed without authentication; whereas, one has to have a user account with appropriate permissions to add, change, or delete a bulletin.

Here's how you can approach the created API:

URL	HTTP Method	Description
http://127.0.0.1:8000/rest-api/bulletin-board/	GET	List bulletins paginated by 100
http://127.0.0.1:8000/rest-api/bulletin-board/	POST	Create a new bulletin if the requesting user is authenticated and authorized to create bulletins
http://127.0.0.1:8000/rest-api/bulletin-board/1/	GET	Get a bulletin with the 1 ID

URL	HTTP Method	Description
`http://127.0.0.1:8000/rest-api/bulletin-board/1/`	PUT	Update a bulletin with the 1 ID, if the user is authenticated and authorized to change bulletins
`http://127.0.0.1:8000/rest-api/bulletin-board/1/`	DELETE	Delete the bulletin with the 1 ID, if the user is authenticated and authorized to delete bulletins

How to use the API practically? For example, if you have the `requests` library installed, you can create a new bulletin in the Django shell as follows:

```
(myproject_env)$ python manage.py shell
>>> import requests
>>> response = requests.post("http://127.0.0.1:8000/rest-api/bulletin-
board/", auth=("admin", "admin"), data={"title": "TEST", "category.
title": "TEST", "contact_person": "TEST", "bulletin_type": "searching",
"description": "TEST"})
>>> response.status_code
201
>>> response.json()
{u'category': {u'id': 6, u'title': u'TEST'}, u'description': u'TEST',
u'title': u'TEST', u'image': None, u'email': u'', u'phone': u'',
u'bulletin_type': u'searching', u'contact_person': u'TEST', u'id': 3}
```

Additionally, Django REST Framework provides you with a web-based API documentation that is shown when you access the API endpoints in a browser. There you can also try out the APIs by integrated forms, as shown in the following screenshot:

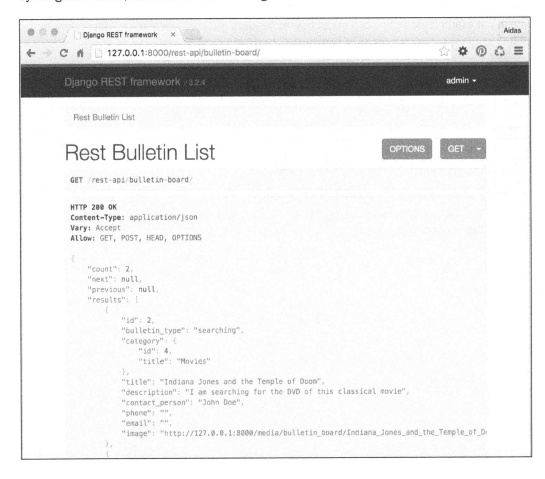

Let's take a quick look at how the code that we wrote works. In the settings, we have set the access to be dependent on the permissions of the Django system. For anonymous requests, only reading is allowed. Other access options include allowing any permission to everyone, allowing any permission only to authenticated users, allowing any permission to staff users, and so on. The full list can be found at `http://www.django-rest-framework.org/api-guide/permissions/`.

Then, in the settings, pagination is set. The current option is to have the `limit` and `offset` parameters like in an SQL query. Other options are to have either pagination by page numbers for rather static content or cursor pagination for real-time data. We set the default pagination to 100 items per page.

Later we define serializers for categories and bulletins. They handle the data that will be shown in the output or validated by the input. In order to handle category retrieval or saving, we had to overwrite the `create()` and `update()` methods of `BulletinSerializer`. There are various ways to serialize relations in Django REST Framework and we chose the most verbose one in our example. To read more about how to serialize relations, refer to the documentation at `http://www.django-rest-framework.org/api-guide/relations/`.

After defining the serializers, we created two class-based views to handle the API endpoints and plugged them in the URL configuration. In the URL configuration, we have a rule (`/api-auth/`) for browsable API pages, login, and logout.

See also

- The *Creating filterable RSS feeds* recipe
- The *Using Tastypie to create API* recipe
- The *Testing API created using Django REST framework* recipe in *Chapter 11, Testing and Deployment*

10

Bells and Whistles

In this chapter, we will cover the following recipes:

- ► Using the Django shell
- ► Using database query expressions
- ► Monkey-patching the slugify() function for better internationalization support
- ► Toggling the Debug Toolbar
- ► Using ThreadLocalMiddleware
- ► Caching the method return value
- ► Using Memcached to cache Django views
- ► Using signals to notify administrators about new entries
- ► Checking for missing settings

Introduction

In this chapter, we will go through several other important bits and pieces that will help you understand and utilize Django even better. You will get an overview of how to use the Django shell to experiment with the code before writing it in the files. You will be introduced to monkey patching, also known as guerrilla patching, which is a powerful feature of dynamical languages such as Python and Ruby. You will learn how to debug your code and check its performance. You will see how to access the currently logged in user and other request parameters from any module. Also, you will learn how to cache values, handle signals, and create system checks. Get ready for an interesting programming experience!

Using the Django shell

With the virtual environment activated and your project directory selected as the current directory, enter the following command in your command-line tool:

```
(myproject_env)$ python manage shell
```

By executing the preceding command, you will get in an interactive Python shell configured for your Django project, where you can play around with the code, inspect classes, try out methods, or execute scripts on the fly. In this recipe, we will go through the most important functions that you need to know in order to work with the Django shell.

Getting ready

You can either install IPython or bpython using one of the following commands, which will highlight the syntax for the output of your Django shell and add some other helpers:

```
(myproject_env)$ pip install ipython
(myproject_env)$ pip install bpython
```

How to do it...

Learn the basics of using the Django shell by following these instructions:

1. Run the Django shell by typing the following command:

   ```
   (myproject_env)$ python manage.py shell
   ```

   The prompt will change to In [1]: or >>>, depending on whether you use IPython or not. If you use bpython, the shell will be shown in full terminal window with the available shortcuts at the bottom (similar to the nano editor) and you will also get code highlighting and text autocompletion when typing.

2. Now, you can import classes, functions, or variables and play around with them. For example, to see the version of an installed module, you can import the module and then try to read its __version__, VERSION, or version variables, as follows:

   ```
   >>> import re
   >>> re.__version__
   '2.2.1'
   ```

3. To get a comprehensive description of a module, class, function, method, keyword, or documentation topic, use the help() function. You can either pass a string with the path to a specific entity, or the entity itself, as follows:

   ```
   >>> help("django.forms")
   ```

This will open the help page for the `django.forms` module. Use the arrow keys to scroll the page up and down. Press *Q* to get back to the shell.

 If you run `help()` without the parameters, it opens an interactive help. Here you can enter any path of a module, class, function, and so on and get information on what it does and how to use it. To quit the interactive help press *Ctrl + D*.

4. This is an example of passing an entity to the `help()` function. This will open a help page for the `ModelForm` class, as follows:

```
>>> from django.forms import ModelForm
>>> help(ModelForm)
```

5. To quickly see what fields and values are available for a model instance, use the `__dict__` attribute. Also, use the `pprint()` function to get the dictionaries printed in a more readable format (not just one long line), as shown in the following:

```
>>> from pprint import pprint
>>> from django.contrib.contenttypes.models import ContentType
>>> pprint(ContentType.objects.all()[0].__dict__)
{'_state': <django.db.models.base.ModelState object at
0x10756d250>,
 'app_label': u'bulletin_board',
 'id': 11,
 'model': u'bulletin',
 'name': u'Bulletin'}
```

Note that using `__dict__`, we don't get many-to-many relationships. However, this might be enough for a quick overview of the fields and values.

6. To get all the available properties and methods of an object, you can use the `dir()` function, as follows:

```
>>> dir(ContentType())
['DoesNotExist', 'MultipleObjectsReturned', '__class__', '__
delattr__', '__dict__', '__doc__', '__eq__', '__format__',
'__getattribute__', '__hash__', '__init__', u'__module__', '__
ne__', '__new__', '__reduce__', '__reduce_ex__', '__repr__',
'__setattr__', '__sizeof__', '__str__', '__subclasshook__', '__
unicode__', '__weakref__', '_base_manager', '_default_manager',
'_deferred', '_do_insert', '_do_update', '_get_FIELD_display', '_
get_next_or_previous_by_FIELD', '_get_next_or_previous_in_order',
'_get_pk_val', '_get_unique_checks', '_meta', '_perform_date_
checks', '_perform_unique_checks', '_save_parents', '_save_table',
'_set_pk_val', '_state', 'app_label', 'clean', 'clean_fields',
```

```
'content_type_set_for_comment', 'date_error_message', 'delete',
'full_clean', 'get_all_objects_for_this_type', 'get_object_for_
this_type', 'id', 'logentry_set', 'model', 'model_class', 'name',
'natural_key', 'objects', 'permission_set', 'pk', 'prepare_
database_save', 'save', 'save_base', 'serializable_value',
'unique_error_message', 'validate_unique']
```

To get these attributes printed one per line, you can use the following:

```
>>> pprint(dir(ContentType()))
```

7. The Django shell is useful to experiment with `QuerySets` or regular expressions before putting them in your model methods, views, or management commands. For example, to check the e-mail validation regular expression, you can type the following in the Django shell:

```
>>> import re
>>> email_pattern = re.compile(r"[^@]+@[^@]+\.[^@]+")
>>> email_pattern.match("aidas@bendoraitis.lt")
<_sre.SRE_Match object at 0x1075681d0>
```

8. If you want to try out different `QuerySets`, you need to execute the setup of the models and apps in your project, as shown in the following:

```
>>> import django
>>> django.setup()
>>> from django.contrib.auth.models import User
>>> User.objects.filter(groups__name="Editors")
[<User: admin>]
```

9. To exit the Django shell, press *Ctrl + D* or type the following command:

```
>>> exit()
```

How it works...

The difference between a normal Python shell and the Django shell is that when you run the Django shell, `manage.py` sets the `DJANGO_SETTINGS_MODULE` environment variable to the project's settings path, and then all the code in the Django shell is handled in the context of your project.

See also

▶ The *Using database query expressions* recipe

▶ The *Monkey-patching the slugify() function for better internationalization support* recipe

Using database query expressions

Django **Object-relational mapping** (**ORM**) comes with special abstraction constructs that can be used to build complex database queries. They are called **Query Expressions** and they allow you to filter data, order it, annotate new columns, and aggregate relations. In this recipe, we will see how that can be used in practice. We will create an app that shows viral videos and counts how many times each video has been seen on mobile and desktop devices.

Getting ready

To start with, install `django-mobile` to your virtual environment. This module will be necessary to differentiate between desktop devices and mobile devices:

(myproject_env)$ pip install django-mobile

To configure it, you will need to modify several project settings as follows. Besides that, let's create the `viral_videos` app. Put both of them under `INSTALLED_APPS`:

```
# conf/base.py or settings.py
INSTALLED_APPS = (
    # ...
    # third party
    "django_mobile",

    # project-specific
    "utils",
    "viral_videos",
)

TEMPLATE_CONTEXT_PROCESSORS = (
    # ...
    "django_mobile.context_processors.flavour",
)

TEMPLATE_LOADERS = (
    # ...
    "django_mobile.loader.Loader",
)

MIDDLEWARE_CLASSES = (
    # ...
    "django_mobile.middleware.MobileDetectionMiddleware",
    "django_mobile.middleware.SetFlavourMiddleware",
)
```

Next, create a model for viral videos with a creation and modification timestamps, title, embedded code, impressions on desktop devices, and impressions on mobile devices, as follows:

```python
# viral_videos/models.py
# -*- coding: UTF-8 -*-
from __future__ import unicode_literals
from django.db import models
from django.utils.translation import ugettext_lazy as _
from django.utils.encoding import python_2_unicode_compatible
from utils.models import CreationModificationDateMixin, UrlMixin


@python_2_unicode_compatible
class ViralVideo(CreationModificationDateMixin, UrlMixin):
    title = models.CharField(
        _("Title"), max_length=200, blank=True)
    embed_code = models.TextField(_("YouTube embed code"), blank=True)
    desktop_impressions = models.PositiveIntegerField(
        _("Desktop impressions"), default=0)
    mobile_impressions = models.PositiveIntegerField(
        _("Mobile impressions"), default=0)

    class Meta:
        verbose_name = _("Viral video")
        verbose_name_plural = _("Viral videos")

    def __str__(self):
        return self.title

    def get_url_path(self):
        from django.core.urlresolvers import reverse
        return reverse(
            "viral_video_detail",
            kwargs={"id": str(self.id)}
        )
```

How to do it...

To illustrate the query expressions, let's create the viral video detail view and plug it in the URL configuration, as shown in the following:

1. Create the `viral_video_detail()` view in the `views.py`, as follows:

```python
# viral_videos/views.py
# -*- coding: UTF-8 -*-
```

```
from __future__ import unicode_literals
import datetime
from django.shortcuts import render, get_object_or_404
from django.db import models
from django.conf import settings
from .models import ViralVideo

POPULAR_FROM = getattr(
    settings, "VIRAL_VIDEOS_POPULAR_FROM", 500
)


def viral_video_detail(request, id):
    yesterday = datetime.date.today() - \
        datetime.timedelta(days=1)

    qs = ViralVideo.objects.annotate(
        total_impressions=\
            models.F("desktop_impressions") + \
            models.F("mobile_impressions"),
        label=models.Case(
            models.When(
                total_impressions__gt=OPULAR_FROM,
                then=models.Value("popular")
            ),
            models.When(
                created__gt=yesterday,
                then=models.Value("new")
            ),
            default=models.Value("cool"),
            output_field=models.CharField(),
        ),
    )

    # DEBUG: check the SQL query that Django ORM generates
    print(qs.query)

    qs = qs.filter(pk=id)
    if request.flavour == "mobile":
        qs.update(
            mobile_impressions=\
                models.F("mobile_impressions") + 1
        )
    else:
        qs.update(
```

```
                desktop_impressions=\
                    models.F("desktop_impressions") + 1
            )

        video = get_object_or_404(qs)

        return render(
            request,
            "viral_videos/viral_video_detail.html",
            {'video': video}
        )
```

2. Define the URL configuration for the app, as shown in the following:

```
# viral_videos/urls.py
# -*- coding: UTF-8 -*-
from __future__ import unicode_literals
from django.conf.urls import *
urlpatterns = [
    url(
        r"^(?P<id>\d+)/",
        "viral_videos.views.viral_video_detail",
        name="viral_video_detail"
    ),
]
```

3. Include the URL configuration of the app in the project's root URL configuration, as follows:

```
# myproject/urls.py
# -*- coding: UTF-8 -*-
from __future__ import unicode_literals
from django.conf.urls import include, url
from django.conf import settings
from django.conf.urls.i18n import i18n_patterns

urlpatterns = i18n_patterns("",
    # ...
    url(r"^viral-videos/", include("viral_videos.urls")),
)
```

4. Create a template for the `viral_video_detail()` view, as shown in the following:

```
{# templates/viral_videos/viral_video_detail.html #}
{% extends "base.html" %}
```

```
{% load i18n %}

{% block content %}
    <h1>{{ video.title }}
        <span class="badge">{{ video.label }}</span>
    </h1>
    <div>{{ video.embed_code|safe }}</div>
    <div>
        <h2>{% trans "Impressions" %}</h2>
        <ul>
            <li>{% trans "Desktop impressions" %}:
                {{ video.desktop_impressions }}</li>
            <li>{% trans "Mobile impressions" %}:
                {{ video.mobile_impressions }}</li>
            <li>{% trans "Total impressions" %}:
                {{ video.total_impressions }}</li>
        </ul>
    </div>
{% endblock %}
```

5. Set up administration for the `viral_videos` app and add some videos to the database.

How it works...

You might have noticed the `print()` statement in the view. It is there temporarily for debugging purposes. If you run local development server and access the first video in the browser at `http://127.0.0.1:8000/en/viral-videos/1/`, you will see the following SQL query printed in the console:

```
SELECT "viral_videos_viralvideo"."id", "viral_videos_
viralvideo"."created", "viral_videos_viralvideo"."modified", "viral_
videos_viralvideo"."title", "viral_videos_viralvideo"."embed_code",
"viral_videos_viralvideo"."desktop_impressions", "viral_videos_
viralvideo"."mobile_impressions", ("viral_videos_viralvideo"."desktop_
impressions" + "viral_videos_viralvideo"."mobile_impressions") AS
"total_impressions", CASE WHEN ("viral_videos_viralvideo"."desktop_
impressions" + "viral_videos_viralvideo"."mobile_impressions") >
500 THEN popular WHEN "viral_videos_viralvideo"."created" > 2015-
11-06 00:00:00 THEN new ELSE cool END AS "label" FROM "viral_videos_
viralvideo"
```

Then, in the browser, you will see a simple page similar to the following image, showing the title of a video, label of the video, embedded video, and impressions on desktop devices, mobile devices and in total:

Zach King Best Vines Compilation 2015

Impressions

- Desktop impressions: 1159
- Mobile impressions: 302
- Total impressions: 1461

The `annotate()` method in Django `QuerySets` allows you to add extra columns to the `SELECT SQL` statement as well as on-the-fly created properties for the objects retrieved from `QuerySets`. With `models.F()`, we can reference different field values from the selected database table. In this example, we will create the `total_impressions` property, which is the sum of the impressions on the desktop devices and the impressions on mobile devices.

With `models.Case()` and `models.When()`, we can return the values depending on different conditions. To mark the values, we are using `models.Value()`. In our example, we will create the `label` column for SQL query and the property for the objects returned by `QuerySet`. It will be set to *popular* if it has more than 500 impressions, *new* if it has been created today, and *cool* otherwise.

At the end of the view, we have the `qs.update()` methods called. They increment `mobile_impressions` or `desktop_impressions` of the current video, depending on the device used by the visitor. The incrementation happens at the SQL level. This solves the so-called race conditions, when two or more visitors are accessing the view at the same time and try to increase the impressions count simultaneously.

See also

- ▸ The *Using the Django shell* recipe
- ▸ The *Creating a model mixin with URL-related methods* recipe in *Chapter 2, Database Structure*
- ▸ The *Creating a model mixin to handle creation and modification dates* recipe in *Chapter 2, Database Structure*

Monkey-patching the slugify() function for better internationalization support

Monkey patch or guerrilla patch is a piece of code that extends or modifies another piece of code at runtime. It is not recommended to use monkey patch often; however, sometimes, it is the only possible way to fix a bug in third-party modules without creating a separate branch of the module. Also, monkey patching might be used to prepare functional or unit tests without using complex database or file manipulations. In this recipe, you will learn how to exchange the default `slugify()` function with the one from the third-party `awesome-slugify` module, which handles German, Greek, and Russian words smarter and allows to create customized slugs for other languages. As a quick reminder, we uses the `slugify()` function to create a URL-friendly version of the object's title or the uploaded filename; it strips the leading and trailing whitespace, converts the text to lowercase, removes nonword characters, and converts spaces to hyphens.

Getting ready

To get started, execute the following steps:

1. Install `awesome-slugify` in your virtual environment, as follows:

   ```
   (myproject_env)$ pip install awesome-slugify
   ```

2. Create a `guerrilla_patches` app in your project and put it under `INSTALLED_APPS` in the settings.

How to do it...

In the `models.py` file of the `guerrilla_patches` app, add the following content:

```python
# guerrilla_patches/models.py
# -*- coding: UTF-8 -*-
from __future__ import unicode_literals
from django.utils import text
from slugify import slugify_de as awesome_slugify
awesome_slugify.to_lower = True
text.slugify = awesome_slugify
```

How it works...

The default Django `slugify()` function handles German diacritical symbols incorrectly. To see this for yourself, run the following code in the Django shell without the monkey patch:

(myproject_env)$ python manage.py shell

>>> from django.utils.text import slugify

>>> slugify("Heizölrückstoßabdämpfung")

u'heizolruckstoabdampfung'

This is incorrect in German as the letter ß is totally stripped out instead of substituting it with ss and the letters ä, ö, and ü are changed to a, o, and u; whereas, they should be substituted with ae, oe, and ue.

The monkey patch that we did loads the `django.utils.text` module at initialization and assigns the callable instance of the `Slugify` class as the `slugify()` function. Now, if you run the same code in the Django shell, you will get different but correct results, as follows:

(myproject_env)$ python manage.py shell

>>> from django.utils.text import slugify

>>> slugify("Heizölrückstoßabdämpfung")

u'heizoelrueckstossabdaempfung'

To read more about how to utilize the `awesome-slugify` module, refer to the following: https://pypi.python.org/pypi/awesome-slugify.

There's more...

Before creating any monkey patch, we need to completely understand how the code that we want to modify works. This can be done by analyzing the existing code and inspecting the values of different variables. To do this, there is a useful built-in Python debugger pdb module, which can temporarily be added to the Django code or any third-party module to stop the execution of a development server at any breakpoint. Use the following code to debug an unclear part of a Python module:

```
import pdb
pdb.set_trace()
```

This launches the interactive shell, where you can type the variables to see their values. If you type c or continue, the code execution will continue until the next breakpoint. If you type q or quit, the management command will be aborted. You can learn more commands of the Python debugger and how to inspect the traceback of the code at https://docs.python.org/2/library/pdb.html.

Another quick way to see a value of a variable in the development server is to raise a warning with the variable as a message, as follows:

raise Warning, some_variable

When you are in the DEBUG mode, the Django logger will provide you with the traceback and other local variables.

Don't forget to remove the debugging functions before committing the code to a repository.

See also

- ▶ The *Using the Django shell* recipe

Toggling the Debug Toolbar

While developing with Django, you will want to inspect request headers and parameters, check the current template context, or measure the performance of SQL queries. All this and more is possible with the Django Debug Toolbar. It is a configurable set of panels that displays various debug information about the current request and response. In this recipe, I will guide you on how to toggle the visibility of the Debug Toolbar, depending on a cookie, set by bookmarklet. A bookmarklet is a bookmark of a small piece of JavaScript code that you can run on any page in a browser.

Getting ready

To get started with toggling the visibility of the Debug Toolbar, take a look at the following steps:

1. Install the Django Debug Toolbar to your virtual environment:

   ```
   (myproject_env)$ pip install django-debug-toolbar==1.4
   ```

2. Put `debug_toolbar` under `INSTALLED_APPS` in the settings.

How to do it...

Follow these steps to set up the Django Debug Toolbar, which can be switched on or off using bookmarklets in the browser:

1. Add the following project settings:

   ```
   MIDDLEWARE_CLASSES = (
       # ...
       "debug_toolbar.middleware.DebugToolbarMiddleware",
   )

   DEBUG_TOOLBAR_CONFIG = {
       "DISABLE_PANELS": [],
       "SHOW_TOOLBAR_CALLBACK": \
           "utils.misc.custom_show_toolbar",
       "SHOW_TEMPLATE_CONTEXT": True,
   }

   DEBUG_TOOLBAR_PANELS = [
       "debug_toolbar.panels.versions.VersionsPanel",
       "debug_toolbar.panels.timer.TimerPanel",
   ```

```
    "debug_toolbar.panels.settings.SettingsPanel",
    "debug_toolbar.panels.headers.HeadersPanel",
    "debug_toolbar.panels.request.RequestPanel",
    "debug_toolbar.panels.sql.SQLPanel",
    "debug_toolbar.panels.templates.TemplatesPanel",
    "debug_toolbar.panels.staticfiles.StaticFilesPanel",
    "debug_toolbar.panels.cache.CachePanel",
    "debug_toolbar.panels.signals.SignalsPanel",
    "debug_toolbar.panels.logging.LoggingPanel",
    "debug_toolbar.panels.redirects.RedirectsPanel",
]
```

2. In the `utils` module, create a `misc.py` file with the `custom_show_toolbar()` function, as follows:

```
# utils/misc.py
# -*- coding: UTF-8 -*-
from __future__ import unicode_literals

def custom_show_toolbar(request):
    return "1" == request.COOKIES.get("DebugToolbar", False)
```

3. Open the Chrome or Firefox browser and go to **Bookmark Manager**. Then, create two new JavaScript links. The first link shows the toolbar. It looks similar to the following:

```
Name: Debug Toolbar On
URL: javascript:(function(){document.cookie="DebugToolbar=1;
path=/";location.reload();})();
```

4. The second JavaScript link hides the toolbar and looks similar to the following:

```
Name: Debug Toolbar Off
URL: javascript:(function(){document.cookie="DebugToolbar=0;
path=/";location.reload();})();
```

How it works...

The `DEBUG_TOOLBAR_PANELS` setting defines the panels to show in the toolbar. The `DEBUG_TOOLBAR_CONFIG` dictionary defines the configuration for the toolbar, including a path to the function that is used to check whether or not to show the toolbar.

By default, when you browse through your project the Django Debug Toolbar will not be shown. However, as you click on your bookmarklet, **Debug Toolbar On**, the DebugToolbar cookie will be set to 1, the page will be refreshed, and you will see the toolbar with debugging panels. For example, you will be able to inspect the performance of SQL statements for optimization, as shown in the following screenshot:

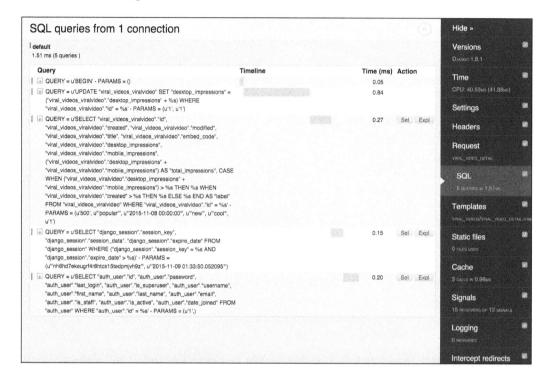

You will also be able to check the template context variables for the current view, as shown in the following screenshot:

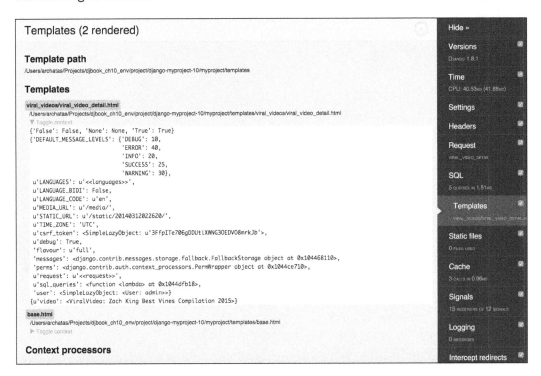

▶ The *Getting detailed error reporting via e-mail* recipe in *Chapter 11, Testing and Deployment*

Using ThreadLocalMiddleware

The `HttpRequest` object contains useful information about the current user, language, server variables, cookies, session, and so on. As a matter of fact, `HttpRequest` is provided in the views and middlewares, and then you can pass it or its attribute values to forms, model methods, model managers, templates, and so on. To make life easier, you can use the `ThreadLocalMiddleware` middleware that stores the current `HttpRequest` object in the globally-accessed Python thread. Therefore, you can access it from model methods, forms, signal handlers, and any other place that didn't have direct access to the `HttpRequest` object previously. In this recipe, we will define this middleware.

Getting ready

Create the `utils` app and put it under `INSTALLED_APPS` in the settings.

How to do it...

Execute the following two steps:

1. Add a `middleware.py` file in the `utils` app with the following content:

    ```python
    # utils/middleware.py
    # -*- coding: UTF-8 -*-
    from threading import local
    _thread_locals = local()

    def get_current_request():
        """ returns the HttpRequest object for this thread """
        return getattr(_thread_locals, "request", None)

    def get_current_user():
        """ returns the current user if it exists
            or None otherwise """
        request = get_current_request()
        if request:
            return getattr(request, "user", None)

    class ThreadLocalMiddleware(object):
        """ Middleware that adds the HttpRequest object
            to thread local storage """
        def process_request(self, request):
            _thread_locals.request = request
    ```

2. Add this middleware to `MIDDLEWARE_CLASSES` in the settings:

    ```python
    MIDDLEWARE_CLASSES = (
        # ...
        "utils.middleware.ThreadLocalMiddleware",
    )
    ```

How it works...

The `ThreadLocalMiddleware` processes each request and stores the current `HttpRequest` object in the current thread. Each request-response cycle in Django is single threaded. There are two functions: `get_current_request()` and `get_current_user()`. These functions can be used from anywhere to grab the current `HttpRequest` object or the current user.

For example, you can create and use `CreatorMixin`, which saves the current user as the creator of a model, as follows:

```python
# utils/models.py
# -*- coding: UTF-8 -*-
from __future__ import unicode_literals
from django.db import models
from django.utils.translation import ugettext_lazy as _

class CreatorMixin(models.Model):
    """
    Abstract base class with a creator
    """
    creator = models.ForeignKey(
        "auth.User",
        verbose_name=_("creator"),
        editable=False,
        blank=True,
        null=True,
    )

    def save(self, *args, **kwargs):
        from utils.middleware import get_current_user
        if not self.creator:
            self.creator = get_current_user()
        super(CreatorMixin, self).save(*args, **kwargs)
    save.alters_data = True

    class Meta:
        abstract = True
```

See also

▶ The *Creating a model mixin with URL-related methods* recipe in *Chapter 2, Database Structure*

▶ The *Creating a model mixin to handle creation and modification dates* recipe in *Chapter 2, Database Structure*

▶ The *Creating a model mixin to take care of meta tags* recipe in *Chapter 2, Database Structure*

▶ The *Creating a model mixin to handle generic relations* recipe in *Chapter 2, Database Structure*

Caching the method return value

If you call the same model method with heavy calculations or database queries multiple times in the request-response cycle, the performance of the view might be very slow. In this recipe, you will learn about a pattern that you can use to cache the return value of a method for later repetitive use. Note that we are not using the Django cache framework here, we are just using what Python provides us by default.

Getting ready

Choose an app with a model that has a time-consuming method that will be used repetitively in the same request-response cycle.

How to do it...

This is a pattern that you can use to cache a method return value of a model for repetitive use in views, forms, or templates, as follows:

```
class SomeModel(models.Model):
    # ...
    def some_expensive_function(self):
        if not hasattr(self, "_expensive_value_cached"):
            # do some heavy calculations...
            # ... and save the result to result variable
            self._expensive_value_cached = result
        return self._expensive_value_cached
```

For example, let's create a `get_thumbnail_url()` method for the `ViralVideo` model that we created in the *Using database query expressions* recipe earlier in this chapter:

```python
# viral_videos/models.py
# -*- coding: UTF-8 -*-
from __future__ import unicode_literals
import re
# ... other imports ...


@python_2_unicode_compatible
class ViralVideo(CreationModificationDateMixin, UrlMixin):
    # ...
    def get_thumbnail_url(self):
        if not hasattr(self, "_thumbnail_url_cached"):
            url_pattern = re.compile(
                r'src="https://www.youtube.com/embed/([^"]+)"'
            )
            match = url_pattern.search(self.embed_code)
            self._thumbnail_url_cached = ""
            if match:
                video_id = match.groups()[0]
                self._thumbnail_url_cached = \
                    "http://img.youtube.com/vi/{}/0.jpg".format(
                        video_id
                    )
        return self._thumbnail_url_cached
```

How it works...

The method checks whether the `_expensive_value_cached` attribute exists for the model instance. If it doesn't exist, the time-consuming calculations are done and the result is assigned to this new attribute. At the end of the method, the cached value is returned. Of course, if you have several weighty methods, you will need to use different attribute names to save each calculated value.

You can now use something like `{{ object.some_expensive_function }}` in the header and footer of a template, and the time-consuming calculations will be done just once.

In a template, you can use the function in both, the {% if %} condition, and output of the value, as follows:

```
{% if object.some_expensive_function %}
    <span class="special">
        {{ object.some_expensive_function }}
    </span>
{% endif %}
```

In this example, we are checking the thumbnail of a YouTube video by parsing the URL of the video's embed code, getting its ID, and then composing the URL of the thumbnail image. Then, you can use it in a template as follows:

```
{% if video.get_thumbnail_url %}
    <figure>
        <img src="{{ video.get_thumbnail_url }}"
            alt="{{ video.title }}" />
        <figcaption>{{ video.title }}</figcaption>
    </figure>
{% endif %}
```

See also

▸ Refer to *Chapter 4, Templates and JavaScript* for more details

Using Memcached to cache Django views

Django provides a possibility to speed up the request-response cycle by caching the most expensive parts such as database queries or template rendering. The fastest and most reliable caching natively supported by Django is the memory-based cache server, Memcached. In this recipe, you will learn how to use Memcached to cache a view for our viral_videos app that we created in the *Using database query expressions* recipe earlier in this chapter.

Getting ready

There are several things to do in order to prepare caching for your Django project:

1. Install Memcached server, as follows:

```
$ wget http://memcached.org/files/memcached-1.4.23.tar.gz
$ tar -zxvf memcached-1.4.23.tar.gz
$ cd memcached-1.4.23
$ ./configure && make && make test && sudo make install
```

2. Start Memcached server, as shown in the following:

```
$ memcached -d
```

3. Install Memcached Python bindings in your virtual environment, as follows:

```
(myproject_env)$ pip install python-memcached
```

How to do it...

To integrate caching for your specific views, perform the following steps:

1. Set CACHES in the project settings, as follows:

```
CACHES = {
    "default": {
        "BACKEND": "django.core.cache.backends."
            "memcached.MemcachedCache",
        "LOCATION": "127.0.0.1:11211",
        "TIMEOUT": 60,  # 1 minute
        "KEY_PREFIX": "myproject_production",
    }
}
```

2. Modify the views of the viral_videos app, as follows:

```
# viral_videos/views.py
# -*- coding: UTF-8 -*-
from __future__ import unicode_literals
from django.views.decorators.vary import vary_on_cookie
from django.views.decorators.cache import cache_page


@vary_on_cookie
@cache_page(60)
def viral_video_detail(request, id):
    # ...
```

How it works...

Now, if you access the first viral video at http://127.0.0.1:8000/en/viral-videos/1/ and refresh the page a few times, you will see that the number of impressions changes only once a minute. This is because for every visitor, caching is enabled for 60 seconds. Caching is set for the view using the @cache_page decorator.

Memcached is a key-value store and by default for each cached page, the full URL is used to generate the key. When two visitors access the same page simultaneously, the first visitor will get the page generated by the Python code and the second one will get the HTML code from the Memcached server.

In our example, to ensure that each visitor gets treated separately even if they access the same URL, we are using the `@vary_on_cookie` decorator. This decorator checks the uniqueness of the `Cookie` header of the HTTP request.

Learn more about Django's cache framework from the official documentation at `https://docs.djangoproject.com/en/1.8/topics/cache/`.

See also

▸ The *Using database query expressions* recipe

▸ The *Caching the method return value* recipe

Using signals to notify administrators about new entries

Django framework has a concept of signals, which are similar to events in JavaScript. There is a handful of built-in signals that you can use to trigger actions before and after initialization of a model, saving or deleting an instance, migrating the database schema, handling a request, and so on. Moreover, you can create your own signals in your reusable apps and handle them in other apps. In this recipe, you will learn how to use signals to send emails to administrators whenever a specific model is saved.

Getting ready

Let's start with the `viral_videos` app that we created in the *Using database query expressions* recipe.

How to do it...

Follow these steps to create notifications to administrators:

1. Create the `signals.py` file with the following content:

```python
# viral_videos/signals.py
# -*- coding: UTF-8 -*-
from __future__ import unicode_literals
from django.db.models.signals import post_save
from django.dispatch import receiver
from .models import ViralVideo


@receiver(post_save, sender=ViralVideo)
def inform_administrators(sender, **kwargs):
```

```
        from django.core.mail import mail_admins
        instance = kwargs["instance"]
        created = kwargs["created"]
        if created:
            context = {
                "title": instance.title,
                "link": instance.get_url(),
            }
            plain_text_message = """
A new viral video called "%(title)s" has been created.
You can preview it at %(link)s.""" % context
            html_message = """
<p>A new viral video called "%(title)s" has been created.</p>
<p>You can preview it <a href="%(link)s">here</a>.</p>""" %
context

            mail_admins(
                subject="New Viral Video Added at example.com",
                message=plain_text_message,
                html_message=html_message,
                fail_silently=True,
            )
```

2. Create the `apps.py` file with the following content:

    # viral_videos/apps.py
    ```
    # -*- coding: UTF-8 -*-
    from __future__ import unicode_literals
    from django.apps import AppConfig
    from django.utils.translation import ugettext_lazy as _


    class ViralVideosAppConfig(AppConfig):
        name = "viral_videos"
        verbose_name = _("Viral Videos")

        def ready(self):
            from .signals import inform_administrators
    ```

3. Update the `__init__.py` file with the following content:

    # viral_videos/__init__.py
    ```
    # -*- coding: UTF-8 -*-
    from __future__ import unicode_literals

    default_app_config = \
        "viral_videos.apps.ViralVideosAppConfig"
    ```

4. Make sure that you have ADMINS set in the project settings, as follows:

```
ADMINS = (
    ("Aidas Bendoraitis", "aidas.bendoraitis@example.com"),
)
```

How it works...

The `ViralVideosAppConfig` app configuration class has the `ready()` method, which will be called when all the models of the project are loaded in the memory. According to the Django documentation, *signals allow certain senders to notify a set of receivers that some action has taken place*. In the `ready()` method, we will import, therefore, registering the `inform_administrators()` signal receiver for the `post_save` signal, and limiting it to handle only signals, where the `ViralVideo` model is the sender. Therefore, whenever we save the `ViralVideo` model, the `inform_administrators()` function will be called. The function checks whether a video is newly created. In that case, it sends an e-mail to the system administrators that are listed in ADMINS in the settings.

Learn more about Django's signals from the official documentation at `https://docs.djangoproject.com/en/1.8/topics/signals/`.

See also

▸ The *Using database query expressions* recipe

▸ The *Creating app configuration* recipe in *Chapter 1, Getting Started with Django 1.8*

▸ The *Checking for missing settings* recipe

Checking for missing settings

Since Django 1.7, you can use an extensible **System Check Framework**, which replaces the old validate management command. In this recipe, you will learn how to create a check if the ADMINS setting is set. Similarly, you will be able to check whether different secret keys or access tokens are set for the APIs that you are using.

Getting ready

Let's start with the `viral_videos` app that we created in the *Using database query expressions* recipe and extended in the previous recipe.

How to do it...

To use System Check Framework, follow these simple steps:

1. Create the `checks.py` file with the following content:

```
# viral_videos/checks.py
# -*- coding: UTF-8 -*-
from __future__ import unicode_literals
from django.core.checks import Warning, register, Tags


@register(Tags.compatibility)
def settings_check(app_configs, **kwargs):
    from django.conf import settings
    errors = []
    if not settings.ADMINS:
        errors.append(
            Warning(
                """The system admins are not set in the project
settings""",
                hint="""In order to receive notifications when new
videos are created, define system admins like ADMINS=(("Admin",
"admin@example.com"),) in your settings""",
                id="viral_videos.W001",
            )
        )
    return errors
```

2. Import the checks in the `ready()` method of the app configuration, as follows:

```
# viral_videos/apps.py
# -*- coding: UTF-8 -*-
from __future__ import unicode_literals
from django.apps import AppConfig
from django.utils.translation import ugettext_lazy as _


class ViralVideosAppConfig(AppConfig):
    name = "viral_videos"
    verbose_name = _("Viral Videos")

    def ready(self):
        from .signals import inform_administrators
        from .checks import settings_check
```

3. To try the check that you just created, remove or comment out the `ADMINS` setting and run the `check` management command in your virtual environment, as shown in the following:

```
(myproject_env)$ python manage.py check
System check identified some issues:


WARNINGS:
?: (viral_videos.W001) The system admins are not set in the
project settings
   HINT: define system admins like ADMINS=(("Admin", "admin@
example.com"),) in your settings


System check identified 1 issue (0 silenced).
```

How it works...

The System Check Framework has a bunch of checks in the models, fields, database, administration, authentication, content types, and security, where it raises errors or warnings if something in the project is not set correctly. Additionally, you can create your own checks similar to what we did in this recipe.

We have registered the `settings_check()` function, which returns a list with a warning if there is no `ADMINS` setting defined for the project.

Besides the `Warning` instances from the `django.core.checks` module, the returned list can also contain instances of the `Debug`, `Info`, `Error`, and `Critical` classes or any other class inheriting from `django.core.checks.CheckMessage`. Debugs, infos, and warnings would fail silently; whereas, errors and criticals would prevent the project from running.

In this example, the check is tagged as a `compatibility` check. The other options are: `models`, `signals`, `admin`, and `security`.

Learn more about System Check Framework from the official documentation at `https://docs.djangoproject.com/en/1.8/topics/checks/`.

See also

- ▸ The *Using database query expressions* recipe
- ▸ The *Using signals to notify administrators about new entries* recipe
- ▸ The *Creating app configuration* recipe in *Chapter 1, Getting Started with Django 1.8*

11

Testing and Deployment

In this chapter, we will cover the following recipes:

- ▶ Testing pages with Selenium
- ▶ Testing views with mock
- ▶ Testing API created using Django REST framework
- ▶ Releasing a reusable Django app
- ▶ Getting detailed error reporting via e-mail
- ▶ Deploying on Apache with mod_wsgi
- ▶ Setting up cron jobs for regular tasks
- ▶ Creating and using the Fabric deployment script

Introduction

At this point, I expect you to have one or more Django projects or reusable apps developed and ready to show to the public. For the concluding steps of development cycle, we will take a look at how to test your project, distribute reusable apps to others, and publish your website on a remote server. Stay tuned for the final bits and pieces!

Testing pages with Selenium

Django provides a possibility to write test suites for your website. Test suites automatically check your website or its components to see whether everything is working correctly. When you modify your code, you can run tests to check whether the changes didn't affect the application's behavior in a wrong way. The world of automated software testing can be divided into five levels: unit testing, integration testing, component interface testing, system testing, and operational acceptance testing. Acceptance tests check the business logic to know whether the project works the way it is supposed to. In this recipe, you will learn how to write acceptance tests with Selenium, which allows you to simulate activities such as filling in forms or clicking on specific DOM elements in a browser.

Getting ready

Let's start with the `locations` and `likes` apps from the *Implementing the Like widget* recipe in *Chapter 4*, *Templates and JavaScript*.

If you don't have it yet, install the Firefox browser from `http://getfirefox.com`.

Then, install Selenium in your virtual environment, as follows:

```
(myproject_env)$ pip install selenium
```

How to do it...

We will test the Ajax-based *liking* functionality with Selenium by performing the following steps:

1. Create the `tests.py` file in your `locations` app with the following content:

```
# locations/tests.py
# -*- coding: UTF-8 -*-
from __future__ import unicode_literals
from time import sleep
from django.test import LiveServerTestCase
from django.contrib.contenttypes.models import ContentType
from django.contrib.auth.models import User
from selenium import webdriver
from selenium.webdriver.support.ui import WebDriverWait
from likes.models import Like
from .models import Location

class LiveLocationTest(LiveServerTestCase):
    @classmethod
    def setUpClass(cls):
```

```python
        super(LiveLocationTest, cls).setUpClass()
        cls.browser = webdriver.Firefox()
        cls.browser.delete_all_cookies()
        cls.location = Location.objects.create(
            title="Haus der Kulturen der Welt",
            slug="hkw",
            small_image="locations/2015/11/"
                "20151116013056_small.jpg",
            medium_image="locations/2015/11/"
                "20151116013056_medium.jpg",
            large_image="locations/2015/11/"
                "20151116013056_large.jpg",
        )
        cls.username = "test-admin"
        cls.password = "test-admin"
        cls.superuser = User.objects.create_superuser(
            username=cls.username,
            password=cls.password,
            email="",
        )

    @classmethod
    def tearDownClass(cls):
        super(LiveLocationTest, cls).tearDownClass()
        cls.browser.quit()
        cls.location.delete()
        cls.superuser.delete()

    def test_login_and_like(self):
        # login
        self.browser.get("%(website)s/admin/login/"
            "?next=/locations/%(slug)s/" % {
            "website": self.live_server_url,
            "slug": self.location.slug,
        })
        username_field = \
            self.browser.find_element_by_id("id_username")
        username_field.send_keys(self.username)
        password_field = \
            self.browser.find_element_by_id("id_password")
        password_field.send_keys(self.password)
        self.browser.find_element_by_css_selector(
            'input[type="submit"]'
        ).click()
```

```
WebDriverWait(self.browser, 10).until(
    lambda x: self.browser.\
        find_element_by_css_selector(
            ".like-button"
        )
)
# click on the "like" button
like_button = self.browser.\
    find_element_by_css_selector('.like-button')
is_initially_active = \
    "active" in like_button.get_attribute("class")
initial_likes = int(self.browser.\
    find_element_by_css_selector(
        ".like-badge"
    ).text)

sleep(2) # remove this after the first run

like_button.click()
WebDriverWait(self.browser, 10).until(
    lambda x: int(
        self.browser.find_element_by_css_selector(
            ".like-badge"
        ).text
    ) != initial_likes
)
likes_in_html = int(
    self.browser.find_element_by_css_selector(
        ".like-badge"
    ).text
)
likes_in_db = Like.objects.filter(
    content_type=ContentType.objects.\
        get_for_model(Location),
    object_id=self.location.pk,
).count()

sleep(2) # remove this after the first run

self.assertEqual(likes_in_html, likes_in_db)
if is_initially_active:
    self.assertLess(likes_in_html, initial_likes)
else:
    self.assertGreater(
```

```
                    likes_in_html, initial_likes
                )

            # click on the "like" button again to switch back
            # to the previous state
            like_button.click()
            WebDriverWait(self.browser, 10).until(
                lambda x: int(
                    self.browser.find_element_by_css_selector(
                        ".like-badge"
                    ).text
                ) == initial_likes
            )

            sleep(2) # remove this after the first run
```

2. Tests will be running in the `DEBUG = False` mode; therefore, you have to ensure that all the static files are accessible in your development environment. Make sure that you add the following lines to your project's URL configuration:

```python
# myproject/urls.py
# -*- coding: UTF-8 -*-
from __future__ import unicode_literals
from django.conf.urls import patterns, include, url
from django.conf import settings
from django.conf.urls.static import static
from django.contrib.staticfiles.urls import \
    staticfiles_urlpatterns

urlpatterns = patterns("",
    # …
)

urlpatterns += staticfiles_urlpatterns()
urlpatterns += static(
    settings.STATIC_URL,
    document_root=settings.STATIC_ROOT
)
urlpatterns += static(
    settings.MEDIA_URL,
    document_root=settings.MEDIA_ROOT
)
```

3. Collect static files to make them accessible by the test server, as follows:

```
(myproject_env)$ python manage.py collectstatic --noinput
```

4. Run the tests for the `locations` app, as shown in the following:

    ```
    (myproject_env)$ python manage.py test locations
    Creating test database for alias 'default'...
    .
    ----------------------------------------------------------
    Ran 1 test in 19.158s


    OK
    Destroying test database for alias 'default'...
    ```

How it works...

When we run these tests, the Firefox browser will open and go to the administration login page at `http://localhost:8081/admin/login/?next=/locations/hkw/`.

Then, the username and password fields will get filled in with `test-admin` and you will get redirected to the detail page of the `Haus der Kulturen der Welt` location, as follows: `http://localhost:8081/locations/hkw/`.

There you will see the **Like** button clicked twice, causing liking and unliking actions.

Let's see how this works in the test suite. We define a class extending `LiveServerTestCase`. This creates a test suite that will run a local server under the `8081` port. The `setUpClass()` class method will be executed at the beginning of all the tests and the `tearDownClass()` class method will be executed after the tests have been run. In the middle, the testing will execute all the methods of the suite whose names start with `test`. For each passed test, you will see a dot (`.`) in the command-line tool, for each failed test there will be the letter `F`, and for each error in the tests you will see the letter `E`. At the end, you will see hints about the failed and erroneous tests. As we currently have only one test in the suite for the `locations` app, you will only see one dot there.

When we start testing, a new test database is created. In `setUpClass()`, we create a browser object, one location, and one super user. Then, the `test_login_and_like()` method is executed, which opens the administration login page, finds the **username** field, types in the administrator's username, finds the **password** field, types in administrator's password, finds the **submit** button, and clicks on it. Then, it waits maximal ten seconds until a DOM element with the `.like-button` CSS class can be found on the page.

As you might remember from the *Implementing the Like widget* recipe in *Chapter 4, Templates and JavaScript*, our widget consists of two elements: a **Like** button and a badge showing the total number of likes. If a button is clicked, either your `Like` is added or removed from the database by an Ajax call. Moreover, the badge count is updated to reflect the number of likes in the database, as shown in the following image:

Further in the test, we check what is the initial state of the button is (whether it has the `.active` CSS class or not), check the initial number of likes, and simulate a click on the button. We wait maximal 10 seconds until the count in the badge changes. Then, we check whether the count in the badge matches the total likes for the location in the database. We will also check how the count in the badge has changed (increased or decreased). Lastly, we will simulate the click on the button again to switch back to the previous state.

The `sleep()` functions are in the test just for you to be able to see the whole workflow. You can safely remove them in order to make the tests run faster.

Finally, the `tearDownClass()` method is called, which closes the browser and removes the location and the super user from the test database.

See also

▸ The *Implementing the Like widget* recipe in *Chapter 4, Templates and JavaScript*

▸ The *Testing views with mock* recipe

▸ The *Testing API created using Django REST Framework* recipe

Testing views with mock

In this recipe, we will take a look at how to write unit tests. Unit tests are those that check whether the functions or methods return correct results. We again take the `likes` app and write tests checking whether posting to the `json_set_like()` view returns `{"success"; false}` in the response for unauthenticated users and returns `{"action": "added", "count": 1, "obj": "Haus der Kulturen der Welt", "success": true}` for authenticated users. We will use the `Mock` objects to simulate the `HttpRequest` and `AnonymousUser` objects.

Getting ready

Let's start with the `locations` and `likes` apps from the *Implementing the Like widget* recipe in *Chapter 4, Templates and JavaScript*.

Install the `mock` module in your virtual environment, as follows:

```
(myproject_env)$ pip install mock
```

How to do it...

We will test the *liking* action with mock by performing the following steps:

1. Create the `tests.py` file in your `likes` app with the following content:

```python
# likes/tests.py
# -*- coding: UTF-8 -*-
from __future__ import unicode_literals
import mock
import json
from django.contrib.contenttypes.models import ContentType
from django.contrib.auth.models import User
from django.test import SimpleTestCase
from locations.models import Location


class JSSetLikeViewTest(SimpleTestCase):
    @classmethod
    def setUpClass(cls):
        super(JSSetLikeViewTest, cls).setUpClass()
        cls.location = Location.objects.create(
            title="Haus der Kulturen der Welt",
            slug="hkw",
            small_image="locations/2015/11/"
                "20151116013056_small.jpg",
            medium_image="locations/2015/11/"
                "20151116013056_medium.jpg",
            large_image="locations/2015/11/"
                "20151116013056_large.jpg",
        )
        cls.content_type = \
            ContentType.objects.get_for_model(Location)
        cls.username = "test-admin"
        cls.password = "test-admin"
        cls.superuser = User.objects.create_superuser(
            username=cls.username,
```

```
        password=cls.password,
        email="",
    )

@classmethod
def tearDownClass(cls):
    super(JSSetLikeViewTest, cls).tearDownClass()
    cls.location.delete()
    cls.superuser.delete()

def test_authenticated_json_set_like(self):
    from .views import json_set_like
    mock_request = mock.Mock()
    mock_request.user = self.superuser
    mock_request.method = "POST"
    response = json_set_like(
        mock_request,
        self.content_type.pk,
        self.location.pk
    )
    expected_result = json.dumps({
        "success": True,
        "action": "added",
        "obj": self.location.title,
        "count": Location.objects.count(),
    })
    self.assertJSONEqual(
        response.content,
        expected_result
    )

def test_anonymous_json_set_like(self):
    from .views import json_set_like
    mock_request = mock.Mock()
    mock_request.user.is_authenticated.return_value = \
        False
    mock_request.method = "POST"
    response = json_set_like(
        mock_request,
        self.content_type.pk,
        self.location.pk
    )
    expected_result = json.dumps({
        "success": False,
```

```
    })
    self.assertJSONEqual(
        response.content,
        expected_result
    )
```

2. Run the tests for the `likes` app, as follows:

```
(myproject_env)$ python manage.py test likes
Creating test database for alias 'default'...
..
---------------------------------------------------------------
Ran 2 tests in 0.093s

OK
Destroying test database for alias 'default'...
```

How it works...

Just like in the previous recipe, when you run tests for the `likes` app, at first, a temporary test database is created. Then, the `setUpClass()` method is called. Later, the methods whose names start with `test` are executed, and finally the `tearDownClass()` method is called.

Unit tests inherit from the `SimpleTestCase` class. In `setUpClass()`, we create a location and a super user. Also, we find out the `ContentType` object for the `Location` model—we will need it for the view that sets or removes likes for different objects. As a reminder, the view looks similar to the following and returns the JSON string as a result:

```
def json_set_like(request, content_type_id, object_id):
    # ...all the view logic goes here...
    return HttpResponse(
        json_str,
        content_type="text/javascript; charset=utf-8"
    )
```

In the `test_authenticated_json_set_like()` and `test_anonymous_json_set_like()` methods, we use the `Mock` objects. They are objects that have any attributes or methods. Each undefined attribute or method of a `Mock` object is another `Mock` object. Therefore, in the shell, you can try chaining attributes as follows:

```
>>> import mock
>>> m = mock.Mock()
>>> m.whatever.anything().whatsoever
<Mock name='mock.whatever.anything().whatsoever' id='4464778896'>
```

In our tests, we use the `Mock` objects to simulate the `HttpRequest` and `AnonymousUser` objects. For the authenticated user, we still need the real `User` object as the view needs the user's ID to save in the database for the `Like` object.

Therefore, we call the `json_set_like()` function and see if the returned JSON response is correct: it returns `{"success": false}` in the response if the visitor is unauthenticated; and returns something like `{"action": "added", "count": 1, "obj": "Haus der Kulturen der Welt", "success": true}` for authenticated users.

In the end, the `tearDownClass()` class method is called that deletes the location and super user from the test database.

See also

▸ The *Implementing the Like widget* recipe in *Chapter 4, Templates and JavaScript*

▸ The *Testing pages with Selenium* recipe

▸ The *Testing API created using Django REST Framework* recipe

Testing API created using Django REST framework

We already have an understanding about how to write operational acceptance and unit tests. In this recipe, we will go through component interface testing for the REST API that we created earlier in this book.

 If you are not familiar with what REST API is and how to use it, you can learn about it at `http://www.restapitutorial.com/`.

Getting ready

Let's start with the `bulletin_board` app from the *Using Django REST framework to create API* recipe in *Chapter 9, Data Import and Export*.

How to do it...

To test REST API, perform the following steps:

1. Create a `tests.py` file in your `bulletin_board` app, as follows:

```
# bulletin_board/tests.py
# -*- coding: UTF-8 -*-
from __future__ import unicode_literals
```

```python
from django.contrib.auth.models import User
from django.core.urlresolvers import reverse
from rest_framework import status
from rest_framework.test import APITestCase
from .models import Category, Bulletin


class BulletinTests(APITestCase):
    @classmethod
    def setUpClass(cls):
        super(BulletinTests, cls).setUpClass()
        cls.superuser, created = User.objects.\
            get_or_create(
                username="test-admin",
            )
        cls.superuser.is_active = True
        cls.superuser.is_superuser = True
        cls.superuser.save()

        cls.category = Category.objects.create(
            title="Movies"
        )

        cls.bulletin = Bulletin.objects.create(
            bulletin_type="searching",
            category=cls.category,
            title="The Matrix",
            description="There is no Spoon.",
            contact_person="Aidas Bendoraitis",
        )
        cls.bulletin_to_delete = Bulletin.objects.create(
            bulletin_type="searching",
            category=cls.category,
            title="Animatrix",
            description="Trinity: "
                "There's a difference, Mr. Ash, "
                "between a trap and a test.",
            contact_person="Aidas Bendoraitis",
        )

    @classmethod
    def tearDownClass(cls):
        super(BulletinTests, cls).tearDownClass()
        cls.category.delete()
        cls.bulletin.delete()
        cls.superuser.delete()
```

2. Add a method to test the API call listing the bulletins as shown in the following:

```
def test_list_bulletins(self):
    url = reverse("rest_bulletin_list")
    data = {}
    response = self.client.get(url, data, format="json")
    self.assertEqual(
        response.status_code, status.HTTP_200_OK
    )
    self.assertEqual(
        response.data["count"], Bulletin.objects.count()
    )
```

3. Add a method to test the API call showing a single bulletin as follows:

```
def test_get_bulletin(self):
    url = reverse("rest_bulletin_detail", kwargs={
        "pk": self.bulletin.pk
    })
    data = {}
    response = self.client.get(url, data, format="json")
    self.assertEqual(
        response.status_code, status.HTTP_200_OK
    )
    self.assertEqual(response.data["id"], self.bulletin.pk)
    self.assertEqual(
        response.data["bulletin_type"],
        self.bulletin.bulletin_type
    )
    self.assertEqual(
        response.data["category"]["id"],
        self.category.pk
    )
    self.assertEqual(
        response.data["title"],
        self.bulletin.title
    )
    self.assertEqual(
        response.data["description"],
        self.bulletin.description
    )
    self.assertEqual(
        response.data["contact_person"],
        self.bulletin.contact_person
    )
```

4. Add a method to test the API call creating a bulletin if the current user is authenticated, as follows:

```python
def test_create_bulletin_allowed(self):
    # login
    self.client.force_authenticate(user=self.superuser)

    url = reverse("rest_bulletin_list")
    data = {
        "bulletin_type": "offering",
        "category": {"title": self.category.title},
        "title": "Back to the Future",
        "description": "Roads? Where we're going, "
            "we don't need roads.",
        "contact_person": "Aidas Bendoraitis",
    }
    response = self.client.post(url, data, format="json")
    self.assertEqual(
        response.status_code, status.HTTP_201_CREATED
    )
    self.assertTrue(Bulletin.objects.filter(
        pk=response.data["id"]
    ).count() == 1)

    # logout
    self.client.force_authenticate(user=None)
```

5. Add a method to test the API call trying to create a bulletin; however, failing as the current visitor is anonymous, as shown in the following:

```python
def test_create_bulletin_restricted(self):
    # make sure the user is logged out
    self.client.force_authenticate(user=None)

    url = reverse("rest_bulletin_list")
    data = {
        "bulletin_type": "offering",
        "category": {"title": self.category.title},
        "title": "Back to the Future",
        "description": "Roads? Where we're going, "
            "we don't need roads.",
        "contact_person": "Aidas Bendoraitis",
    }
    response = self.client.post(url, data, format="json")
    self.assertEqual(
        response.status_code, status.HTTP_403_FORBIDDEN
    )
```

6. Add a method to test the API call changing a bulletin if the current user is authenticated, as follows:

```python
def test_change_bulletin_allowed(self):
    # login
    self.client.force_authenticate(user=self.superuser)

    url = reverse("rest_bulletin_detail", kwargs={
        "pk": self.bulletin.pk
    })

    # change only title
    data = {
        "bulletin_type": self.bulletin.bulletin_type,
        "category": {
            "title": self.bulletin.category.title
        },
        "title": "Matrix Resurrection",
        "description": self.bulletin.description,
        "contact_person": self.bulletin.contact_person,
    }
    response = self.client.put(url, data, format="json")
    self.assertEqual(
        response.status_code, status.HTTP_200_OK
    )
    self.assertEqual(response.data["id"], self.bulletin.pk)
    self.assertEqual(
        response.data["bulletin_type"], "searching"
    )

    # logout
    self.client.force_authenticate(user=None)
```

7. Add a method to test the API call trying to change a bulletin; however, failing as the current visitor is anonymous:

```python
def test_change_bulletin_restricted(self):
    # make sure the user is logged out
    self.client.force_authenticate(user=None)

    url = reverse("rest_bulletin_detail", kwargs={
        "pk": self.bulletin.pk
    })
    # change only title
    data = {
        "bulletin_type": self.bulletin.bulletin_type,
```

```
        "category": {
            "title": self.bulletin.category.title
        },
        "title": "Matrix Resurrection",
        "description": self.bulletin.description,
        "contact_person": self.bulletin.contact_person,
    }
    response = self.client.put(url, data, format="json")
    self.assertEqual(
        response.status_code, status.HTTP_403_FORBIDDEN
    )
```

8. Add a method to test the API call deleting a bulletin if the current user is authenticated, as shown in the following:

```python
def test_delete_bulletin_allowed(self):
    # login
    self.client.force_authenticate(user=self.superuser)

    url = reverse("rest_bulletin_detail", kwargs={
        "pk": self.bulletin_to_delete.pk
    })
    data = {}
    response = self.client.delete(url, data, format="json")
    self.assertEqual(
        response.status_code, status.HTTP_204_NO_CONTENT
    )

    # logout
    self.client.force_authenticate(user=None)
```

9. Add a method to test the API call trying to delete a bulletin; however, failing as the current visitor is anonymous:

```python
def test_delete_bulletin_restricted(self):
    # make sure the user is logged out
    self.client.force_authenticate(user=None)

    url = reverse("rest_bulletin_detail", kwargs={
        "pk": self.bulletin_to_delete.pk
    })
    data = {}
    response = self.client.delete(url, data, format="json")
    self.assertEqual(
        response.status_code, status.HTTP_403_FORBIDDEN
    )
```

10. Run the tests for the `bulletin_board` app, as follows:

```
(myproject_env)$ python manage.py test bulletin_board
Creating test database for alias 'default'...
........
--------------------------------------------------------
Ran 8 tests in 0.081s


OK
Destroying test database for alias 'default'...
```

How it works...

REST API test suite extends the `APITestCase` class. Once again, we have the `setUpClass()` and `tearDownClass()` class methods that will be executed before and after the different tests. Also, the test suite has a `client` attribute of the `APIClient` type that can be used to simulate API calls. It has methods for all standard HTTP calls: `get()`, `post()`, `put()`, `patch()`, `delete()`, `head()`, and `options()`; whereas, in our tests, we are using the GET, POST, and DELETE requests. Also, `client` has methods to authenticate a user by the login credentials, token, or just the `User` object. In our tests, we are authenticating by the third way, just passing a user directly to the `force_authenticate()` method.

The rest of the code is self-explanatory.

See also

▸ The *Using Django REST framework to create API* recipe in *Chapter 9, Data Import and Export*

▸ The *Testing pages with Selenium* recipe

▸ The *Testing views with mock* recipe

Releasing a reusable Django app

Django documentation has a tutorial about how to package your reusable apps so that they can be installed later with `pip` in any virtual environment:

`https://docs.djangoproject.com/en/1.8/intro/reusable-apps/`

However, there is an even better way to package and release a reusable Django app using the **Cookiecutter** tool, which creates templates for different coding projects such as new Django CMS website, Flask website, or jQuery plugin. One of the available project templates is `cookiecutter-djangopackage`. In this recipe, you will learn how to use it to distribute the reusable `likes` app.

Getting ready

Install `Cookiecutter` in your virtual environment:

```
(myproject_env)$ pip install cookiecutter
```

How to do it...

To release your `likes` app, follow these steps:

1. Start a new Django app project, as follows:

   ```
   (myapp_env)$ cookiecutter \
   https://github.com/pydanny/cookiecutter-djangopackage.git
   ```

2. Answer the questions to create the app template:

   ```
   full_name [Your full name here]: Aidas Bendoraitis
   email [you@example.com]: aidas@bendoraitis.lt
   github_username [yourname]: archatas
   project_name [dj-package]: django-likes
   repo_name [dj-package]: django-likes
   app_name [djpackage]: likes
   project_short_description [Your project description goes here]:
   Django-likes allows your website users to like any object.
   release_date [2015-10-02]:
   year [2015]:
   version [0.1.0]:
   ```

3. This will create a file structure, as shown in the following image:

```
django-likes
├── .editorconfig
├── .gitignore
├── .travis.yml
├── AUTHORS.rst
├── CONTRIBUTING.rst
├── HISTORY.rst
├── LICENSE
├── MANIFEST.in
├── Makefile
├── README.rst
├── docs
│   ├── Makefile
│   ├── authors.rst
│   ├── conf.py
│   ├── contributing.rst
│   ├── history.rst
│   ├── index.rst
│   ├── installation.rst
│   ├── make.bat
│   ├── readme.rst
│   └── usage.rst
├── likes
│   ├── __init__.py
│   ├── models.py
│   ├── static
│   │   ├── css
│   │   │   └── likes.css
│   │   ├── img
│   │   │   └── .gitignore
│   │   └── js
│   │       └── likes.js
│   └── templates
│       └── likes
│           └── base.html
├── requirements-test.txt
├── requirements.txt
├── requirements_dev.txt
├── runtests.py
├── setup.cfg
├── setup.py
├── tests
│   ├── __init__.py
│   └── test_models.py
└── tox.ini
```

4. Copy the files of the `likes` app from a Django project, where you are using it, to the `django-likes/likes` directory.

5. Add the reusable app project to the Git repository under GitHub.

6. Explore different files and complete the license, README, documentation, configuration and other files.

7. Make sure that the app passes the tests:

```
(myapp_env)$ pip install -r requirements-test.txt
```

```
(myapp_env)$ python runtests.py
```

8. If your package is closed source, create a shareable release as a ZIP archive:

```
(myapp_env)$ python setup.py sdist
```

This will create a `django-likes/dist/django-likes-0.1.0.tar.gz` file that can be installed or uninstalled with pip, as follows:

```
(myproject_env)$ pip install django-likes-0.1.0.tar.gz
```

```
(myproject_env)$ pip uninstall django-likes
```

9. If your package is open source, register and publish your app on **Python Package Index** (**PyPI**):

```
(myapp_env)$ python setup.py register
```

```
(myapp_env)$ python setup.py publish
```

10. Also, to spread the word, add your app to Django packages by submitting a form at `https://www.djangopackages.com/packages/add/`.

How it works...

Cookiecutter fills in the entered requested data in different parts of the Django app project template. As a result, you get the `setup.py` file ready for distribution to Python Package Index, Sphinx documentation, BSD as the default license, universal text editor configuration for the project, static files and templates included in your app, and other goodies.

See also

▶ The *Creating a project file structure* recipe in *Chapter 1, Getting Started with Django 1.8*

▶ The *Handling project dependencies with pip* recipe in *Chapter 1, Getting Started with Django 1.8*

▶ The *Implementing the Like widget* recipe in *Chapter 4, Templates and JavaScript*

Getting detailed error reporting via e-mail

To perform system logging, Django uses Python's built-in logging module. The default Django configuration seems to be quite complex. In this recipe, you will learn how to tweak it in order to send error e-mails with complete HTML, similar to what is provided by Django in the DEBUG mode when an error happens.

Getting ready

Locate the Django project in your virtual environment.

How to do it...

The following procedure will help you send detailed e-mails about errors:

1. Open the `myproject_env/lib/python2.7/site-packages/django/utils/log.py` file in a text editor and copy the `DEFAULT_LOGGING` dictionary to your project's settings as the `LOGGING` dictionary.

2. Add the `include_html` setting to the `mail_admins` handler, as follows:

```python
# myproject/conf/base.py or myproject/settings.py
LOGGING = {
    "version": 1,
    "disable_existing_loggers": False,
    "filters": {
        "require_debug_false": {
            "()": "django.utils.log.RequireDebugFalse",
        },
        "require_debug_true": {
            "()": "django.utils.log.RequireDebugTrue",
        },
    },
    "handlers": {
        "console": {
            "level": "INFO",
            "filters": ["require_debug_true"],
            "class": "logging.StreamHandler",
        },
        "null": {
            "class": "django.utils.log.NullHandler",
        },
        "mail_admins": {
```

```
                "level": "ERROR",
                "filters": ["require_debug_false"],
                "class": "django.utils.log.AdminEmailHandler",
                "include_html": True,
            }
        },
        "loggers": {
            "django": {
                "handlers": ["console"],
            },
            "django.request": {
                "handlers": ["mail_admins"],
                "level": "ERROR",
                "propagate": False,
            },
            "django.security": {
                "handlers": ["mail_admins"],
                "level": "ERROR",
                "propagate": False,
            },
            "py.warnings": {
                "handlers": ["console"],
            },
        }
    }
}
```

How it works...

Logging configuration consists of four parts: loggers, handlers, filters, and formatters. The following is how they can be described:

- ▶ Loggers are entry points in the logging system. Each logger can have a log level: DEBUG, INFO, WARNING, ERROR, or CRITICAL. When a message is written to the logger, the log level of the message is compared with the logger's level. If it meets or exceeds the log level of the logger, it will be further processed by a handler. Otherwise, the message will be ignored.

- ▶ Handlers are engines that define what happens to each message in the logger. They can be written to a console, sent by an e-mail to the administrator, saved to a log file, sent to the Sentry error logging service, and so on. In our case, we set the include_ html parameter for the mail_admins handler as we want the full HTML with traceback and local variables for the error messages that happen in our Django project.

▸ Filters provide additional control over the messages that are passed from the loggers to handlers. For example, in our case, the e-mails will be sent only when the DEBUG mode is set to `False`.

▸ Formatters are used to define how to render a log message as a string. They are not used in this example; however, for more information about logging, you can refer to the official documentation at `https://docs.djangoproject.com/en/1.8/topics/logging/`.

See also

▸ The *Deploying on Apache with mod_wsgi* recipe

Deploying on Apache with mod_wsgi

There are many options as to how to deploy your Django project. In this recipe, I will guide you through the deployment of a Django project on a dedicated Linux server with Virtualmin.

A dedicated server is a type of Internet hosting, where you lease the whole server that is not shared with anyone else. Virtualmin is a web-hosting control panel that allows you to manage virtual domains, mailboxes, databases, and entire servers without having deep knowledge of the command-line routines of the server administration.

To run the Django project, we will be using the Apache web server with the `mod_wsgi` module and a MySQL database.

Getting ready

Make sure that you have Virtualmin installed on your dedicated Linux server. For instructions, refer to `http://www.virtualmin.com/download.html`.

How to do it...

Follow these steps to deploy a Django project on a Linux server with Virtualmin:

1. Log in to Virtualmin as the root user and set `bash` instead of `sh` as the default shell for the server's users. This can be done by navigating to **Virtualmin | System Customization | Custom Shells**, as shown in the following screenshot:

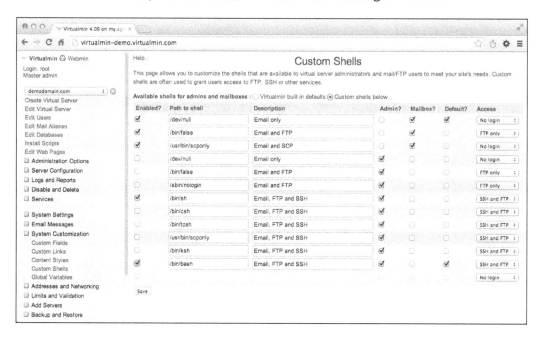

2. Create a virtual server for your project by navigating to **Virtualmin | Create Virtual Server**. Enable the following features: **Setup website for domain?** and **Create MySQL database?**. The username and password that you set for the domain will also be used for the SSH connections, FTP, and MySQL database access, as follows:

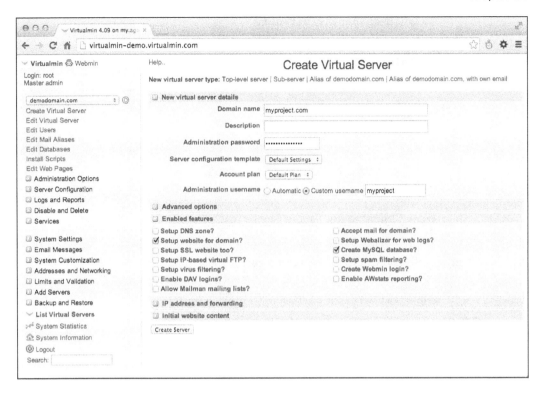

3. Log in to your domain administration panel and set the A record for your domain to the IP address of your dedicated server.

4. Connect to the dedicated server via Secure Shell as the root user and install Python libraries, `pip`, `virtualenv`, `MySQLdb`, and `Pillow` system wide.

5. Ensure that the default MySQL database encoding is UTF-8:

    1. Edit MySQL configuration file on the remote server, for example, using the nano editor:

    ```
    $ ssh root@myproject.com
    root@myproject.com's password:


    $ nano /etc/mysql/my.cnf
    ```

    Add or edit the following configurations:

    ```
    [client]
    default-character-set=utf8


    [mysql]
    ```

```
default-character-set=utf8


[mysqld]
collation-server=utf8_unicode_ci
init-connect='SET NAMES utf8'
character-set-server=utf8
```

2. Press *Ctrl + O* to save the changes and *Ctrl + X* to exit the nano editor.

3. Then, restart the MySQL server, as follows:

```
$ /etc/init.d/mysql restart
```

4. Press *Ctrl + D* to exit Secure Shell.

6. When you create a domain with Virtualmin, the user for that domain is created automatically. Connect to the dedicated server via Secure Shell as a user of your Django project and create a virtual environment for your project, as follows:

```
$ ssh myproject@myproject.com
myproject@myproject.com's password:


$ virtualenv . --system-site-packages
$ echo source ~/bin/activate >> .bashrc
$ source ~/bin/activate
(myproject)myproject@server$
```

 The .bashrc script will be called each time you connect to your Django project via Secure Shell as a user related to the domain. The .bashrc script will automatically activate the virtual environment for this project.

7. If you host your project code on Bitbucket, you will need to set up SSH keys in order to avoid password prompts when pulling from or pushing to the Git repository:

1. Execute the following commands one by one:

```
(myproject)myproject@server$ ssh-keygen
(myproject)myproject@server$ ssh-agent /bin/bash
(myproject)myproject@server$ ssh-add ~/.ssh/id_rsa
(myproject)myproject@server$ cat ~/.ssh/id_rsa.pub
```

2. This last command prints your SSH public key that you need to copy and paste at **Manage Account** | **SSH keys** | **Add Key** on the Bitbucket website.

8. Create a `project` directory, go to it, and clone your project's code as follows:

   **(myproject)myproject@server$ git clone **

   git@bitbucket.org:somebitbucketuser/myproject.git myproject

 Now, your project path should be something similar to the following:
   `/home/myproject/project/myproject`

9. Install the Python requirements for your project, including a specified version of Django, as follows:

   (myproject)myproject@server$ pip install -r requirements.txt

10. Create the `media`, `tmp`, and `static` directories under your project's directory.

11. Also, create `local_settings.py` with settings similar to the following:

```
# /home/myproject/project/myproject/myproject/local_settings.py
DATABASES = {
    "default": {
        "ENGINE": "django.db.backends.mysql",
        "NAME": "myproject",
        "USER": "myproject",
        "PASSWORD": "mypassword",
    }
}
PREPEND_WWW = True
DEBUG = False
ALLOWED_HOSTS = ["myproject.com"]
```

12. Import the database dump that you created locally. If you are using a Mac, you can do that with an app, **Sequel Pro** (`http://www.sequelpro.com/`), using an SSH connection. You can also upload the database dump to the server by FTP and then run the following in Secure Shell:

   **(myproject)myproject@server$ python manage.py dbshell < **

   ~/db_backups/db.sql

13. Collect static files, as follows:

   **(myproject)myproject@server$ python manage.py collectstatic **

   --noinput

14. Go to the `~/public_html` directory and create a `wsgi` file using the nano editor (or an editor of your choice):

```
# /home/myproject/public_html/my.wsgi
#!/home/myproject/bin/python
# -*- coding: utf-8 -*-
```

```
import os, sys, site
django_path = os.path.abspath(
    os.path.join(os.path.dirname(__file__),
    "../lib/python2.6/site-packages/"),
)
site.addsitedir(django_path)
project_path = os.path.abspath(
    os.path.join(os.path.dirname(__file__),
    "../project/myproject"),
)
sys.path += [project_path]
os.environ["DJANGO_SETTINGS_MODULE"] = "myproject.settings"
from django.core.wsgi import get_wsgi_application
application = get_wsgi_application()
```

15. Then, create the `.htaccess` file in the same directory. The `.htaccess` file will redirect all the requests to your Django project set in the `wsgi` file, as shown in the following:

 # /home/myproject/public_html/.htaccess
```
AddHandler wsgi-script .wsgi
DirectoryIndex index.html
RewriteEngine On
RewriteBase /
RewriteCond %{REQUEST_FILENAME} !-f
RewriteCond %{REQUEST_FILENAME}/index.html !-f
RewriteCond %{REQUEST_URI} !^/media/
RewriteCond %{REQUEST_URI} !^/static/
RewriteRule ^(.*)$ /my.wsgi/$1 [QSA,L]
```

16. Copy `.htaccess` as `.htaccess_live`.

17. Then, also create `.htaccess_maintenace` for maintenance cases. This new Apache configuration file will show `temporarily-offline.html` for all the users except you, recognized by the IP address of your LAN or computer. You can check your IP by googling `what's my ip`. The following is how the `.htaccess_maintenance` will look:

 # /home/myproject/public_html/.htaccess_maintenance
```
AddHandler wsgi-script .wsgi
DirectoryIndex index.html
RewriteEngine On
RewriteBase /
RewriteCond %{REMOTE_HOST} !^1\.2\.3\.4$
RewriteCond %{REQUEST_URI} !/temporarily-offline\.html
RewriteCond %{REQUEST_URI} !^/media/
RewriteCond %{REQUEST_URI} !^/static/
```

```
RewriteRule .* /temporarily-offline.html [R=302,L]
RewriteCond %{REQUEST_FILENAME} !-f
RewriteCond %{REQUEST_FILENAME}/index.html !-f
RewriteCond %{REQUEST_URI} !^/media/
RewriteCond %{REQUEST_URI} !^/static/
RewriteRule ^(.*)$ /my.wsgi/$1 [QSA,L]
```

 Replace the IP digits in this file with your own IP.

18. Then, create an HTML file that will be shown when your website is down:

    ```
    <!-- /home/myproject/public_html/temporarily-offline.html -->
    The site is being updated... Please come back later.
    ```

19. Log in to the server as the root user via Secure Shell and edit the Apache configuration:

    1. Open the domain configuration file, as follows:

        ```
        $ nano /etc/apache2/sites-available/myproject.mydomain.conf
        ```

    2. Add the following lines before `</VirtualHost>`:

        ```
        Options -Indexes
        AliasMatch ^/static/\d+/(.*) \
            "/home/myproject/project/myproject/static/$1"
        AliasMatch ^/media/(.*) \
            "/home/myproject/project/myproject/media/$1"
        <FilesMatch "\.(ico|pdf|flv|jpe?g|png|gif|js|css|swf)$">
            ExpiresActive On
            ExpiresDefault "access plus 1 year"
        </FilesMatch>
        ```

    3. Restart Apache for the changes to take effect:

        ```
        $ /etc/init.d/apache2 restart
        ```

20. Set the default scheduled cron jobs. For more information on how to do this, refer to the *Setting up cron jobs for regular tasks* recipe.

How it works...

With this configuration, files in the `media` and `static` directories are served directly from Apache; whereas, all the other URLs are handled by the Django project through the `my.wsgi` file.

Using the `<FilesMatch>` directive in the Apache site configuration, all media files are set to be cached for one year. Static URL paths have a numbered prefix that changes whenever you update the code from the Git repository.

When you need to update the website and want to set it down for maintenance, you'll have to copy `.htaccess_maintenance` to `.htaccess`. When you want to set the website up again, you'll have to copy `.htaccess_live` to `.htaccess`.

There's more...

To find other options for hosting your Django project, refer to: `http://djangofriendly.com/hosts/`.

See also

▸ The *Creating a project file structure* recipe in *Chapter 1, Getting Started with Django 1.8*

▸ The *Handling project dependencies with pip* recipe in *Chapter 1, Getting Started with Django 1.8*

▸ The *Setting up STATIC_URL dynamically for Git users* recipe in *Chapter 1, Getting Started with Django 1.8*

▸ The *Setting UTF-8 as the default encoding for MySQL configuration* recipe in *Chapter 1, Getting Started with Django 1.8*

▸ The *Creating and using the Fabric deployment script* recipe

▸ The *Setting up cron jobs for regular tasks* recipe

Setting up cron jobs for regular tasks

Usually websites have some management tasks to do in the background once in a week, day, or every hour. This can be achieved using cron jobs that are also known as scheduled tasks. These are scripts that run on the server for the specified period of time. In this recipe, we will create two cron jobs: one to clear sessions from the database and another to back up the database data. Both will be run every night.

Getting ready

To start with, deploy your Django project on to a remote server. Then, connect to the server by SSH.

How to do it...

Let's create the two scripts and make them run regularly by following these steps:

1. Create the `commands`, `db_backups` and `logs` directories in your project's home directory:

   (myproject)myproject@server$ mkdir commands

   (myproject)myproject@server$ mkdir db_backups

   (myproject)myproject@server$ mkdir logs

2. In the `commands` directory, create a `cleanup.sh` file with the following content:

   ```bash
   # /home/myproject/commands/cleanup.sh
   #! /usr/bin/env bash
   PROJECT_PATH=/home/myproject
   CRON_LOG_FILE=${PROJECT_PATH}/logs/cleanup.log

   echo "Cleaning up the database" > ${CRON_LOG_FILE}
   date >> ${CRON_LOG_FILE}

   cd ${PROJECT_PATH}
   . bin/activate
   cd project/myproject
   python manage.py cleanup --traceback >> \
   ${CRON_LOG_FILE}   2>&1
   ```

3. Make the following file executable:

   (myproject)myproject@server$ chmod +x cleanup.sh

4. Then, in the same directory, create a `backup_db.sh` file with the following content:

   ```bash
   # /home/myproject/commands/cleanup.sh
   #! /usr/bin/env bash
   PROJECT_PATH=/home/myproject
   CRON_LOG_FILE=${PROJECT_PATH}/logs/backup_db.log
   WEEK_DATE=$(LC_ALL=en_US.UTF-8 date +"%w-%A")
   BACKUP_PATH=${PROJECT_PATH}/db_backups/${WEEK_DATE}.sql
   DATABASE=myproject
   USER=my_db_user
   PASS=my_db_password

   EXCLUDED_TABLES=(
   django_session
   )

   IGNORED_TABLES_STRING=''
   ```

```
for TABLE in "${EXCLUDED_TABLES[@]}"
do :
    IGNORED_TABLES_STRING+=\
    " --ignore-table=${DATABASE}.${TABLE}"
done

echo "Creating DB Backup" > ${CRON_LOG_FILE}
date >> ${CRON_LOG_FILE}

cd ${PROJECT_PATH}
mkdir -p db_backups

echo "Dump structure" >> ${CRON_LOG_FILE}
mysqldump -u ${USER} -p${PASS} --single-transaction \
--no-data ${DATABASE} > ${BACKUP_PATH} 2>> ${CRON_LOG_FILE}

echo "Dump content" >> ${CRON_LOG_FILE}
mysqldump -u ${USER} -p${PASS} ${DATABASE} \
${IGNORED_TABLES_STRING} >> ${BACKUP_PATH} 2>> \
${CRON_LOG_FILE}
```

5. Make the following file executable too:

    (myproject)myproject@server$ chmod +x backup_db.sh

6. Test the scripts to see whether they are executed correctly by running the scripts and then checking the `*.log` files in the `logs` directory, as follows:

    (myproject)myproject@server$ ./cleanup.sh

    (myproject)myproject@server$ ./backup_db.sh

7. In your project's home directory create a `crontab.txt` file with the following tasks:

    00 01 * * * /home/myproject/commands/cleanup.sh

    00 02 * * * /home/myproject/commands/backup_db.sh

8. Install the crontab tasks, as follows:

    (myproject)myproject@server$ crontab -e crontab.txt

How it works...

With the current setup, every night `cleanup.sh` will be executed at 1 A.M. and `backup_db.sh` will be executed at 2 A.M. The execution logs will be saved in `cleanup.log` and `backup_db.log`. If you get any errors, you should check these files for the traceback.

The database backup script is a little more complex. Every day of the week, it creates a backup file for that day called `0-Sunday.sql`, `1-Monday.sql`, and so on. Therefore, you will be able to restore data backed seven days ago or later. At first, the backup script dumps the database schema for all the tables and then it dumps the data for all the tables, except for the ones listed one under each other in `EXCLUDED_TABLES` (currently, that is, `django_session`).

The crontab syntax is this: each line contains a specific period of time and then a task to run at it. The time is defined in five parts separated by spaces, as shown in the following:

- Minutes from 0 to 59
- Hours from 0 to 23
- Days of month from 1 to 31
- Months from 1 to 12
- Days of week from 0 to 7, where 0 is Sunday, 1 is Monday, and so on. 7 is Sunday again.

An asterisk (*) means that every time frame will be used. Therefore, the following task defines `cleanup.sh` to be executed at 1:00 AM every day of a month, every month, and every day of the week:

00 01 * * * /home/myproject/commands/cleanup.sh

You can learn more about the specifics of the crontab at `https://en.wikipedia.org/wiki/Cron`.

See also

- The *Deploying on Apache with mod_wsgi* recipe
- The *Creating and using the Fabric deployment script* recipe

Creating and using the Fabric deployment script

Usually, to update your site, you have to perform repetitive tasks such as setting a maintenance page, stopping cron jobs, creating a database backup, pulling new code from a repository, migrating databases, collecting static files, testing, starting cron jobs again, and unsetting the maintenance page. That's quite a tedious work, where mistakes can occur. Also, you need not forget the different routines for staging site (the one where new features can be tested) and production site (which is shown to the public). Fortunately, there is a Python library called **Fabric** that allows you to automate these tasks. In this recipe, you will learn how to create `fabfile.py`, the script for Fabric, and how to deploy your project on staging and production environments.

The Fabric script can be called from the directory that contains it, as follows:

```
(myproject_env)$ fab staging deploy
```

This will deploy the project on the staging server.

Getting ready

Set up analogous staging and production websites using the instructions in the *Deploying on Apache with mod_wsgi* recipe. Install Fabric on your computer globally or in your project's virtual environment, as follows:

```
$ pip install fabric
```

How to do it...

We will start by creating a `fabfile.py` file in the Django project directory with several functions, as follows:

```python
# fabfile.py
# -*- coding: UTF-8 -*-
from fabric.api import env, run, prompt, local, get, sudo
from fabric.colors import red, green
from fabric.state import output

env.environment = ""
env.full = False
output['running'] = False

PRODUCTION_HOST = "myproject.com"
PRODUCTION_USER = "myproject"

def dev():
    """ chooses development environment """
    env.environment = "dev"
    env.hosts = [PRODUCTION_HOST]
    env.user = PRODUCTION_USER
    print("LOCAL DEVELOPMENT ENVIRONMENT\n")

def staging():
    """ chooses testing environment """
    env.environment = "staging"
    env.hosts = ["staging.myproject.com"]
    env.user = "myproject"
```

```
    print("STAGING WEBSITE\n")

def production():
    """ chooses production environment """
    env.environment = "production"
    env.hosts = [PRODUCTION_HOST]
    env.user = PRODUCTION_USER
    print("PRODUCTION WEBSITE\n")

def full():
    """ all commands should be executed without questioning """
    env.full = True

def deploy():
    """ updates the chosen environment """
    if not env.environment:
        while env.environment not in ("dev", "staging",
            "production"):
            env.environment = prompt(red('Please specify target'
                'environment ("dev", "staging", or '
                '"production"): '))
            print
    globals()["_update_%s" % env.environment]()
```

The `dev()`, `staging()`, and `production()` functions set the appropriate environment for the current task. Then, the `deploy()` function calls the `_update_dev()`, `_update_staging()`, or `_update_production()` private functions, respectively. Let's define these private functions in the same file, as follows:

▶ The function for deploying in the development environment will optionally do the following tasks:

  ❑ Update the local database with data from the production database

  ❑ Download media files from the production server

  ❑ Update code from the Git repository

  ❑ Migrate the local database

Let's create this function in the Fabric script file, as follows:

```
def _update_dev():
    """ updates development environment """
    run("")  # password request
    print

    if env.full or "y" == prompt(red("Get latest "
```

```
            "production database (y/n)?"), default="y"):
        print(green(" * creating production-database "
            "dump..."))
        run("cd ~/db_backups/ && ./backup_db.sh --latest")
        print(green(" * downloading dump..."))
        get("~/db_backups/db_latest.sql",
            "tmp/db_latest.sql")
        print(green(" * importing the dump locally..."))
        local("python manage.py dbshell < "
            "tmp/db_latest.sql && rm tmp/db_latest.sql")
        print
        if env.full or "y" == prompt("Call prepare_dev "
            "command (y/n)?", default="y"):
            print(green(" * preparing data for "
                "development..."))
            local("python manage.py prepare_dev")
    print

    if env.full or "y" == prompt(red("Download media "
        "uploads (y/n)?"), default="y"):
        print(green(" * creating an archive of media "
            "uploads..."))
        run("cd ~/project/myproject/media/ "
            "&& tar -cz -f "
            "~/project/myproject/tmp/media.tar.gz *")
        print(green(" * downloading archive..."))
        get("~/project/myproject/tmp/media.tar.gz",
            "tmp/media.tar.gz")
        print(green(" * extracting and removing archive "
            "locally..."))
        for host in env.hosts:
            local("cd media/ "
                "&& tar -xzf ../tmp/media.tar.gz "
                "&& rm tmp/media.tar.gz")
        print(green(" * removing archive from the "
            "server..."))
        run("rm ~/project/myproject/tmp/media.tar.gz")
    print

    if env.full or "y" == prompt(red("Update code (y/n)?"),
        default="y"):
        print(green(" * updating code..."))
```

```
        local("git pull")
    print

    if env.full or "y" == prompt(red("Migrate database "
        "schema (y/n)?"), default="y"):
        print(green(" * migrating database schema..."))
        local("python manage.py migrate --no-initial-data")
        local("python manage.py syncdb")
    print
```

- ► The function for deploying in a staging environment will optionally do the following tasks:
    - ❑ Set a maintenance screen saying that the site is being updated and the visitors should wait or come back later
    - ❑ Stop scheduled cron jobs
    - ❑ Get the latest data from the production database
    - ❑ Get the latest media files from the production database
    - ❑ Pull code from the Git repository
    - ❑ Collect static files
    - ❑ Migrate the database schema
    - ❑ Restart the Apache web server
    - ❑ Start scheduled cron jobs
    - ❑ Unset the maintenance screen

Let's create this function in the Fabric script, as follows:

```
def _update_staging():
    """ updates testing environment """
    run("")   # password request
    print

    if env.full or "y" == prompt(red("Set under-"
        "construction screen (y/n)?"), default="y"):
        print(green(" * Setting maintenance screen"))
        run("cd ~/public_html/ "
            "&& cp .htaccess_under_construction .htaccess")
    print

    if env.full or "y" == prompt(red("Stop cron jobs "
        " (y/n)?"), default="y"):
        print(green(" * Stopping cron jobs"))
        sudo("/etc/init.d/cron stop")
```

```
print

if env.full or "y" == prompt(red("Get latest "
    "production database (y/n)?"), default="y"):
    print(green(" * creating production-database "
        "dump..."))
    run("cd ~/db_backups/ && ./backup_db.sh --latest")
    print(green(" * downloading dump..."))
    run("scp %(user)s@%(host)s:"
        "~/db_backups/db_latest.sql "
        "~/db_backups/db_latest.sql" % {
            "user": PRODUCTION_USER,
            "host": PRODUCTION_HOST,
        }
    )
    print(green(" * importing the dump locally..."))
    run("cd ~/project/myproject/ && python manage.py "
        "dbshell < ~/db_backups/db_latest.sql")
    print
    if env.full or "y" == prompt(red("Call "
        " prepare_staging command (y/n)?"),
        default="y"):
        print(green(" * preparing data for "
            " testing..."))
        run("cd ~/project/myproject/ "
            "&& python manage.py prepare_staging")
print
if env.full or "y" == prompt(red("Get latest media "
    " (y/n)?"), default="y"):
    print(green(" * updating media..."))
    run("scp -r %(user)s@%(host)s:"
        "~/project/myproject/media/* "
        " ~/project/myproject/media/" % {
            "user": PRODUCTION_USER,
            "host": PRODUCTION_HOST,
        }
    )
print

if env.full or "y" == prompt(red("Update code (y/n)?"),
    default="y"):
    print(green(" * updating code..."))
    run("cd ~/project/myproject "
        "&& git pull")
```

```
print

if env.full or "y" == prompt(red("Collect static "
    "files (y/n)?"), default="y"):
    print(green(" * collecting static files..."))
    run("cd ~/project/myproject "
        "&& python manage.py collectstatic --noinput")
print

if env.full or "y" == prompt(red('Migrate database "
    " schema (y/n)?'), default="y"):
    print(green(" * migrating database schema..."))
    run("cd ~/project/myproject "
        "&& python manage.py migrate "
        "--no-initial-data")
    run("cd ~/project/myproject "
        "&& python manage.py syncdb")
print

if env.full or "y" == prompt(red("Restart webserver "
    "(y/n)?"), default="y"):
    print(green(" * Restarting Apache"))
    sudo("/etc/init.d/apache2 graceful")
print

if env.full or "y" == prompt(red("Start cron jobs "
    "(y/n)?"), default="y"):
    print(green(" * Starting cron jobs"))
    sudo("/etc/init.d/cron start")
print

if env.full or "y" == prompt(red("Unset under-"
    "construction screen (y/n)?"), default="y"):
    print(green(" * Unsetting maintenance screen"))
    run("cd ~/public_html/ "
        "&& cp .htaccess_live .htaccess")
print
```

▶ The function for deploying in a production environment will optionally do the following tasks:

   ❑ Set the maintenance screen telling that the site is being updated and the visitors should wait or come back later

   ❑ Stop scheduled cron jobs

- ❑ Back up the database
- ❑ Pull code from the Git repository
- ❑ Collect static files
- ❑ Migrate the database schema
- ❑ Restart the Apache web server
- ❑ Start scheduled cron jobs
- ❑ Unset the maintenance screen

Let's create this function in the Fabric script, as follows:

```python
def _update_production():
    """ updates production environment """
    if "y" != prompt(red("Are you sure you want to "
        "update " + red("production", bold=True) + \
        " website (y/n)?"), default="n"):
        return

    run("")  # password request
    print

    if env.full or "y" == prompt(red("Set under-"
        "construction screen (y/n)?"), default="y"):
        print(green(" * Setting maintenance screen"))
        run("cd ~/public_html/ "
            "&& cp .htaccess_under_construction .htaccess")
    print
    if env.full or "y" == prompt(red("Stop cron jobs"
        " (y/n)?"), default="y"):
        print(green(" * Stopping cron jobs"))
        sudo("/etc/init.d/cron stop")
    print

    if env.full or "y" == prompt(red("Backup database "
        "(y/n)?"), default="y"):
        print(green(" * creating a database dump..."))
        run("cd ~/db_backups/ "
            "&& ./backup_db.sh")
    print

    if env.full or "y" == prompt(red("Update code (y/n)?"),
        default="y"):
        print(green(" * updating code..."))
        run("cd ~/project/myproject/ "
```

```
                "&& git pull")
    print

    if env.full or "y" == prompt(red("Collect static "
        "files (y/n)?"), default="y"):
        print(green(" * collecting static files..."))
        run("cd ~/project/myproject "
            "&& python manage.py collectstatic --noinput")
    print

    if env.full or "y" == prompt(red("Migrate database "
        "schema (y/n)?"), default="y"):
        print(green(" * migrating database schema..."))
        run("cd ~/project/myproject "
            "&& python manage.py migrate "
            "--no-initial-data")
        run("cd ~/project/myproject "
            "&& python manage.py syncdb")
    print

    if env.full or "y" == prompt(red("Restart webserver "
        "(y/n)?"), default="y"):
        print(green(" * Restarting Apache"))
        sudo("/etc/init.d/apache2 graceful")
    print
    if env.full or "y" == prompt(red("Start cron jobs "
        "(y/n)?"), default="y"):
        print(green(" * Starting cron jobs"))
        sudo("/etc/init.d/cron start")
    print

    if env.full or "y" == prompt(red("Unset under-"
        "construction screen (y/n)?"), default="y"):
        print(green(" * Unsetting maintenance screen"))
        run("cd ~/public_html/ "
            "&& cp .htaccess_live .htaccess")
    print
```

How it works...

Each non-private function in a `fabfile.py` file becomes a possible argument to be called from the command-line tool. To see all the available functions, run the following command:

```
(myproject_env)$ fab --list
Available commands:
    deploy      updates the chosen environment
    dev         chooses development environment
    full        all commands should be executed without questioning
    production  chooses production environment
    staging     chooses testing environment
```

These functions are called in the same order as they are passed to the Fabric script, therefore you need to be careful about the order of the arguments when deploying to different environments:

- To deploy in a development environment, you would run the following command:

  ```
  (myproject_env)$ fab dev deploy
  ```

  This will ask you questions similar to the following:

  ```
  Get latest production database (y/n)? [y] _
  ```

  When answered positively, a specific step will be executed.

- To deploy in a staging environment, you would run the following command:

  ```
  (myproject_env)$ fab staging deploy
  ```

- Finally, to deploy in a production environment, you would run the following command:

  ```
  (myproject_env)$ fab production deploy
  ```

For each step of deployment, you will be asked whether you want to do it or skip it. If you want to execute all the steps without any prompts (except the password requests), add a `full` parameter to the deployment script, as follows:

```
(myproject_env)$ fab dev full deploy
```

The Fabric script utilizes several basic functions that can be described as follows:

- `local()`: This function is used to run a command locally in the current computer
- `run()`: This function is used to run a command as a specified user on a remote server

- ▶ `prompt()`: This function is used to ask a question
- ▶ `get()`: This function is used to download a file from a remote server to a local computer
- ▶ `sudo()`: This function is used to run a command as the root (or other) user

Fabric uses the Secure Shell connection to perform tasks on remote servers. Each `run()` or `sudo()` command is executed as a separate connection; therefore, when you want to execute multiple commands at once, you have to either create a `bash` script on the server and call it from Fabric or you have to separate the commands using the `&&` shell operator, which executes the next command only if the previous one was successful.

We are also using the `scp` command to copy files from the production server to the staging server. The syntax of `scp` for recursively copying all the files from a specified directory is similar to the following:

```
scp -r myproject_user@myproject.com:/path/on/production/server/* \
/path/on/staging/server/
```

To make the output more user-friendly, we are using colors, as follows:

```
print(green(" * migrating database schema..."))
```

The deployment script expects you to have two management commands: `prepare_dev` and `prepare_staging`. It's up to you to decide what to put in these commands. Basically, you could change the super user password to a simpler one and change the site domain there. If you don't need such functionality, just remove that from the Fabric script.

The general rule of thumb is not to store any sensitive data in the Fabric script if it is saved in the Git repository. Therefore, for example, to make a backup of the database, we call the `backup_db.sh` script on the remote production server. The content of such a file could be something similar to the following:

```
# ~/db_backups/backup_db.sh
#!/bin/bash
if [[ $1 = '--latest' ]]
then
    today="latest"
else
    today=$(date +%Y-%m-%d-%H%M)
fi
mysqldump --opt -u my_db_user -pmy_db_password myproject > \
    db_$today.sql
```

You can make it executable with the following:

```
$ chmod +x backup_db.sh
```

When the preceding command is run without parameters, it will create a database dump with the date and time in the filename, for example, db_2014-04-24-1400.sql, as follows:

```
$ ./backup_db.sh
```

When the --latest parameter is passed, the filename of the dump will be db_latest.sql:

```
$ ./backup_db.sh --latest
```

There's more...

Fabric scripts can be used not only for deployment, but also for any routine that you need to perform on remote servers, for example, collecting translatable strings when you are using the Rosetta tool to translate *.po files online, rebuild search indexes when you are using Haystack for full-text searches, create backups on demand, call custom management commands, and so on.

To learn more about Fabric, refer to the following URL: http://docs.fabfile.org/en/1.10/.

See also

▸   The *Deploying on Apache with mod_wsgi* recipe

Index

A

add_arguments() method
  about 255
  URL 255
admin actions
  creating 180-185
administrators
  notifying, signals used 308-310
aggregation functions
  URL 187
Ajax
  images, uploading 141-149
Apache
  deploying on, with mod_wsgi 335-342
API key
  URL 259
app
  configuration, creating 30-32
  converting, to CMS app 214, 215
Application Program Interface (API)
  creating, Django REST framework
        used 278-284
  creating, Tastypie used 274-278
  testing, Django REST framework
        used 323-329
attachable menus
  URL 218
authorized files
  downloading 79-82
awesome-slugify module
  URL 296

B

base.html template
  arranging 116-118
Bootstrap
  URL 74

C

cache framework
  URL 308
category administration interface
  creating, with django-mptt-admin 236-239
  creating, with
        django-mptt-tree-editor 240-242
category selection
  single selection field, used in forms 245-247
change form
  map, inserting 192-203
change list page
  columns, customizing 175-180
  filters, developing 185-187
checkbox list
  used, for multiple category selection
        in forms 247-251
class-based views
  composing 95-98
CMS app
  app, converting 214, 215
CMS page
  fields, adding 224-230
columns
  customizing, in change list page 175-180

comma-separated values (CSV) 253
compatible code
  creating, with Python 2.7 and Python 3 9
  reference link 11
continuous scroll
  implementing 132-134
Cookiecutter tool 330
cron jobs
  reference link 345
  setting up, for regular tasks 342-345
CSV library
  URL 256
custom CMS plugin
  creating 219-224
custom navigation
  attaching 216-218
custom template filters
  conventions, following 152, 153
custom template tags
  conventions, following 152, 153

D

database query expressions
  using 289-295
data importing
  from external JSON file 259-264
  from external XML file 264-268
  from local CSV file 253-256
  from local Excel file 256-258
data migration 57
Debug Toolbar
  toggling 298-301
default admin settings
  customizing 188-192
detailed error report
  obtaining, via e-mail 333, 334
development environment
  settings, configuring 14-16
Django CMS
  about 205
  templates, creating 206-210
  URL 206
django-crispy-forms
  used, for creating form layout 74-79
Django migrations
  South migrations, switching to 58, 59

django-mptt app 233
django-mptt-admin
  category administration interface,
    creating with 236-239
django-mptt-tree-editor
  category administration interface,
    creating with 240-242
Django REST framework
  URL 284
  used, for creating API 278-284
  used, for testing API 323-329
Django shell
  using 286-288

E

ElementTree
  reference link 268
  XPath syntax component 268
e-mail
  detailed error report, obtaining via 333, 334
external dependencies
  including 12-14
external JSON file
  data, importing 259-264
external XML file
  data, importing 264-268

F

Fabric
  about 345
  deployment script, creating 345-356
  deployment script, using 345-356
  URL 356
filterable RSS feeds
  creating 269-274
foreign key
  modifying, to many-to-many field 59-61
form
  checkbox list, used for multiple category
    selection 247-251
  HttpRequest, passing 64, 65
  layout, creating with
    django-crispy-forms 74-79
  save method, utilizing 66-68
  single selection field, used for category
    selection 245-247

format() method
reference link 192

G

generic relations
model mixin, creating for 45-49
get function 354
Git ignore file
creating 26-28
Git users
STATIC_URL, setting 20-22
guerrilla patch. *See* **monkey patch**

H

Haystack
multilingual search, implementing 105-114
hierarchical categories
creating 233-236
rendering, in template 243-245
HTML5 data attributes
using 122-127
HttpRequest
passing, to form 64, 65

I

images
uploading 68-73
uploading, by Ajax 141-149

J

JavaScript settings
including 119-121
jScroll plugin
URL 132
JSON endpoint
URL 259

L

Like widget
implementing 134-141
local CSV file
data, importing 253-256

local Excel file
data, importing 256-258
local function 354
local settings
creating 17-19
including 17-19

M

many-to-many field
foreign key, modifying to 59-61
map
inserting, into change form 192-203
Memcached
used, for caching Django views 306, 307
method return value
caching 304, 305
migrations
data migration 57
schema migration 57
using 56, 57
mock
views, testing with 319-322
modal dialog
object details, opening 127-131
model mixin
creating, for creation and modification
dates 40-42
creating, for generic relations 45-49
creating, for meta tags 42-44
creating, URL-related methods used 37-39
using 36, 37
Modified Preorder Tree
Traversal (MPTT) 231-233
mod_wsgi
used, for deploying on Apache 335-342
monkey patch
about 295
used, with slugify() function 295-297
multilingual fields
handling 50-55
multilingual search
implementing, with Haystack 105-114
MySQL configuration
UTF-8, setting as default encoding 22, 23

N

NavigationNode class
attr parameter 218
parent_id parameter 218
parent_namespace parameter 218
visible parameter 218

O

object lists
filtering 83-91
Object-relational mapping (ORM) 289
overwritable app settings
defining 33, 34

P

page menu
structuring 210-213
paginated lists
managing 91-94
PDF documents
generating 98-104
pip
URL 2, 9
used, for handling project dependencies 7-9
production environment
settings, configuring 14-16
project dependencies
handling, with pip 7-9
project file structure
creating 4, 5
prompt function 354
Python 2.7
compatible code, creating 9-11
Python 3
compatible code, creating 9-11
Python-compiled files
deleting 28
Python files
import order, maintaining 29, 30
Python Package Index (PyPI) 12

Q

QueryDict objects
URL 172

Query Expressions 289

R

regular expressions
reference link 157
relative paths
defining, in settings 16, 17
REST API
URL 323
reusable Django app
releasing 329-332
URL 329
run function 354

S

save method
utilizing, of form 66-68
schema migration 57
Selenium
used, for testing pages 314-319
Sequel Pro
URL 339
signals
URL 310
used, for notifying administrators 308-310
single selection field
used, for category selection
in forms 245-247
slugify() function
monkey patch, used with 295-297
South migrations
switching, to Django migrations 58, 59
staging environment
settings, configuring 14-16
STATIC_URL
setting, dynamically for Git users 20-22
setting, dynamically for
Subversion users 19, 20
Subversion ignore property
setting 23-26
sudo function 354
System Check Framework
about 310
URL 312
used, for checking settings 310-312

T

Tastypie
about 274
URL 278
used, for creating API 274-278
template
creating, for Django CMS 206-210
hierarchical categories, rendering 243-245
template filter
creating, for calculation of time differences
since post was published 153-155
creating, for extraction of first
media object 155-157
creating, for humanization of URLs 157, 158
template tag
creating, for inclusion of another
template 158-161
creating, for loading QuerySet in
template 162-166
creating, for modification of request query
parameters 169-173
creating, for parsing content as
template 166-168
reference link 212
testing environment
settings, configuring 14-16
ThreadLocalMiddleware
using 301-303
tree data structure
about 231
ancestors node 232
descendants node 231
leaf node 232
parent node 231
siblings node 232
tree_info filter
URL 245
tree manager methods
URL 236

U

URL-related methods
used, for creating model mixin 37-40
UTF-8
setting, MySQL configuration 22, 23

V

views
testing, with mock 319-322
caching, Memcached used 306, 307
virtual environment
working with 2, 3
Virtualmin
about 335
URL 335

X

XPath
reference link 268
syntax component 268

Thank you for buying
Web Development with Django Cookbook
Second Edition

About Packt Publishing

Packt, pronounced 'packed', published its first book, *Mastering phpMyAdmin for Effective MySQL Management*, in April 2004, and subsequently continued to specialize in publishing highly focused books on specific technologies and solutions.

Our books and publications share the experiences of your fellow IT professionals in adapting and customizing today's systems, applications, and frameworks. Our solution-based books give you the knowledge and power to customize the software and technologies you're using to get the job done. Packt books are more specific and less general than the IT books you have seen in the past. Our unique business model allows us to bring you more focused information, giving you more of what you need to know, and less of what you don't.

Packt is a modern yet unique publishing company that focuses on producing quality, cutting-edge books for communities of developers, administrators, and newbies alike. For more information, please visit our website at www.packtpub.com.

About Packt Open Source

In 2010, Packt launched two new brands, Packt Open Source and Packt Enterprise, in order to continue its focus on specialization. This book is part of the Packt open source brand, home to books published on software built around open source licenses, and offering information to anybody from advanced developers to budding web designers. The Open Source brand also runs Packt's open source Royalty Scheme, by which Packt gives a royalty to each open source project about whose software a book is sold.

Writing for Packt

We welcome all inquiries from people who are interested in authoring. Book proposals should be sent to author@packtpub.com. If your book idea is still at an early stage and you would like to discuss it first before writing a formal book proposal, then please contact us; one of our commissioning editors will get in touch with you.

We're not just looking for published authors; if you have strong technical skills but no writing experience, our experienced editors can help you develop a writing career, or simply get some additional reward for your expertise.

Web Development with Django Cookbook

ISBN: 978-1-78328-689-8   Paperback: 294 pages

Over 70 practical recipes to create multilingual, responsive, and scalable websites with Django

1. Improve your skills by developing models, forms, views, and templates.

2. Create a rich user experience using Ajax and other JavaScript techniques.

3. A practical guide to writing and using APIs to import or export data.

Django Essentials

ISBN: 978-1-78398-370-4   Paperback: 172 pages

Develop simple web applications with the powerful Django framework

1. Get to know MVC pattern and the structure of Django.

2. Create your first webpage with Django mechanisms.

3. Enable user interaction with forms.

4. Program extremely rapid forms with Django features.

Please check **www.PacktPub.com** for information on our titles

Instant Django 1.5 Application Development Starter

ISBN: 978-1-78216-356-5   Paperback: 78 pages

Jump into Django with this hands-on guide to practical web application development with Python

1. Learn something new in an Instant! A short, fast, focused guide delivering immediate results.

2. Work with the database API to create a data-driven app.

3. Learn Django by creating a practical web application.

4. Get started with Django's powerful and flexible template system.

Django 1.2 E-commerce

ISBN: 978-1-84719-700-9   Paperback: 244 pages

Build powerful e-commerce applications using Django, a leading Python web framework

1. Build all the components for an e-commerce store, from product catalog to shopping cart to checkout processor.

2. Build a high quality e-commerce site quickly and start making money.

3. All the examples in the book will run smoothly for all the versions of Django 1.x.

4. Follow a tutorial format to build many components from scratch while leveraging the open-source community to enhance functionality.

Please check **www.PacktPub.com** for information on our titles